Christianity

A SHORT GLOBAL HISTORY

OTHER BOOKS IN THIS SERIES

RELATED TITLES PUBLISHED BY ONEWORLD

Christianity

A SHORT GLOBAL HISTORY

Frederick W. Norris

ONEWORLD

OXFORD

CHRISTIANITY: A SHORT GLOBAL HISTORY

Oneworld Publications
(Sales and Editorial)
185 Banbury Road
Oxford OX2 7AR
England
www.oneworld-publications.com

ISBN 1–85168–296–1

Cover design by Design Deluxe
Typeset by Saxon Graphics Ltd, Derby
Printed and bound in Britain by Bell & Bain Ltd, Glasgow

For the teams that didn't play:
    Dana, David, Joe, Kees, Ken, Michael, Penny, Saphir, Scott,
        and especially Andrew

CONTENTS

INTRODUCTION

'I believe because it is impossible,' said the North African theologian Tertullian (*fl.* AD 200) about Christian faith.

Anyone writing a short global history of Christianity knows that the task is impossible, yet believes it is necessary. Each author selects what appear to be the most important aspects of the history and tries to make them attractive, knowing full well that all readers will be disappointed because things they hold dear are absent. Sadly such is the beast.

The term 'Christianity' is an abstraction. Perhaps more helpful than the unwieldy term 'Hinduism', it still tells us much less than we want to know. In this book Christians are the focus. They seek to practice the virtues of Jesus Christ. Those virtues are fruit of the Spirit growing within communities of character bound together in the grace of God. Jesus is their example as well as their Master and Savior. Christian groups have been marked by particular kinds of spirituality, service and evangelism. They pray, they assist others and they tell the story of Jesus.

The Oneworld series on religions includes *Christianity: A Short Introduction* by Keith Ward, which presents a contemporary account of major Christian doctrines. Thus the present volume is freed to concentrate heavily on the lives of Christians. Some doctrinal reflection must occupy this work, but the emphasis falls on who Christians were and what they did. The plan is to look through the centuries and global regions at believers who tried to follow Christ. After appropriate introductory matter, each chapter will attempt to give reasons why the lives of Christians took those shapes. It is hoped that important themes are treated in such a way that peoples' interests during other eras and our twenty-first-century issues may intersect. Three broad questions form the outline of every chapter: (1) What kinds of relationships have Christians had with people of other faiths? (2) How have Christians functioned within various cultures? (3) Have Christians over the centuries developed a single core of practices and beliefs that make them recognizable? When answers to these questions are treated as transparent overlays, they tell most of the Christian story. The discipline of separating them for study remains difficult because they are so interrelated. Often people and themes could be properly treated under more than one of the questions.

A majority of Christians have confessed a series of beliefs intricately involved in their way of life. The Creator God, both all powerful and good, loves and forgives people. God calls God's children to personify such love and forgiveness in communities. Jesus Christ is both divine and human, God incarnate; after his death and resurrection he is now ascended to heaven where he rules with God the Father. The Holy Spirit, the third member of the Trinity, dwells within the Christian community and also works outside it. God is both three and one.

Throughout the church's history, however, some naming themselves Christians have questioned the character of a God who allows so much evil in this life. Some have seen Jesus Christ as only human, but an exceptional prophet, teacher or healer; others have viewed him as singularly divine, not fully human. Some have found the conception of Trinity incoherent. Still others have wanted to follow Jesus but have found his teachings to be unrealistic and thus in need of serious reformulation in terms of their own contemporary categories. More than a few have questioned talk about a Holy Spirit.

Like Buddhists before them and Muslims after them, Christians try to incarnate a missionary faith. Beginning in the Middle East within a pluralistic Jewish and Graeco–Roman religious environment, they became dominant for over a thousand years in Western Europe, yet their history tells a different global tale. Outside the West they have often been small religious groups faced by many larger ones. Christians have existed nearly anywhere in spite of pressure or persecution and have translated their sacred scriptures and practices into the many languages and cultures in which they have lived. At different times some Christian professional missionaries have nearly smothered the message under the culture of their home civilizations, but better missionaries and believers have insisted on something else. Christians remain Nigerian, Chinese, Indian, Brazilian, etc., a part of the country in which they convert; they can live within nearly any culture and still be followers of Christ's way. Of course, Christian zealots have viewed all religions but their own as totally false; yet some believers have discovered at least a modicum of truth among groups who trust other gods. Because there is only one God to be worshipped, any who speak of gods must be trying to talk about God. Still other Christians have insisted that all religions are equally truthful.

Christ's disciples have organized themselves in diverse ways but have frequently understood that they needed to worship within community in order to exist in the world. They have handed down their approaches to devotion and life through tradition and practice, have flourished or floundered in quite disparate relationships to economic and political powers, and have appropriated or developed a series of institutions to embody their ways. For most Christians the church has not been an appendix; rather it has been the organism necessary for sustaining existence. They believe that only within its nurturing atmosphere can full human development occur. Being a Christian by oneself is impossible; even hermits may be said to live within the larger community of faith.

Two technical terms appear frequently in this volume: 'contextualization' and 'inculturation'. They speak about the attempts by various Christians to deal with the three questions. Followers of Christ must always be aware of their contexts, their relationships with people and things that form their worlds. No description of Christian life and belief or anything like a core is neutral, unaffected by its convictions or its environment. The word 'culture' itself has often been employed broadly enough that the three questions could be included particularly under the term 'inculturation'.

All Christian communities must study and decide what aspects of the world in which they find themselves can be appropriated even to the point that some of them enhance while others change their understanding of central practices and faith. They also must discern what characteristics of their world endanger their life together and must be resisted. For example, numerous nineteenth- and twentieth-century missionaries to India recognized that Christians could claim attributes of Indian life and spirituality. But they still rejected the rite of *sati*, the burning of the widow with the body of her husband. They also questioned the foundations of the caste system whereas the indigenous

Thomas Christians for hundreds of years had operated within it as a separate local caste. Some twentieth-century German Christians supported the Nazi programs as both German and Christian. Other Germans (and people from other European countries) were clearly counter-cultural and fought the Nazis at every possible point. Yet even those protesters were inculturating what they understood as the gospel into German or European cultural forms. Counter-cultural movements respond specifically to their larger culture and are best understood within it. The contextualization or inculturation process is terribly messy and always open to other judgments.

Historians propose time periods that are seldom recognized by the people who go to and fro within them. Such folk are too busy staying alive. The old standard of early, medieval, Reformation and modern church history fitted the demands of a two-semester university or seminary course, but it operated primarily on the false assumption that Christians belong to a Western religion that moved from Jerusalem to London or New York through continental Europe. That sense of things leaves out the very regions where many of the most interesting materials lie. How can we get the best information about Christians' relations with Buddhists, Hindus and Muslims if we ignore the places in which the most contact occurred? In a nearly two-thousand-year history we will miss much about the lives of Christians if we do not look at their failures and near annihilations as well as their apparent successes. The Christian story is not one of continuous victory. At times Christian communities seem to expand at the boundaries of the places where they are strong and to shrivel toward death at their aging centers. Sometimes the new groups are anything but widely praised and well established in the regions where they emerge.

Nearly all the earth has felt Christian presence. From the seventh until the late fifteenth century, the geographical center of Christianity was in Sogdiana (Turkmenistan and Uzbekistan), a small country on the Silk Road in Central Asia. Perhaps as many as two-thirds of twenty-first-century Christians live in the less developed south. Most of the world's Roman Catholics reside in Latin America, where some of the more intense growth among Protestant pentecostals is now taking place. The sum total of Christians in Africa is greater than the sum total of all people living in the United States. Christians, therefore, cannot be thought of first as members of a Western religion most at home in Europe, Canada and the United States. Although European Christians are experiencing some renewal, this does not match the vitality of churches in Africa or Latin America. Congregations in the United States hardly keep pace with population growth, but Asian Christians are recovering from near extinction at the end of the thirteenth-century Mongolian peace. They are a tiny minority in China, yet thirty million believers (a conservative estimate) can hardly be deemed insignificant. Those realities demand a different look at the history of Christians, one that appears eccentric in relation to standard Western church histories but one that flows from the center of things. All history is written within sets of questions that periodically change. A popular book should attempt to deal with contemporary concerns.

A few arbitrary decisions have been made. For the short space in which they are needed, 'AD' and 'BC' are here brought back as the way to speak of time periods because 'CE' and 'BCE' make less and less sense. Using a calendar that employs the assumed date of Jesus' birth as its starting point could be called the 'Christian era' and could designate the previous period as 'before (the) Christian era', but the 'CE' in these abbreviations sometimes means 'the common era'. Many countries and religions of the world have their own reckonings. I do not attempt to make that clear by for example citing Muslim and Chinese dates for people from those communities. But trying to avoid Eurocentrism or North American dominance while speaking of 'CE' as 'the common era' boggles the mind. There is no world 'common era'. 'AD' and 'BC' only indicate that I have adopted a Christian calendar, not that I am convinced that there is a singularly universal one.

Places are identified in the early chapters by their ancient names with the modern ones in parenthesis: thus 'Bithynia (north-western Turkey)'. That should help the reader find the locations. Perhaps the most difficult of these designations is 'Palestine (Israel)', in many ways an odd choice but one that allows the first to be the historical name and the second the modern one.

Individual people form the backbone of this story but not because history moves solely through its greatest leaders. Often those leaders are out front only because the crest of a movement sent them surfing. Yet biographical vignettes make a book human.

Finally one apology seems appropriate. Paying attention to Christians round the world emphasizes that they belong to a non-Western religion. That does present difficulties for any book, particularly a short one with a popular audience in view. Many strange names for countries, cities and people must appear. Indeed it is precisely these stories that remind us of Christians' long and far-flung history. The tale of Christ's followers living out their faith should never be told without some accounts of those outside the Middle East (never a thoroughly Western region), Europe and 'first-world' North America.

For further information please visit www.oneworld-publications.com/christianityhistory.

Frederick W. Norris

10 December 2001 (anniversary of Thomas Merton's death in 1968)

1 LITTLE-KNOWN TO PERSECUTED MINORITY: BEGINNINGS TO 313

Jesus loved people, particularly the diseased, the poor and the oppressed. His household in Palestine (Israel) was unassuming. Its head, Joseph, worked either as a carpenter or a small contractor to support a family of children. A trip to Egypt with an expected return perhaps planned to escape King Herod's slaughter of little ones suggests that some discretionary funds were available. Later village life in Nazareth in Galilee meant that Jesus grew up among people scratching out a meager livelihood, but nearby Sepphoris was a bustling Roman town. The adults in Jesus' inner circle were small-businessmen, fishermen and others, even a well-to-do tax collector, all of whom held low or negative status in their communities. Showing his good sense of humor, Jesus said it was more difficult for the rich to enter heaven than it was for a camel to pass through the eye of a needle, but he also remarked that it was possible with God. Indeed, wealthy women financially underwrote his efforts. But the message about God that he preached dealt most often with the plight of those trodden underfoot. Probably the most remarkable part of his ministry was that some Jewish and Roman leaders discovered his deeds and words speaking to them. His descriptions of the kingdom of God detailed not only a hospitality to strangers and those less fortunate but also a freedom for those whose higher position and station brought uncertain fulfillment. To recognize life as having a purpose that included care for others, to see that after death there was existence in which injustices were rectified, was good news. Jesus' deeds of mercy and power (loving the unlovable, healing the sick and attacking the religiously arrogant), his stories, and finally his death and resurrection gave hope to both rich and poor who had found their days filled with little expectation or painful drudgery. Jesus was impressed with a widow who gave her last penny at the temple; he belittled a rich farmer who thought his crop was his to handle as he saw fit.

The New Testament says that Jesus wrote in sand, but we have no documents from his hand. Information about him is limited yet more than we have for many ancient figures. A few Roman historians knew about Christians and a bit about Christos or Chrestos, as they named him. Most Western scholars accept that we know much of what Aristotle taught although the great manuscripts of his writings are not dated earlier than about twelve hundred years after his death. Yet the collections of Jesus' deeds and words, probably first written and compiled within a generation or two of his death, come from people who believed in him, probably from some who had lived alongside him. The New Testament contains pieces completed by the end of the first century AD. Textual fragments of the Christian Gospels have been dated to the second or even the first century AD. Full manuscripts from the fourth century still exist. Even the most ancient writings containing the teachings of Buddha are not dated as close to his death as the Christian Gospels are to Jesus' demise.

Whether the Christian Gospels included in the New Testament come from the hands of his disciples or of some of their followers, the stories depict that original band of twelve apostles in anything but a good or a defensive light. They look like bumblers who seldom got the point on their first try; they were both prejudiced toward others and driven by their own self-interests. Unless the skeptic can make the case that the stories represent a quite sophisticated hoax, the writings about Jesus make a claim for their authenticity because they have the breath of real people struggling to understand their leader. Tatian, a second-century AD Syrian writer, constructed a single account of Jesus' life called the *Diatessaron*, 'from the four', that attempted to remove the overlap and smooth the differences he found in his sources. Successful in Syria and western Persia (Iraq), it eventually lost out to the four Gospels despite their warts. John Chrysostom (*c.* 347–407), bishop of Constantinople, insisted that in the main the four were in agreement. Their disagreements only enhanced the authenticity of their stories. Had they always said the same things in the same way, Christians' opponents would have rightly declared that the books had been cooked.

Nearly any reader of the Gospels finds Jesus to be an interesting teacher and something of a prophet. Today fewer critics attack the tales of miracle and healing; the sense of what is possible has been at least partially freed from the stranglehold of Western Enlightenment scientific categories without becoming unscientific. Other central figures of world religions have such scenes depicting their powers. The primary battleground over what is possible remains the claims for Jesus' remarkable birth and his resurrection from the dead. The Muslim Qur'an accepts his virgin birth; its problem is with his death and resurrection. But some second-century Jewish literature and a non-Christian author of that period, Celsus in his *True Discourse*, depicted Jesus as an accomplished liar and manipulative magician. Eusebius of Caesarea (*c.* 260–*c.* 339), Christian apologist and church historian, responded by warning (tongue in cheek) that people seldom follow someone they know to be a charlatan. That would be especially true when following him involved both impugning honored religious traditions and being placed in danger of beatings or death. Yet according to Eusebius there was no knock-down argument for the superiority of Christian practice and faith. Conversion depended on the power of God.

Armed with a sense that the Christian gospel could be put into another language and culture without losing its center – they had already moved it from Aramaic to Greek, from Israel to other parts of the Mediterranean – Christians spread rapidly along trade routes. At the first Christian Pentecost, Jews living outside Palestine (Israel) came from Elam, Media, Mesopotamia and Parthia (Iraq and Iran), the Roman provinces of Asia, Cappadocia, Pamphilia and Phrygia (all in modern Turkey), Egypt, and Italy to celebrate the Jewish Passover in Jerusalem. They heard the gospel of Christ in their own tongues. About two decades later Paul traveled through the countries lying on the northern Mediterranean littoral. He spent time in what are now Israel, Syria, Turkey, Greece and Italy, and perhaps traveled to Spain. The church at Rome, started by unnamed leaders, was there to meet him. Christians like Apollos, probably from Alexandria, along with Aquila and Priscilla from Rome and Corinth, took advantage of Roman peace to move around. Legends about the journeys of the eleven apostles into Europe and farther east do not command general acceptance, but the travels of Thomas to India, described in the *Acts of Thomas*, suggest that he or someone like him did take Christian faith there. Some information makes such a trip likely. Before the first century AD there were recognized shipping routes from Egypt to India and back supported by a yearly shift of trade winds. First-century coins from a region just west of India, one ruled by twin kings, give credence to the mention of such brothers in the *Acts of Thomas*. Odd-sized bricks used to build Roman ports on the western Indian coast were employed in Thomas's tomb at Madras near India's eastern shore. They are not common anywhere else in India or in any other time period. By the end of the second century, Christian missionaries served in France, North Africa, Iraq and Iran. Tertullian of Carthage (*fl.* 200) knew a tradition about Christians in Britain.

CHRISTIANS AND PEOPLE OF OTHER FAITHS

Most of the first Christians were *Jews* who thought of Jesus as the Jewish Messiah. Both Jesus and the apostle Paul called the Jews of their time to repentance and reform. They left the earliest Christians a mixed legacy. Both men loved their own people: Jesus wept over Jerusalem, Paul was willing to die for his kin. But they also had deep disdain for major Jewish religious leaders who, in their view, had badly tainted both practice and faith. They also felt strong disappointment that many Jews followed those leaders. The prophetic intensity of Jesus and Paul brought them into conflict with Jewish authorities and, through the troublesome agitation of those relationships, also with Roman authorities. Jesus was killed as a Jewish blasphemer who threatened Roman peace; Paul was executed as a rabble-rouser with a history that made him dangerous to the established order.

Reading about the early antagonism between Jews and Christians is especially troublesome when we think of the atrocities in later centuries that Jews suffered at the hands of people who called themselves Christians. Because during this early period the Jewish diaspora was widespread and primarily urban, it was (as we see in Paul's various missions) a logical place to preach Jesus as the Messiah. Hatred between the members of these two groups probably is best explained by the suggestion that Christians were at first part of the Jewish community, a sect that became a new cult against its own family. Even in the Jewish heartland Christians had experienced considerable success. Evidently thousands of Jews in Palestine (Israel) had become Christians and were still puzzled by what to do about their previous practices. Issues involving Jewish ritual and custom continued to be problematic in Jerusalem despite the apparent settlement, in a previous Jerusalem council, of what could be required by Jewish Christians of new gentile converts. Not circumcision, the clearest sign of Jewish covenant, but careful avoidance of treating the food laws flippantly formed part of advised Christian practice for gentiles.

In Antioch members of this new cult were first called 'Christians'. The emergence of this name probably involved a bitter pogrom in the 40s AD, one carried out against the Jews whose circus teams had won a stunning victory in the horse races. Crowds of Antiochene citizens burst out of the stadium and began looting Jewish homes and businesses. Many Jews died during the attacks. Evidently, as the authorities tried to restore peace, they had to find some name for these new believers who insisted that they were not Jews. Early in Jerusalem Christians had referred to themselves as people of 'the Way'. But now they probably were given the name 'Christians'.

Irenaeus (c. 115–c. 202) and others battled to keep Jewish scripture as part of the Christian Bible. Marcion of Sinope (died c. 154) and a number of Gnostic teachers had found those ancient writings to be stories about a far different God from the one whom Jesus revealed. But many Christians insisted that they could not understand their Christ if they did not interpret him in terms of Jewish scripture, which they called the 'Old Testament'. Thus the terrible relations between Jews and Christians at various times in their histories are probably best understood in terms of warring clans from the same tribe. As their own scriptures attest, Jews had had success in wooing converts from outside the ranks of those born to Jewish mothers. The strange tales in the early centuries AD of gentiles attaching themselves to synagogues in some outer circle called 'God-fearers' show the synagogues' appeal to those who did not grow up in Jewish communities. Jews may not have been as openly missionary as Christians, but the story of neither of these groups can be told in full measure without noticing that at any time either one, or the other, or both were winning the allegiance of those who began in the other camp.

Jewish Christians as a group may have been mortally weakened even as early as the first century AD, but they left a legacy that needed to be investigated. Melito, bishop of Sardis in the late second century, presents perhaps the most fevered early attack on Jews. He charges them with responsibility for the death of Christ and uses vitriolic language in describing their way of life. A twenty-first-century audience of anti-Semites would agree with him; others with tolerance and love toward the often persecuted Jews would find his words appalling.

Melito was interested in what scripture Jews in Palestine (Israel) used; he traveled there to answer the question for himself. He evidently thought he needed all the weaponry for his battle that he could acquire. Melito's Christian community was small; twentieth-century excavations of Sardis's Jewish synagogue (well located and regularly enlarged), however, suggest that the Jewish community was larger and did not feel itself pressured in ways that the Christians evidently did.

The Sardis bishop had reasons for his words; thus they are understandable, but unforgivable. Neither Christian minorities who felt threatened by Jews nor Christian majorities with other agendas may be excused for such revolting attacks. As we look back on Christian history we sadly know how far anti-Semitism spread its tentacles among Christian communities. Fathoming the pain or frustration of a Christian community helps explain part of its sensitivities. But neither Jesus nor Paul lost his deep love for his own flesh and blood as well as the heritage given to Christians by Jews. Their occasionally sharp words against certain Jews form no foundation for fanaticism against all Jews.

Deep distrust of and anger at Jews marked some, but not all, Christians. The prominent church historian Eusebius of Caesarea (c. 260–339) points out the Christian leaders in the first three centuries AD who understood Hebrew. His knowledge is not global and he names only a few. One of those he mentions, however, is the great Christian theologian Origen (c. 185–c. 251). The Alexandrian created an edition of the Old Testament called the Hexapla that laid out the texts in six columns. The first was a Hebrew text of the Hebrew Bible, the second was that text transliterated into Greek letters, followed by four Greek translations – including not only the Septuagint made by Jews but also three made by individual Christians who became Jews: Aquila, Symmachus and Theodotian.

Because of Origen's reputation in later centuries as a heretic, and the vagaries of textual transmission, we have only a small collection of his biblical commentaries. But those we still possess present strong resemblances in various places to comments of Jewish leaders on their scriptures. Evidently in Alexandria and in Palestinian Caesarea, Origen carried on fruitful conversations with Jews, perhaps both by reading their works and by talking with them. For him there was no question but that the Christian Old Testament, works shared with the Jews, should be part of Holy Writ and should be viewed at least part of the time through a Jewish lens.

Direct contact with *Graeco-Roman religions* appears only obliquely in Jesus' career. He found remarkable faith in a Syro-Phoenician woman and a Roman centurion as well as interest among a group of Greeks, but there are no records of extensive discussions with any of them about their religious practices or beliefs. Paul's response to believers in gods of the Graeco-Roman pantheon is more clearly depicted. Once he and Silas were mistaken for appearances by Zeus and Hermes. They tore their clothes and vigorously denied that they represented what their audience hoped they were. In a series of comments in his epistles and in the Acts of the Apostles, Paul brought forward the usual charges from Jews that Graeco-Roman religions were idolatrous and immoral and offered his own interesting adjustments. Nothing in the meat offered to idols made it unholy. The slaughter of animals to remove the debt of guilty people was crude and unnecessary. Sins there were, but Christ had paid the penalty on the cross. This new faith did not involve animal sacrifices as almost all of the neighboring religions did.

Pagan temples were the butcher shops and restaurants of the time. Eating with non-Christian friends surely brought the occasion of fare that came from the temples. But the issue did not demand that one believe the gods actually existed, rather it called for attention to the weak who could be led astray if the strong did not always remember such immaturity in the faith. Christians previously had been liars and thieves, purveyors of magic, all such things before their conversions. Now they were to take on Jesus' way of life.

In the New Testament book of Romans, in the midst of a scathing rebuke focused on the depths of depravity to which humans had descended, the apostle Paul insisted that people without the Jewish law might know much of that law in their consciences and act according to it. On the day of God's judgment they would be examined on the basis of what they knew and how they had lived. Their thoughts would either accuse or excuse them. In Athens Paul voiced his hatred of idolatry but used a statue dedicated to an unknown god and quotations from Greek poets to preach his gospel. He acknowledged truth where he found it. He could argue that some virtues were particularly commendable because there had never been any laws against them. Because those virtues had not been condemned, they must have been honored in the cultures known to Paul. During a riot at Ephesus fomented by fearful artisans who saw the threat Christians presented to their successful business of making and selling idols, both Christians and Paul's friends who were pagan priests pleaded with him not to speak in the arena because he might be killed.

Christian apologists of the second and third centuries used most of their arguments to attack what they viewed as pagan practices. Idols made by human hands could not compare to the God of creation who made all things. Surely the stories about those gods, even the major ones from Olympus – whether designated by Greek or Roman names – clearly depicted their character. They lived in such terrible ways that they should not be honored. Zeus turned himself into many forms in order to seduce women. Within that Olympian court, intrigue, jealousy, and hatred even to the point of murder marked the relationships. Why worship gods who are worse than many of the most vicious humans?

We must avoid the old saw that says Christians denied the presence of any truth in other religions at the same time that they found the philosophers of Greece and Rome to be teachers of morality. A number of Graeco-Roman philosophers did ridicule the traditional religions. Thus some of the apologists tried to separate philosophy and religion. Justin Martyr (died c. 165), impressed with the philosophers, said that they could lead non-Jews toward the truth of the Christian gospel just as Jewish scripture had led Jews to Jesus. Justin had followed that philosophical journey himself. While on it he discovered the truth of the Christian message on the basis of yearnings both partially met and missed in his previous studies.

Sprinkled through early Christian literature is another view, a sometimes begrudging, sometimes admiring respect for what people in non-Christian religions had accomplished. Clement of Alexandria (c. 160–215) offered accurate descriptions of *Buddhists* in Bactria and India. Origen, who followed Clement as the teacher in Alexandria's Christian academy, seems to have known a bit about the Buddha. Ammonius Sacca(s) is thought by some to be Ammonius the Sakka, i.e. one from the same tribe as Buddha, who was called 'Sayka Muni', sage from the Sayka tribe or Sakka people. He taught Origen among others. His views well may be a connection between various Neoplatonic and Buddhist doctrines like transmigration. Perhaps Clement's teacher, Pantaenus, traveled to India and there acquired a few pearls of *Indian wisdom*. Travel routes to and from the East occasionally brought Indian gurus to Alexandria. Information about these Eastern approaches to life appears in contexts of both praise and blame.

Christians borrowed from the religions around them. The statuary depicting Mary and the suckling baby Jesus closely resembles statues of

Isis. Both Clement and Origen did not insist that syncretism was the greatest danger. The point was to take over the religious riches that pagans had to offer. After all, it was God who told the Israelites to plunder their Egyptian owners' possessions. Origen had his students read all kinds of philosophers – nearly all of them except those atheists who denied providence and God. Many of their philosophies had good religious elements.

Christians also found *Gnostics* in their world as well as among their believers and some of their leaders. We do not know exactly what Gnosticism might have been because the writings are so varied. The discovery of buried texts at Nag Hammadi in Egypt in the twentieth century has given us more information but not all the answers. What have been called proto-Gnostic views existed in the first century AD, sometimes as a background to certain New Testament texts. But whether developed systems emerged before Christian Gnostic teachers in the second half of the second century is difficult to tell. The Christian Gnostic teachings, perhaps never tightly structured systems, appeared in Egypt, Palestine (Israel), Syria, Jordan, Asia Minor (Turkey) and Rome. They often emphasized the imprisonment of the soul in the human body and the need for a savior to provide the secret knowledge necessary to escape this present evil world. The character of the savior and the number of passwords and gates to be opened varied. Gnostics sometimes divided the human race into three groups: (1) those capable of salvation; (2) those incapable of rescue; and (3) those in between who might or might not respond properly. Gnostic ethics could include the disciplining of the body to serve the needs of the soul or a wild debauchery that destroyed the flesh.

The names of some second-century Gnostic leaders have come down to us: Basileides, Cerinthus, Valentinus. We may even have a writing from the last, *The Gospel of Truth*. The Gnostics were a strong force among Christians, people opposed at times in certain regions by smaller groups of more orthodox followers of Christ. The development of confessions of faith and the strengthening of regional leaders like bishops in large cities who banded together to confront these teachings have left their mark most clearly on Catholic, Orthodox and Anglican Christians. Serapion of Antioch and other second-century leaders warned that a group of gospels and tracts with strong Gnostic themes should not be read within the churches. A church at Rhossus near Antioch in Syria (Antakya, Turkey) had asked Serapion if they should read a gospel written by Peter. He responded that surely they should use it; but then they sent him a copy. When he read it, he insisted that they were never to employ it again.

Gnostic themes and teachers were not limited to Christian communities. When the Greek philosophers Plotinus (c. 205–69/70) and Porphyry (c. 232–c.305) attacked such positions, they did not always connect them directly to Christians. Porphyry in particular had a quite different strategy in opposing Christians than the one he used in confronting Gnostics.

In Egypt during both the second and third centuries governmental financial support of temples devoted to the Graeco-Roman pantheon had decreased. But Maximus of Tyre (c. 125–85), a pagan philosopher, gives us a better idea of just how pluralistic the religious situation of the Mediterranean was. He guessed that people in the eastern Mediterranean worshipped about thirty thousand gods. That leaves open how many were honored in the rest of the region. His contemporary, Pausanius (fl. 150), writing about his travels through Greece, insisted that one important aspect of any shrine or temple was its local significance. All that it meant could not be contained in its name as yet another sacred site for Zeus or any other god. Emphasis was often placed on the plurality of the deities, not their unity. And when that opposite theme of unity was emphasized in works like Apuleius's (born c. 123) The Golden Ass, it tended to serve the interests of a few in trying to work through the myriad of gods. Furthermore the expansion of Eastern cults like those of Isis and Mithra throughout the Roman Empire strengthens the observation that early Christians lived in the midst of widespread and deeply rooted religious pluralism.

Both Jewish apologists and Graeco-Roman polytheists attacked not only the character of Christian communities but also the character of Jesus. The New Testament speaks of Jews who explained that the Christ was not raised from the dead; the guards had been bribed when his body was stolen from the tomb. In the late second century, Celsus, a defender of Graeco-Roman traditional religion who was familiar with Jewish critiques and parts of what we now call the New Testament, used both sources to pursue his own purposes. For Celsus, Jesus was the illegitimate son of Mary and a Roman soldier stationed in Egypt. He became an immoral, lying, Egyptian-trained magician who should have been rejected by any sensible person. The Christians themselves were primarily women and children, slaves and the untrustworthy. They hated education and taught tales that were incoherent. How could a father be good if he sent his own son to die in his place? How could he be all powerful if he needed assistance? The Christian god was clearly inferior.

Origen responded to Celsus by denying that his charges made sense. Jesus was good and the God he preached was good also. That can be seen in the effects the gospel had on the people who accepted it. Christians came from all levels of society, not just the lower ones. God loved the poor and downtrodden; the church did God's will when it served them. Christian faith, however, held attractions for many, not merely the emotional and the uneducated. But only those of higher attainment were put in positions of authority and were responsible for preaching and teaching.

In this period the followers of *Mani* (216–76) became a world religion in their own right, one that lasted a thousand years. They began during the third century in Persia (Iran) when the prophet Mani appeared. Only recently with the discovery of Chinese texts in Turkmenistan has it become clear that this religion began as a Christian sect. Mani was surely a man of power and visions. He was forced by the Zoroastrians in Persia (Iran) from his home in Seleucia-Ctesiphon to a life of wandering that led him to India. When he returned, he proved to be so influential that at first the ruler Sapor I supported him. But Sapor's successor had him flayed alive, hung his stuffed skin on an important gate of the city, and banished his followers.

Manichaeans had a dualistic religion emphasizing the struggle between light and darkness. In their view many previous leaders had offered assistance in freeing small bits of light from their imprisonment in darkness. Among them were Buddha, the Jewish prophets, Jesus and of course Mani.

We might expect this religion to have made its way through the East along the Silk Road to India and then on to China. But it also moved west. Augustine (354–430) in North Africa accepted its principles only to become disenchanted with the Manichaean Faustus's ability to explain the determinism that marked its view of salvation. Christians saw the disciples of Mani as significant competitors, ones they mentioned regularly in lists of their enemies.

CHRISTIANS AND THEIR CULTURES

At their beginning Christians faced more than one powerful culture: *Jewish* communities were their cradle, but *Graeco-Roman* believers rocked it. Not every disciple of Jesus thought that the great cities of the

Mediterranean were works of Satan. They were home to most Christians. The countryside was more likely to be the stronghold of 'paganism' (the Latin word *pagos* means 'rural' or 'village district'). The apostle Paul praised the Augustan peace established by the Romans and used its protection of travel as a way to spread the faith. Priscilla and Aquila also journeyed at least from Rome to Ephesus; they had some contact with the Christian from Alexandria, Apollos, who appeared during their stay in Ephesus. Paul invoked his Roman citizenship as a good. He used his education, in both Jewish scripture and Hellenistic rhetoric, to his advantage. Like a good rhetorician he uttered warnings about the problems of philosophy but employed it well in his writings.

The cultural struggles of this first period were complex. Most Christians found ways to adapt within the societies in which they lived. Their adjustments sometimes appear in the Gospels, but particularly in the New Testament book of Acts, the epistles and the apocalypse called Revelation. Some Christians were slaves, but urban slaves who could go to meetings after their work was finished; others were tentmakers or craftsmen. A few owned houses big enough for group meetings and held important positions in either Roman government or Jewish religious organizations. Even during their earliest existence in Galilee and Jerusalem, they were not solely a proletarian or agrarian movement attractive only to lower, less powerful classes. The lowest in society (slaves in galleys and mines, peasants and slaves on small farms) either did not find this new religion appealing or had no one to tell their stories often enough to become a part of historical memory. Two reasons for the spotty persecution of Christians in the first three hundred years of the religion's existence seem plausible. First, they well may have included just enough established people, such as the Roman citizen Paul, that the authorities were often uncertain about what their intentions were and what the consequences of putting them in jail might be. Second, some figures outside Christian groups thought they should be noted, even investigated, but they did not seem to be that numerous or dangerous. Pliny the younger (*c.* 61–*c.* 112), a governor in Bithynia (north-western Turkey) tortured some Christian deaconesses (women leaders) and found that the group was basically harmless. They took oaths not to steal or lie and seemed to come from all strata of society, low and high. They shared a benign common meal. If necessary they could be suppressed. Lucian of Samosata (born *c.* 120) thought them silly. They were so gullible that they even fed their members who had been justly imprisoned.

Because of their reputation for taking care of their own and offering assistance to others and the fearlessness of at least some in the face of persecution, Christians were not easily suppressed. Perhaps they survived epidemics that devastated parts of the Roman Empire because they were so committed to nursing their sick. Modern medicine is well aware of how much the loving climate of a tightly woven family can mean to health. Some other religious communities or work guilds had not prepared their members to take care of ill and dying compatriots. Such a lack of care may have made Christian prayer and friendship seem more powerful. Continuous assistance to any in need must also have seemed impressive. As epidemics weakened various group relationships, perhaps even destroyed others, this new religion seemed to be a better bet. It not only dealt with bodily breakdown; it also provided views of afterlife that tried to make sense of earthly troubles and death.

Christian groups were usually small, often meeting in homes. When the earliest persecutors imprisoned or killed the identified leaders, others rose up. In the second century, impoundment of Christians' sacred books and devotional aids did not stop their worship because much teaching had been committed to memory and simple rituals could be enacted without any particular finery.

Irenaeus (c. 115–c.202) is a witness to another cultural aspect. A second-century missionary in Gaul (France), he knew the ways of his home in Asia Minor (Turkey), but he also warned that it was now difficult to write in Greek because he had been preaching so long in the local language. But he returned to that tongue to make his arguments against the Gnostics whom he had met in Gaul. A contemporary, Tatian from Syria (Iran), scathingly rebuked Greek learning and championed the ancient wisdom of his home and of the Jews. Yet he did so while writing in Greek, employing the best of Hellenistic rhetoric and proving that he had a fuller education in Hellenistic philosophy than his contemporary, Justin (died c. 165). Reading him in a modern translation makes his attack on things Hellenistic appear to be a diatribe against all things Greek. He never rejected everything Greek culture provided.

Tertullian of Carthage (fl. 200), who was a mature Christian leader at the turn of the third century, was a critic of his own culture. He did not like the Roman games and their connections with the temples. At the same time he was a master of Latin, so proficient that either he or early translators of the New Testament into Latin – perhaps both – formed much of the theological vocabulary for subsequent Latin theology. He had been educated so well in rhetoric and law that his apologies to the Roman government were probably the most difficult for any Roman authority to read – if they ever read them – and definitely the most pleasing for Latin Christians to hear. His main argument was that Christians were persecuted because of their name and not because of any thorough investigation, as prescribed by Roman law, into their practices and teachings. Roman authorities should follow their laws. If they did, they would not persecute Christians.

Time and again in this period Christian communities turned their scriptures into the local language and employed the logic of the indigenous cultures to argue their case. The importance of this *translation principle* for Christians is seen as well when it is ignored as when it is followed. Punic tribes in North Africa surely came into contact with the Latin-speaking cities and at times may have lived within them. Yet somehow the great Latin leaders of the North Africa churches did not support the translation of Christian scripture into the Punic language and culture. They referred to them as 'Berbers', 'barbarians' who either did not speak Latin or did not speak it well. Christians in North Africa (Algeria, Tunisia and Libya) seem not to have taken their desert neighbors seriously. Their leaders did not suffer from Irenaeus's problem with fading Greek because they evidently did not daily use Punic. They had no trouble preaching and writing in Latin because they had seldom, if ever, spoken in 'Berber' long enough for operating in Latin to become difficult.

The tragedy of much Roman Catholic missiology until Vatican II (1962–5) was the penchant for offering Christian worship everywhere in Latin. That has meant that the Berber model – dismissing the need for translations into local languages – has been adopted for reasons of perceived beauty and unity while the heart languages of many peoples were deemed incapable of bearing Christian truth.

We have little data about what kind of *art and architecture* the earliest Christians produced. As we see in the stories about Jesus and the letters of Paul the communities often included people of wealth and station. Only a few of the elite classes are mentioned, but only a few such folk existed in the Mediterranean world. The book of James speaks of one whose ring marked him as a man of power and influence in the Roman upper class. Churches meeting in the houses of the well-to-do were common. By the third century, however, we have an interesting example of a house converted into a house church in Dura Europas, a Roman military station in Syria. Built up against the town's outer defensive wall, it was partially destroyed as engineers filled it with rubble. Rome's enemies in the region were masters of tunneling under walls, bracing them with timbers and then setting the timbers ablaze. Unsupported, the walls fell down. But if the Roman engineers created supports behind them and covered that rubble and earth with a substance that made the occasional rain squalls run off without damage, the walls would settle down, not fall in or out. Thus the Dura Europas Christian house church was well preserved by steps taken for far different purposes than saving an early worship center. The murals on the walls show some quality in depicting the shepherd with a sheep on his shoulders. A baptistery was also in place. A Jewish synagogue at Dura Europas with remarkable frescoes indicates that the Christian symbols are in line with the art of other religions in the town. Both worship centers have a Persian flavor.

Varieties of buildings can be found in ancient Christian heartlands, particularly in Italy, Greece, Turkey, Israel, Syria, Jordan and Iraq. Some of those churches were dedicated to famous martyrs and thus were tied into the more difficult lives of previous Christians. The ruins that remain are built of stone or brick and take not only the shape of the Roman oblong basilica, but also shapes like the cross or the octagon. Ones paid for by richer members were adorned with mosaic floors that near the end of the third century began to have quality. At an earlier time floors and sarcophagi have cruder art than those of neighboring buildings, but as more upper class families became Christian the money became available to hire the best artisans.

Some of the earliest Christian art appears in the Roman catacombs. Because a few depictions can be dated as early as the third century, the development from rather crude representations to more refined work offers evidence of the emergence of Christians among the more wealthy and powerful. Yet because Christian communities seldom if ever excluded the poor, their catacomb burials became important to the downtrodden. The poor would have been thrown into open pits had they not been Christians, Jews or members of other religious organizations who took care of their bodies. Near the turn of the third century we have some information about Christian burial practices and the veneration of sites where martyrs were buried.

Christian sculpture has been more difficult to find. Eusebius spoke of an early brass statue of Jesus in Caesarea Philippi that depicted the Savior stretching out his hand evidently to the woman healed there.

Other writers implied that such a statue was erected in Edessa. The third-century pieces at the Cleveland, Ohio art museum are of excellent quality and demonstrate how important the figure of Jonah being regurgitated by the large fish was as a symbol of Christ's three-day stay in the tomb and his resurrection.

Christians very early faced a series of *social institutions*, both Jewish and Graeco-Roman, that caught their attention. Some of Jesus' followers in Jerusalem adopted a communal style of living in which those with plenty helped those more needy; they apparently lived together from shared funds. The apostle Paul commented on the institution of slavery in an oblique way by reminding both a runaway slave, Onesimus, and his owner, Philemon, that the most important relationship in their lives was that of being brothers in Christ. Recognizing such a reality meant that Philemon would not treat Onesimus only as a slave and that Onesimus would not serve Philemon only as his master. Ancient slavery was different from the nineteenth-century servitude more familiar to twenty-first-century readers. Imprisonment in the mines or on the galleys meant terrible suffering and almost certain death, and slavery anywhere else was always much more than a minor inconvenience. But there are numerous stories of and inscriptions about slaves who were educated and put in a position to either earn or purchase their freedom.

Christians worked against the institution of slavery mostly outside the Roman legal system. One remarkable comment from the second-century figure Ignatius of Syrian Antioch (Antakya, Turkey) emphasized that buying the freedom of every slave who became a Christian was not necessary. That statement makes little sense unless there was a deep understanding that leaving anyone enslaved was a heavy burden of conscience. Evidently a constant stream of slaves became Christians in the hope of leaving their situation. During even the first period of Christian growth, the fact of brothers and sisters in Christ being in bondage put strong pressure on the institution of slavery. It weakened. Slaves were still a part of conquest in war; the inability to pay one's debts also could require menial servitude. But even on the economic level Christian distaste for collecting interest on debts came into play as a buffer against the enslavement of the poor.

Clement of Alexandria (c. 160–215) wrote his *Instructor* primarily for upper class Christians who were looking for specific, almost legalistic, guidance in changing their lifestyles. The new faith demanded new practices. Various kinds of clothing and jewelry, household fineries, and

lk. True worship of God was his goal. But he also said just
a case to be made depicting him as a political rebel. He
Jewish Zealot party's hope of driving the Roman armies into
he loss of that hope, however, may lie behind his apostle
rayal of him. With Jesus' death his followers were marked as
ers. Thus the Christian faith first preached at Pentecost
angerous to safely ensconced political leaders. Some of the
re imprisoned in Jerusalem. Paul, the missionary, was beaten
cities where he traveled; once he had to be let down from a
er to escape because the gates were being watched.

h Christian groups grew rapidly, they continued to incur
rsecution. Their earliest legal standing occurred in some of the
ies, particularly Rome, as burial societies. They were illegal as
ews represented an ancient faith with certain rights in various
an centers, but Christians struggled with their Jewish heritage.
of the second century, Ignatius, bishop of Antioch, was
the Roman authorities and taken to Rome. Evidently the
wers thought that by removing the identified leaders of Chris-
, they could suppress them. Ignatius believed he would be
ons in the famed city and looked forward to such a death as
unity to demonstrate his faith. In this period martyrdom
ebated pattern of Christian life. Should faithful followers of
death as a witness to life? Should they become inconspicuous
hey flee? Much depended on the ways in which Roman law
and enforced. Often, provincial governors distant from Rome
t to search out and imprison or kill people who they thought
lly harmless. Pliny the Younger, governor in Bithynia (north-
rkey), was convinced that the Christians could be crushed if

ficult problem for Christians was that some caesars were
oon seeing their predecessors or even themselves as gods.
an leaders thought that the authority of the state depended
raeco-Roman pantheon, which individual caesars could join
worshipped. They tolerated nearly any religion that would
ice to the gods who protected the state. Even Jews were
many cities as those who embodied an ancient religion that
eeply upon continuous sacrifices. But a religious group like
ns, who did not give allegiance to those gods and did not
l sacrifices to their own god, threatened the state.

what might be called 'manners' were spelled out in detail. Wealth and its
trappings endangered the soul. The force of his work was so strong that
he also thought he should make clear in a different book that rich folk
could be saved, certainly a question raised in the Bible and in response
to his detailed account of the Christian life.

Tertullian of Carthage in North Africa spelled out a series of *social
careers* that Christians should not pursue. Stone masons, plasterers and
painters made statuary or pictures of idols and thus supported idolatry.
Craftsmen like cobblers or makers of dinnerware might be accepted, but
only with careful investigation. They too often made frivolous pieces that
signified misspent wealth. Tertullian and others could hardly stomach the
growing urban thirst for entertainment, in either the less expensive theater
or the gaudy circus. Large amounts of money were spent in collecting
animals to fight with each other and with humans. City rulers held such
'games' throughout the empire, not only in Italy and North Africa. Gladiatorial contests began to look shameful to Christians; they seem not to
have been as frequent in Constantinople – the city of Byzantium renamed
and expanded after Constantine's conversion. Jesus urged Christians not
to kill. Even contemplating it amounted to defeat before temptation.

Tertullian did not want Christians to be soldiers, but Eusebius
(*c.* 260–*c.* 339), the church historian, tells us of a third-century legion
composed primarily of Christians who served well. Jesus had not
rebuked the Roman centurion for his professional work but admired
his sense of how commands needed to be obeyed. Christian principle
against killing, whether in war or in other circumstances, was strong,
but some believers tried to justify their involvement in taking human
life as part of their duty.

Christians adopted another institution from the Jewish and Graeco-
Roman cultures surrounding them: the conclave or *council*. Only a few
years after Jesus' death, leaders assembled to talk about what was central
to their faith. Such discussion began in Jerusalem when Jewish Christian
leaders there wanted to hear about the apostle Paul's practice and
preaching. In Asia Minor (Turkey) during the second century, a regional
council gathered to determine the truth of prophecies collected by Montanists, Christians who thought that the spiritual life of the church was
drifting and that prophecy was just as important as ever. The assembled
bishops said that prophecy was not the question – ecstatic prophecy was.
It had no claim to authenticity. But the way was opened to view most
prophecy as ecstatic and thus not a Christian practice.

The same kind of ambiguities faced Christians when they considered *gender roles and family*. The *pater familias* of Roman life began to strike disciples of Christ as overbearing. The power to decide whether or not a newborn lived was too dreadful a decision for a father to make. He was the head of the house as Christ was the head of the church, but Christ gave up his life for that church. Abortion was viewed in similar ways; it was infanticide. Taking various medicines for that purpose or performing manual surgery was forbidden. Children were gifts from God.

God ordained marriage for the creation of family. Divorce was not allowed even as it had been under Jewish law. Women were highly valued, but the dominance of males in the relationship was usually often viewed as divinely sanctioned. Early on Christian marriage was administered by civil authorities and blessed by the church. Only later did it become a church ceremony that had ecclesiastical status.

The writer of the New Testament epistle to the Ephesians – some say Paul – pointed out that marriage is a partnership in which both the man and the woman are to submit to one another in reverence for Christ. The author assumed that women knew submission from their culture, whether it be primarily Jewish or Graeco-Roman. But he demanded that men think about loving their wives in the same ways that they loved their bodies. Christ loved the church and died for it. So should they love their wives. This represented a deep challenge to the *pater familias*. If in Christian marriage the partners lived in mutual submission because of their sense of what Christ did for people, then female children and women could emerge as more significant.

Women appear to have been more important among early Christians than is sometimes supposed. The Virgin Mary holds place as the significant parent to the point that some speculatively posit an early death for Mary's husband, Joseph. The passage in Luke's Gospel that is called the Magnificat depicts her as a deeply virtuous disciple who knew how to serve by bending humbly to God's will. Rich women supplied the money to keep Jesus and his band alive and teaching. Paul has been read as always keeping women silent and placing them in positions of servitude rather than leadership, but he recognized important women in his circle and others. Phoebe was a deacon in a church at Cenchreae near Corinth, a powerful patron and supporter of others. The woman Junia was of note among apostles like Barnabas (not one of the twelve), a Christian before Paul was converted. Priscilla, along with her husband Aquila, taught Apollos a fuller understanding of the faith.

There is evidence from Jewish ins were leaders in Hellenistic synagogues and the money to serve in those capac woman like Lydia, a seller of purple in Christian congregation. The four pro have practiced their gifts in service martyrs could be quite influential. As over have experienced, various spi empower them to take positions of le dence that as the church developed the deacons as the primary levels of auth and at least one was a bishop. The M upon prophecy, had women leaders. I the second century formed part of th Christian communities were squeeze ence. The other important source of of some Christian male leaders for tak in ancient Greek writers like Aristot irrational. The depiction of the husb head of the family also encouraged t Christian groups

Most ethical codes from Christia widows and orphans. The insistence a recognition of their vulnerability w tures. Worship manuals include com They often spell out provisions for th bishop or presbyter and under the were not to be immediately enrolled church; they should be encouraged t free to do so. Gossiping and backbiti but frowned upon. How much th depended upon Graeco-Roman views

The earliest glimpse of Christians Jewish sect and thus shared some of t faced under Roman rule in Palestine words appeared to be threats to b Roman political power, he was cruci mark of shame. Jesus attacked some abandoning their faith and becom

common f enough fo rejected the the seas. Judas's bet troublemak appeared apostles w in various wall in ord

Althoug random pe empire's cit a religion. metropolit At the tur arrested by political po tian group eaten by li an opport became a Christ seek or should was stated did not wa were basic western Tu necessary.

One di insistent u Many Ron upon the and then b offer sacri treated in depended the Christi offer anim

The Epistle to Diognetus, written perhaps in the second century, argued that any threat from Christians to the state or to the society was quite minor. Christians neither lived in special sections of Greek and barbarian cities nor spoke their own dialect. They followed the customs where they lived, eating and dressing as others did. Their practices were not outwardly extraordinary (particularly not in any evil sense); in fact they displayed a character that was peaceful and stabilizing. They married and bore children but did not expose any of their young to deadly weather and starvation. Indeed they offered hospitality as well as protected their moral purity. They obeyed the laws but their lives surpassed the things required by law. Other early apologists, while rejecting the Jewish and Graeco-Roman religions as the writer of *The Epistle to Diognetus* did, also described Christians as basically benign or better – helpful to their communities. But at various times such Christian claims fell on deaf ears.

One reason Christians lived to become the established religion in the Roman Empire was that persecution was not pursued diligently across the whole empire. It came in waves and then receded. When it occurred, some Christians had to face it. A number in various areas met it head on, at times called to courage perhaps because they were not quick enough or powerful enough to escape. Irenaeus, a missionary in Gaul (France), knew of martyrs in Lyons. Eusebius, bishop of Caesarea in Palestine (Israel), wrote about their suffering.

At the beginning of the third century, after the emperor Septimus Severus had outlawed conversions, two North African Christian women, Perpetua and Felicitas, were killed. Later a basilica dedicated to them became one of the most important places of worship in Carthage. The famous bishop of that city, Cyprian (*c*.200–58), first fled but later submitted to *martyrdom*. Sermons on the martyrs and calls to martyrdom appear regularly in early Christian writings. Origen (*c.* 185–*c.* 251) escaped martyrdom in his home town, Alexandria, only because his mother hid his clothes when his father was arrested and slain. But as an older man in Caesarea, Palestine (Israel), Origen encouraged those waiting in various prisons to remain faithful even in death. He noted that the whole drama was played out before God and previous martyrs as well as Satan and his demons. Origen himself died after severe torture.

Wherever suppression was intense, a large proportion of Christians offered sacrifices and prayed to the pagan gods in order to stay alive. When oppression abated, many of those believers regretted their actions and sought to be readmitted to the churches. Bitter struggles erupted within the communities over whether such folks could return, first to membership and later to leadership. Was purity of life so necessary that forgiveness could not be invoked?

Not every Christian leader had to decide about taking a stand against Roman authority. Paul of Samosata, bishop of Antioch of Syria (Antakya, Turkey) about 260–8, was unseated by a council of bishops, not so much for his beliefs as for his practices. He had acquired wealth and influence as a Roman procurator. He went to the market with a bodyguard, put a high throne in the Christian basilica as his honored seat, and constructed a secret room in the sanctuary in which he and his cronies could decide what was best for the church. He questioned hymns sung in honor of Christ but had others composed that honored him. The council deposing him claimed that disciples of Christ did not act that way. But as legal status as a religion was granted and then establishment began, by custom and eventually by law under Theodosius, bishops regularly became political powers within and outside the church. Paul of Samosata's innovative reconfiguring of the architecture and furniture in the sanctuary became commonplace. The choosing of bishops who already had credentials in the Roman political system also became a more natural decision. Experience in wielding power seemed desirable for Christian leadership.

A CHRISTIAN CORE

Spirituality, evangelism and service have been central to Christian life since its beginning. The word 'spirituality' has a twenty-first-century flavor because it is used in so many contexts from religion to pop psychology. But it is dominant in determining the core of Christianity. The Latin aphorism 'lex orandi, lex credendi' generally proved true: people's prayer lives shaped how and what they believed. Jesus appropriated much of Jewish spirituality. He prayed to God, he worshipped in the synagogue, he studied the Hebrew scriptures. His model prayer, called the Lord's Prayer, became a frequent component of public Christian liturgy. The opening and closing sections of Paul's letters were marked both by praise to God for the Christians to whom the epistle was written and by specific prayers for persons in those communities. As far as we can tell, other apostles did much the same. Prayers offered and hymns sung were so closely intertwined as to be almost inseparable; furthermore some of the most significant phrases in the New Testament epistles about who

Jesus is are themselves hymns sung in the congregations. The apostle Paul deftly uses such a hymn in Philippians 2, a call to become like the Christ in his serving and self-emptying attitudes.

Christian community in this earliest period included the fervent *evangelism* that marked Christians as members of a missionary religion. Friends and acquaintances looked for occasions to talk with others about these deep convictions. Merchants and trades people traveled about and found opportunities to practice and speak about their faith. Professional missionaries appeared later. Seldom if ever did the earliest Christians who lived without political preference or establishment rely on political, economic or social coercion. Although their initial success was primarily among Jews, their persecutors were also Jewish authorities, like Saul (who became the apostle Paul). The horrifying later holocaust perpetrated by Christians when they had power, so much more destructive than any Jewish acts, does not take away this Jewish mistreatment of Christians. The Romans raised their own concerns for social stability such that martyrdom became a factor in Christian life. Even in death, disciples of Christ could tell the story of Jesus and urge others to join in communities who followed him.

Another significant feature of Christian groups was their passion for the poor and the sick. *Service* mattered. Each Christian lived in a subversive relationship to the larger communities in which they worked. The documents that form the New Testament, particularly the Gospels, revolve around deepening the life of faith by meditating on the highest values through proper care for the self and for others. Loving your neighbor as yourself in a lifetime of selfless service stood out.

Beginning in Galilee and Judaea (Israel), where Greek was already a language that stood alongside Aramaic on gravestones, Christians soon adopted the lingua franca of the Roman Mediterranean. To call their Jesus the Messiah made sense to Jews immersed in Hebrew, but even its *translation* into Greek as *Christos*, 'Christ', made little immediate sense to Hellenists. *Kurios*, 'Lord', was different. It not only appeared in the Septuagint Greek translation of the Hebrew Bible; it was also a word of exceptional honor used for the highest-ranking Graeco-Roman gods. Already by the time of the apostle Paul, theological reflections on who Jesus was and what his gospel meant were underway as the church collected stories and wrote hymns about him. This former Jewish apologist, an apostle well versed in both Jewish and Hellenistic practices and beliefs, further shaped the message for both Jews and Greeks. He and others attacked some Jewish views and leaders for their narrowness, but neither Paul nor Jesus hated Jews. Certainly one of the tragic losses Christians sustained in the early centuries was the demise of Jewish Christian communities. Jews had existed for centuries within Hellenistic culture. In the work of people like Philo (c. 20 BC to AD 50) they had found ways to make Jewish life more understandable to their Graeco-Roman neighbors. Philo used Greek philosophical and religious categories to explain ancient Jewish wisdom; his work was salvaged primarily by early Christians who found it helpful in their attempts to claim the good in Greek life and thought.

During this period Christian congregations developed their so-called 'traditional' and distinctive *teachings*. How to view Jesus presented a series of conundrums. Paul broke the great Jewish confession called the Shema – 'The Lord our God is one Lord' – into two pieces, one which referred to God the Father and one which referred to Jesus Christ. A daring division indeed. In the Gospel of John, Thomas calls Jesus both 'Lord' and 'God'. Hymns or hymn fragments elsewhere in the New Testament praise Christ with the highest names possible. Pliny the Younger (c. 61–112) noted that Christians sang hymns to Christ 'as to a god.' His investigations had uncovered that such a confession was a strong emphasis in their worship.

Yet there was always a sense that believers in Christ confessed only *one God*; talking about Jesus with such language struck some as odd or even threatening. Wasn't he primarily a human prophet and teacher? Didn't reference to him as God destroy monotheism?

From about 180 to 230 three significant Christian leaders spoke of a single *rule of faith* shared by most believers, one that dealt with some of these questions. Irenaeus (c. 115–c. 202), a native of Asia Minor (Turkey) who was a missionary in Gaul (France), Tertullian (fl. 200) of North Africa, and Origen (c. 185–c. 251) of Egypt and Palestine (Israel) took similar positions. God is *Father, Son and Holy Spirit*. The Father created heaven and earth; the Son assisted. The Son, incarnate as both God and man, was born of a virgin, died, was resurrected and ascended to heaven in order that people might be saved. The Spirit comforts and makes people holy who believe the good news of Christian faith.

The three leaders had different emphases. Irenaeus seemed most interested in expressing broader views within his succinct account of restoring humanity to God. Tertullian almost invented Latin words used to describe how Father, Son and Spirit were one God and how Jesus

Christ was both man and God. He used his legal training to argue the consistency of his views. Origen emphasized monotheism more strongly than the other two and expanded the statement of faith to fend off legalistic readers of scripture, to confront those who did not think that Jesus was really human and to attack determinists. Even the more philosophical Origen still depended deeply on biblical language and concepts. Thus by the early third century there was a cadre of Christian leaders who tried to arrange scriptural insights into small, compact statements whose meaning was rooted in Holy Writ and worship.

Confessional summaries like these, however, were not constructed within groups of believers who had none among them or near them who would disagree. As early as the first century there is evidence of dispute. Some Jewish Christians found Jesus remarkable but were unsure that he should be seen as God. Others not easily categorized found that his ability to appear in a room through a locked door meant that he did not have a human body. Such folk insisted that they were Christians.

Certain religious rites were quite important to most churches. One of these was *baptism*, at first an immersion in water for cleansing from sins. New Testament texts distinguish Christian baptism from various types of washing among Jews, such as in a sect like the Essenes and the baptism for repentance offered by the prophet John the Baptist. In the beginning, Christian communities offered baptism to new converts almost immediately after their profession of faith. But in the second century, when a majority of new believers were coming out of Graeco-Roman religious groups quite different from the Jews, church leaders set up a period of instruction for converts before their baptism. In Rome and in North Africa those to be baptized were taught for as long as three years and then examined on the night before Easter Sunday, the day celebrating Jesus' resurrection from the dead. Leaders prayed that the Holy Spirit would descend on the waters. The candidate undressed, renounced the Devil and his deeds, and was anointed with oil to drive away wicked spirits. Moving into the water, the person confessed the Trinity – Father, Son and Holy Spirit – and was immersed three times, once following each profession. Anointed with oil twice more, once as a sign of receiving the Holy Spirit, and given the kiss of peace, the new believer then participated in the Lord's Supper, the Eucharist, a sharing of bread and wine representing the broken body and shed blood of Christ. In Syria at least one difference had arisen: there was no anointing before the immersions.

Some variations were allowed. When water was too limited for immersion, pouring it on a person three times was sufficient. People too ill for immersion could be cared for in a similar manner on their sickbed, but immersion remained a common practice. Baptism of infants does not seem to have been frequent until the beginning of the third century, perhaps a bit earlier. Tertullian opposed it as a recent innovation, but Origen defended it as an apostolic practice. This act apparently reflected the desire of parents to have their children share in the blessings the Christian life offered in the rite. It is not likely that the parents viewed their babies as evil enough to need remission of their sins. Infants so often died that the protection provided by infant baptism must have been quite consoling. Inscriptions often record their baptism near their death. Yet during this period adult immersion remained the norm.

Those who administered the rite were usually bishops, singular heads of churches, but presbyters and deacons, those of lesser orders, could do so if selected by the bishop. In emergencies any man could baptize, but women were often forbidden to do so. Yet in Syria deaconesses offered assistance to women candidates for baptism, most likely because of issues concerning modesty.

In the third century, Cyprian, bishop of Carthage, and Stephen, bishop of Rome, argued over the validity of baptism performed by a heretic. Cyprian opposed it; Stephen said that the water and the confession of the Trinity overpowered any deficiency of the one administering the rite.

The *Eucharist*, the memorial to the death and resurrection of Christ celebrated by eating and drinking consecrated bread and wine, was also common in Christian communities. Jesus established such a supper himself. Paul warned that participating in the Eucharist haphazardly had brought sickness and death. The apostle knew of similar meals held in both Graeco-Roman and Jewish gatherings. The Jewish sabbath eve meals and the Passover feast provided close parallels to the Christian observance.

In the early second century, Pliny, the governor of Bithynia (northwest Turkey), tortured deaconesses, women leaders of the church, in order to find out the truth. He discovered that Christians met for what appeared to him to be a rather bland meal. In that same period, however, Ignatius of Antioch insisted on its importance by calling it 'the medicine of immortality'. By that time it had come to be called the 'Eucharist', a thanksgiving rite. Only Christians could participate although the bread and wine could be taken to those unable to attend the service. Bishops presided, offered a prayer of thanksgiving sometimes for both creation and redemption in Christ, while deacons handed out the elements. The *Apostolic Tradition* of Hippolytus (died *c.* 236) indicates that the custom in Rome had developed further. Deacons brought the bread and wine. The bishop led a dialogue with the people. Then he put his hands on the elements, offered a prayer that told a story of salvation similar to the narrative learned in the pre-baptismal teaching, then repeated Jesus' words of institution. He called for remembrance of Christ's death and resurrection, gave the bread and wine to the deacons and finally asked for the Holy Spirit to bring unity in the church.

According to the final scene in the Gospel of Matthew, Jesus commended his disciples to baptize in the name of the Father, the Son and the Holy Spirit. The Eucharistic prayer of the bishop centered the faith of the people on what God had done for them in Jesus Christ and was doing for them in the Holy Spirit. It renewed that sense of the faith. Confession of sin, however, was somewhat different although clearly linked to the confession of faith. By the time of Tertullian the North African churches had developed a practice of acknowledging their failings, asking for God's assistance and declaring their trust in God's mercy. During the third-century persecution under emperor Decius myriads of Christians renounced their faith in their God and sacrificed to the Graeco-Roman gods in order to avoid torture or death. Thus any penitential act looked to many like a godsend. Those deeply regretting their misdeeds could confess, be reconciled and received back into the church.

CONCLUSION

Christians emerged in Palestine (Israel) near the eastern edges of the Roman Empire that were also the western edges of Asia. The apostle Paul took the new religion west, perhaps even to Spain; the apostle Thomas may have taken it east to India. Only for a few decades were Christians totally a Western faith. Communities of the Way, as they were orginally called, were at first closely connected with Jews but at the end of this period they were surrounded by thousands of gods in the West and hundreds of thousands of gods in the East. Christians lived within strong religious pluralism.

The first generation of Christians moved into the Greek language and Hellenistic culture for the purpose of mission in the larger Graeco-

Roman world. Translation into the heart language of various peoples became a principle taken with them on their travels into countries outside the Roman Empire. Christian faith and practice fit into all cultures in some ways. Followers of Christ honored both families and the solitary life; they fought oppressions such as slavery, hunger and disease. Their message moved both rich and poor. Their communities struggled with all kinds of social ills. Seldom did they have recognition or support from governments.

As monotheists, they had to think hard about Jesus Christ as God. Hymns, rules of faith (small confessions), prayers and worship rites – all based in remembrances of his life, death and resurrection – led them to see him as divine. At the same time they saw in him various human aspects. As they wrote and collected their sacred scriptures, they also discussed the place of the Holy Spirit. At the end of this period they were moving toward Trinitarian belief.

2 PERSECUTED AND PERSECUTING, 300–630

Before the reign of Constantine (306–37) Christians had lived primarily either as a somewhat politically protected religion under the tent of recognized Jewish communities or as an illicit faith that could be attacked at any time for nearly any reason. The Diocletian persecution at the turn of the fourth century was different. Its intent was to exterminate Christians. Believers in the imperial court were driven out. Pagan priests said that they could not read the divine signs, such as the entrails of birds, because Christians were present. Diocletian had to know the will of the gods for his campaign in Persia, so he banished the Christians. He saw threats elsewhere. Some of his generals in Antioch and people from the same families who served on that city's council were Christians who resisted the emperor's religion. They were dangerous, in a position to wreck his staging area and keep supplies from reaching his armies during the war. So he sent them to imprisonment and death in Egypt. Once the persecution was underway, Christians in other regions felt the power of Caesar to reach into their communities and pluck out those who were recognized leaders only within the church as well as those who held positions within the state.

Constantine dramatically changed that, although the fuller attempts at establishment did not appear until the reign of Theodosius II (408–50). Constantine, while serving in the north-western sections of the Roman Empire, fought other generals to obtain rule. At the Milvian bridge, legend says that he saw a vision of the Christian cross, a sign from the Christian God that he would win the victory. Something of that nature may well have occurred because Christians in the western part of the empire were neither well enough positioned politically nor numerous enough for him to have supported their deity on those grounds.

When during his reign Christians at first were tolerated and then became members of a religion legally recognized throughout the empire, some of them were almost ecstatic. Eusebius of Caesarea (c. 260–c. 339) wrote a fawning treatise of praise in which he suggested that Constantine was the Christian bishop for those outside the faith. Anyone like Eusebius who had a long view of Christian history must have been overjoyed that the ever-looming possibility of persecution was lifted. But Constantine's support was always a mixed blessing. He continued to have members of his family killed when they emerged in his mind as threats. He attended worship services and considered himself a believer, but postponed his baptism – as many did – until his deathbed. His new capital in the east, Constantinople, still had a marked non-Christian presence. Even in 326 he underwrote the journey to Egypt of a leader in the Eleusinian mystery religion. For the empire to function properly, Constantine thought that pagans should also be supported.

The privileges and riches he lavished on Christians, however, were considerable. His mother, Helena, visited holy sites in Jerusalem and had imposing churches built there. Constantine provided the funds for the expensive task of copying Bibles. The new copies were sent to important churches. Legislation allowed Christians to recover property taken from them during persecutions; it also excused their leaders from various taxes and military service. Constantine, like other emperors before him, viewed religion as an important pillar of the state. He began to attend or call church councils early in his reign. The most imposing was the Council of Nicea (325), which he funded and attended in order to influence it. According to the emperor, Christians should not be distracted by doctrinal disputes that disunited them. The state needed their unity. Because of his limited vision and that of many participants, the council did not represent the full global character of the faith; a few representatives from the East attended, but Christians in places as near as Armenia (between the Black and Caspian Seas) did not appear in numbers because in so many ways this was an affair of the Roman Empire.

It is difficult to slight the importance of Constantine's recognition of Christians. Pagans continued to follow their ways of life and worship, but Catholic and Orthodox Christians lived for well over a thousand years in this climate of preference. Members of other religions, including the Jews, were opposed by the powers of the state. Saintly figures like the great Augustine (354–430) would soon debate whether Christians should invoke imperial troops to suppress their heretical opponents.

As members of the Roman Empire's preferred religion, however, Christians were perceived as a fifth column in countries east of the empire's boundaries. Many Persians were convinced that Persian Christians posed an internal political threat. Indeed, aspects of religious life in Europe became alien to Christians of the East, whether in Persia (Iran), India, on the Silk Road or in China. They had to survive in situations that offered little political favor and thus often developed deeper commitment. Persecution could be dreadful. Christians remained tiny minorities in those areas and at times seem to have been almost annihilated.

For nearly three hundred years followers of Christ had lived around the Mediterranean without such lavish financial and political privilege. And they had grown. Christians had moved north in Europe, particularly through the mission efforts of [W]ulfila (c. 311–c. 383). The child of a Cappadocian mother and a Gothic father, he was ordained by an Arian bishop for mission among the Goths who lived along the Danube. Driven out into Moesia (Bulgaria), he used Greek, Latin and Gothic runic characters to create a written Gothic language. He and his helpers translated much of scripture into Gothic but purposely left out the Old Testament books of Kings. In their view, it would have supported the ferocious warring life of the Goths.

Further east in Syria and Persia (Jordan, Syria, Iraq and Iran) Christians had made inroads, perhaps even banding together in small enclaves all along the Silk Road. But in those places they were surely few in number, perhaps such tiny groups that they attracted little attention from the authorities. They moved south into Ethiopia through the efforts of Frumentius and Aedesius, youths shipwrecked on a voyage along the Red Sea, who ended up serving in the palace of Ezana, the king of Aksum. Frumentius was allowed to travel back to Alexandria and was there consecrated as bishop by Athanasius (c. 300–73). He well may have been the person responsible for the conversion of Ezana.

Christians were becoming a Coptic-speaking community in Egypt. Athanasius was able to avoid some governmental attempts to send him into exile (others succeeded) by blending into the Coptic population. He wrote his famous treatises in Greek but probably spoke the indigenous language of his people. In both Egypt and Ethiopia Christians organized their assemblies around strong leadership. They translated scripture and other important church documents into their native tongues.

Led by traders and monks from Egypt, Christians had moved into Nubia (Sudan) by the fifth century. There they met some of the same pagan deities they had seen in Egypt. A famous temple of Isis located at Philae had a strong influence as a pilgrimage site until 540. Then it was closed without major opposition. The Ballana kings of this era evidently did not establish an official religion. Their allegiances were multiple. Although they practiced a form of human sacrifice that disgusted their neighbors, their tombs include luxurious items marked with Christian symbols like the cross. Their tolerance of different religions seems to have well served the spread of Christianity in the country. In the sixth century the Byzantine emperor Justinian organized a mission to Nubia that was more concerned with political alliances than religious conversion. He wanted to insure Byzantine rule in Egypt and enhance the promises he had made to Christian Ethiopia that he would provide troops from among the Nobatae (northern Nubians) and the Blemmyes, both well-known warrior peoples. Because religion served as an important pillar that supported political rule, he did send Christian missionaries. His wife, Theodora, saw to it that among those missionaries were Christians who believed that Christ had only one divine nature rather than exclusively those believers, whom Justinian preferred, who confessed that Jesus Christ had both divine and human natures. Justinian defamed the 'Monophysites' as heretics and supported the 'Dyphysites' as orthodox. But the crafty Theodora once more outflanked the interests of her husband. Her protégés, Julian and Longinus, arrived first and began the conversion of Nobatia (northern Nubia).

The fifth-century church historian, Sozomen, collected tales of Christians' movement into areas of Europe and the Middle East, often as slaves or captives in war, unnamed people whose moral lives and well-timed miracles led the rich and powerful to ask them for prayer and guidance.

It appears that a Christian slave girl, known later as St. Nina, who served in the royal house of Georgia was active in Georgia's conversion around 330. At first connected with the see of Antioch in Syria (Antakya, Turkey), Georgian Christians primarily held Chalcedonian views of Jesus (divine and human natures united in one person). They went through a period in the sixth century when they followed more Monophysite teachings about him (one divine nature controlling his person), as did the Christian community in neighboring Armenia. But during the seventh century Chalcedonian emphasis returned.

Sometimes more formal missionary efforts are known to us. In Armenia Gregory the Illuminator (*c.* 240–332), a member of the royal family, returned to his homeland after growing up in exile among Cappadocian Christians. With the conversion of King Tiridates (*c.* 238–314) Christians enjoyed the privileges of an official religion. Gregory was ordained as a metropolitan by the bishop of Caesarea in Cappadocia; his son, Aristakes, set to follow him, seems to have attended the Council of Nicaea in 325. However, the connection with Greek-speaking, particularly Cappadocian, Christians was broken in 374 when the Armenians declared their church to be independent. In 390 the country was divided into separate regions of Byzantine and Persian political control. The fifth-century reformation of the Armenian Bible, liturgy and church was based on Christian Syriac documents translated into Armenian. Armenians had no representative at the Council of Chalcedon in 451 and at the turn of the sixth century they rejected its findings. That decision most probably was reached because of the difficulties Christians in the Persian sector would have had with confessions and canon laws that were Byzantine. Although often tagged as professing a Monophysite Christology (one divine nature), Armenians never allied themselves with churches that officially took Monophysite positions.

To the west, Christians moved into the British Isles and were particularly strong in Ireland. Tribes in England and in northern continental Europe were evangelized in the sixth and seventh centuries as early waves of Irish Celtic missionaries roamed the earth for God.

After Thomas the apostle, Christian leaders from Syriac-speaking churches strengthened communities in India. In about 300 David, bishop of al Basra (Bassarah) in Persia (Iraq), resigned his position and went to India, where he had considerable success. The modern Indian church has a story of Thomas of Cana, a Syrian trader, who in 354 (the date is disputed) arrived with about four hundred people at Craganore, north of the modern Chochin, on the western coast of India. During 425 at Edessa in Syria (Iraq), Mar Komai and a colleague named Daniel the Indian were translating the apostle Paul's epistle to the Romans from Greek into Syriac. Around 470, Mana, bishop of Rew' Ardashir in Persia (Iran), sent to India copies of all the books he had translated from Greek into Syriac. Gregory of Tours (died 593/4), a leader in Gaul, spoke of a man named Theodore who visited an unnamed Christian center in India that had both a church and a monastery. The traveler and geographer Cosmas Indicopleustes (*c.* 547) knew of Christians in Taprobane, a land that is perhaps the present Sri Lanka or the eastern coast of India. The royal chronicle of Sri Lanka, a set of stone inscriptions very difficult to decipher, seems to know about Christians who served in the court from 471 to 508.

Christians also were traveling along the Silk Road all the way to China. The North African apologist Arnobius (died *c.* 327) mentions Christians among the Seres, the Chinese. We have no idea what his source was. Mar Sergis, an East Syrian leader, perhaps was the earliest named missionary to China. By 578 he had settled in Lint'ao, a center on the Silk Road about three hundred miles west of the Chinese capital, Chang'an (Xi'an). In 591 Byzantine mercenaries in northern Persia (Iran) captured Turkic soldiers who had crosses tattooed on their heads. Their explanation was that some of their people were Christians and the crosses had proved to be successful in warding off disease.

CHRISTIANS AND PEOPLE OF OTHER FAITHS

During this period Christians continued to have various types of relations with believers in other religions. Constantine's preferential treatment was not nearly as effective as some scholars have assumed. Constantine did put the Christian faith in place as an acknowledged religion of the empire. Belief in Christ as the savior of the world received growing emphasis, but the roots of other religions were deep and healthy. During his two-year reign the emperor Julian (died 363) showed some sympathy with Jews; at least they still made sacrifices to their god. But the 'Galileans', as he called Christians, stood against all other religions in believing that no more sacrifices were needed. Only an explosion at the site (probably gas seeping from underground set off by some spark) coupled with his early death kept him from having the Jerusalem temple rebuilt. Jews throughout the Roman Empire had sections in various cities where by law they pursued their way of life. They were a significant part of the population in both Alexandria and Rome. Excavations in the twentieth century discovered there was a thriving Jewish community at Sardis in Asia Minor (Turkey). Its leaders used both wealth and political power to make their presence known. They owned property well located in the city and during this period kept refurbishing or enlarging the synagogue on the site.

John Chrysostom (*c.* 347–407) is often viewed as one of the Christian leaders who most vehemently attacked the *Jews*. Any reader could select passages in his orations against Jews that are truly hair raising. But there are other factors that inform a historical reading of his works. Chrysostom lived in Antioch of Syria (Antakya, Turkey) when he wrote his most blistering rebuke of the Jews; that metropolis held a large and influential Jewish community. The Christian community in the fourth largest city of the ancient world received support from governmental establishment, but even Chrysostom and his church found Antiochene Jewry to be both strong and attractive to Christians. John raved against Christians who visited the Jewish synagogues at the time of various festivals. He was stung by the continuing conversion of some Christians to Jewish communities. Nothing excuses the fire in his utterances that later were used to enflame Christian hatred of Jews, but his position was not one in which an overwhelming Christian majority would do nearly anything to enforce its will on the helpless Jewish minority. It was the continued success of the Jews that so angered Chrysostom.

Not all Christian bishops were so scathing in their treatment of Jews. Aphrahat, a church official in Persia during the 330s and 340s, wrote twenty-three treatises in Syriac on theological topics. Some of them debate with a living or fictional Jew about his understanding of circumcision, the Passover, the sabbath and food laws, as well as the Messiah, the place of the gentiles, the teaching about virginity, and the Jewish expectation of being properly reunited. Although Aphrahat clearly knew Jewish traditions – he had strong contacts at least with Persian Jews – he showed no rancor toward them. His Christian faith is Semitic in form, dependent on neither Greek nor Latin categories.

During the mid fourth century, the emperor Julian (died 363) worked to dislodge if not destroy the favored position held by Christians. Raised within a Christian context in which important members of his family had been killed by other Christians, he secretly turned to the *Graeco-Roman* pagan way of life that some of his teachers espoused. When he came to power, he encouraged exiled Christian bishops, whose beliefs did not square with the orthodoxy of the time, to return to their cities. His clear intent was to disrupt the Christian faith he despised. He had simple laws passed that stressed religious toleration and allowed pagan worshippers to reclaim the stone slabs and columns that were parts of their temples. The result was that if the laws were enforced, Christian churches throughout the empire would be pulled down, for they had claimed those expensive building materials as free supplies for their houses of worship. When they had become the larger group with political power they had pulled down pagan temples as houses of false worship and used their stones to build churches.

A large group of Christian bishops were thrilled when Julian was killed in battle. Some of the tales of his death insist that a Christian in his own army was responsible, not the Persians. The vitriol of orations written against Julian is remarkable. Although these bishops could use their rhetorical talents in struggling with each other over questions of doctrine, nothing like the level of ridicule and rebuke marked those debates as it did their attacks on Julian. Gregory of Nazianzus (*c.* 329–90) wrote two such treatises, both brimming with bile. Ephraem the Syrian (*c.* 306–73) also found Julian appalling. The pagan emperor and his attempted revival of pagan communities were widely perceived as an enormous threat to Christian communities. They should not have suffered such fears. In Antioch, where Graeco-Roman religions had been so strong, Julian prepared his troops for battle with the Persians. He went expectantly to a scheduled major festival of Apollo only to find a single old priest ready to sacrifice a lone goose.

In the late fourth century in theological orations apparently focused on Christian disputes, Gregory of Nazianzus also mentioned pagan worshippers but treated them in a much milder manner. He warned that non-Christians would have difficulty understanding the begetting of the Son by the Father. They pictured the birth of gods through tales like those of Triptolemus, who brought forth lesser gods from his thigh and then gobbled them up when he thought they were a threat. But pagan cults made good sense when they kept much of their deepest teaching from the general public and taught it primarily to those already initiated into the community. Christians would do well to ease converts into the mysteries of the faith as those religions did. Gregory also found genuine piety among those worshipping the Graeco-Roman pantheon. Anyone who could pray all night in the cold and rain, as one pagan did, could teach Christians many things about contemplation. Indeed Gregory insisted that his father, a member of the Hypsistarii – an Iranian and Jewish religious mix in Gregory's eyes – had virtually belonged to the Christian church before his conversion. His deeds were exemplary. Some in the church did not live as disciples of Christ; some outside did what Jesus taught without knowing of him. What those apparent outsiders needed was the name disclosed in baptism. They were already inside, as evidenced by their actions.

The contact with other religions was more than just a battle to the death that Christians had already won. John Chrysostom noticed that pagan practices and myths still had power. His contemporary, Porphyry of Gaza in Palestine (Israel), indicated that his city contained only a small minority of Christians. Its greatest festivals were frequented by little groups of Jews and Christians but were dominated by large groups of pagan worshippers. Conditions at Mamre in Palestine seem to have been quite similar. Before the emergence of Christians, Jews had not subdued people who lived within the non-Jewish religions of those centers.

Neither did the outlawing of the ancient Graeco-Roman religious traditions in the law code of Theodosius II in 438 totally squash such worship. Laws are not written unless the lawbreakers are still active. Christian persecution of pagan believers put coercion into conversion, pressure in place of persuasion. Those who resisted were sometimes crucified in a symbolic retaliation for the treatment of Jesus that surely frightened others. But the enforcement of Theodosius's decrees varied locally. Some communities had large enough 'pagan' populations that they could quietly resist. Any close reading of Christian hagiography, the stories about Christian saints, up to at least the seventh century shows how often bishops and monks returned to the high places in order to stamp out the embers of pagan sacrificial fires and put the tops back on Christian sarcophagi. Using the building materials of pagan temples to construct churches on those sites, even employing the land as Christian cemeteries, did not stop the worship of other gods. At night their worshippers would come and reclaim their sacred space. Their celebrations fit the sociological euphemism of existing 'underground' but might be better said to be up high and under dark.

Manichaeans, who originally emerged from a Christian sect, thrived during this period. They described the world primarily in terms of an eternal dualistic conflict between good and evil, light and darkness. All of creation was a gloomy mixture of the two; indeed the god responsible for creation was an evil force. That basic belief led this religion to find much of the Old Testament depicting a different god from the one it worshipped. Manichaeans had difficulty with some aspects of the New Testament as well. A number of Christian theologians attacked this growing religion. Alexander of Lycopolis and Serapion of Thumius, two fourth-century Egyptian theologians, wrote against Mani and his teachings. Serapion did so with some skill. The *Acta Archelaus* is a fictional account, written in the fourth century, of the debate between Archelalus, a Mesopotamian bishop, and Mani himself. It circulated widely and provided information for many anti-Manichaean treatises. Titus of Bostra in the Roman province of Arabia (died 371) defended the justice of God against Mani's followers and attributed evil to human decision. God's providence would prevail because neither evil nor matter was eternal. Both the Old and the New Testaments were good and inspired by the Holy Spirit. He charged that Manichaeans had revised their texts of scripture to fit their needs. The incarnation of the Son, born of the Virgin Mary, provides evidence of the Devil's weakness. Diodore of Tarsus (died c. 390) wrote a large work against the Manichaeans, one devoted primarily to refuting their interpretations of Christian scripture. Ephraem the Syrian, a prominent writer of exquisite Syriac hymns, also wrote a treatise against four dangers: Mani, Marcion, Bardesanes, and the astrologers.

The major Western opponent of this Christian heresy that had become a world religion was Augustine in North Africa. One of the major foci of his work concerns this faith to which he had belonged for nine years. Manichaeans shared his distaste for scripture, both its flawed style and its contradictions. Their ascetic demands intrigued him and suggested a higher sense of virtue. They, like him, also enjoyed debate and insisted that the church had imposed its belief on people rather than encouraging each to join in the search for truth. But other influences eventually moved him away from his commitments to this religion. His mother, Monica, pleaded with him to leave the sect. A Manichaean friend converted to Christian faith, but he soon died. That death forced Augustine to ask many questions of both religions. Manichaean leaders suggested that Augustine wait until the great leader Faustus appeared to answer his queries.

By the time Faustus appeared, Augustine's questions were too deep to be turned aside even by this skilled debater. With his powerful intellect, Augustine set up a series of reasons why this deterministic syncretistic religion was false. The Manichaean religion was strong in his hometown, Carthage, and this gave him the opportunity to watch its members live out their faith. Over time he saw they were not morally superior. They posited perfection but offered no steadfast rules for life, only what struck him as absurd, contradictory advice. Augustine found the Manichaean doctrine of God to be illogical because the contradictions of good and evil powers did not allow for one consistent, supreme divinity. Other types of either/or problems arose. Was the soul both good and evil? Was the will marked also by that dual character? Augustine's study of Neoplatonic philosophers pointed out defects in Mani's teachings and opened him up to Christian faith during his contact with Ambrose (c 339–97) in Milan. There the brilliant preaching of the bishop, based on allegorical interpretations of the Old Testament, finally made sense of scripture for Augustine and took away the last sets of concerns that he had shared with the Manichaeans.

Other Christians worked diligently to refine their own identity over against different religious communities in their world. That tension led the *Syrian* bishop Philoxenus of Mabbug (*c.* 440–523) shockingly to tear out the symbols of the dove in his church. Such an image should remind believers of the Holy Spirit, as it did in Christian scripture at the baptism of Jesus. But Philoxenus insisted that when most Christians in Mabbug saw the dove in their church, they actually thought of the pagan sacred pool and its pigeons that were located near the basilica. Until they rejected those old pagan beliefs, no dove would be represented in his sanctuary. It was a blatant invasion of another religion into their worship.

In *China* one of the most important Christian figures appeared at the end of this period. Alopen, an East Syrian (Nestorian) missionary, reached the Chinese capital of Chang'an (Xi'an) in about 635. He carried with him Christian sacred books and was officially recognized by the emperor, who read translations of the texts and ordered that this religion of the Way (Tao) should be taught. The emperor had an officer of the government build a monastery to house twenty-one Syrian (Ta Ch'in) Christian monks in the capital and paint his imperial portrait on one monastery wall. A later inscription claimed that the emperor built many East Syrian monasteries in other cities and regions. That emperor, T'ai-tsung, had taken control in 626 by having his brother, the first son, killed and demanding that his father abdicate. The father, Kao-tsu, earlier in that year had begun a large-scale persecution of *Buddhists* and *Taoists* and increased privileges for *Confucians*. T'ai-tsung reversed that edict and tried to give equal attention to these three major religious influences then prominent in his realm. That policy of mutual toleration opened up opportunities for new religions from further west. It is also possible that the new emperor was himself an amateur scholar with interests in all kinds of learning. During 631 at least one other religion, named *Hsien* (Heaven-Spirit) – which appears to have been either a Manichaean or Zoroastrian sect from Persia – had made its way along the Silk Road and been welcomed.

Near the turn of the twentieth century, documents that perhaps include one of Alopen's 'sutras' (scriptures) were discovered in a Buddhist library at Dunhuang in north-western China. Buddhist temples there had been carved into a single large rock formation. These Chinese renderings of Christian texts are intriguing because they show that considerable effort went into putting Christian practice and faith into terms of Chinese life and thought. The *Jesus Messiah Sutra* has an opening section that praises much of Chinese social life in concepts that would have been supported by Buddhists, Confucians and Taoists. Christian scripture is called a 'sutra' – a Buddhist word for 'scripture'. Jesus is referred to as Buddha or a Buddha. The translation is somewhat mangled, with remarkable effect. First, it may represent the misunderstandings of a Syrian missionary-translator who still struggled with Chinese, a rather common problem for such initial projects in any language. Second, it renders certain words quite wrongly. For instance, the attempt to represent the word 'Messiah' phonetically results in calling Jesus the 'Remove-Rat-Confusing-Teacher'. Perhaps the text was prepared with the help of a Buddhist monk translator and was purposely sabotaged to make it ridiculous. Or third, it may be the sometimes bumbling attempt of a Christian who wishes to make his views palatable by injecting them into the language of Chinese Buddhists so that they can be taken seriously by that community. This third option is an intriguing one because that is most probably why the group of texts was kept in a Buddhist library: to a Buddhist monastic audience they seemed to be appropriate Buddhist texts for further study.

CHRISTIANS AND THEIR CULTURES

During this period Christians continued to adapt to a myriad of cultures. In terms of education within the standard systems of *Hellenistic* culture, Gregory Nazianzus (*c.* 329–90) from Cappadocia (central Turkey) had a rich mastery of Greek *paideia*, 'education'. He traveled to Caesarea in Palestine (Israel), then to Alexandria, and finally spent ten years in Athens absorbing the best of Greek learning. He wrote seventeen thousand verses of Greek poetry in styles taken directly from classical and Hellenistic forms. He was such a master of rhetoric, as evidenced in his orations, that later Byzantine rhetorical textbooks replaced quotations from the renowned ancient Greek figure Demosthenes with quotations from Gregory. Thus Byzantine education was thoroughly Greek as well as Christian.

Basil of Caesarea (330–79) in Cappadocia (central Turkey) like Gregory was educated in Athens and had also studied in Constantinople.

He used his position of wealth and privilege to do much for the church. Gregory of Nazianzus said that Basil's letters were better examples of great Greek literature than his own epistles. Yet Basil chafed under the weight of Greek education and never praised it as did his friend Gregory. Both of them, however, employed the examples and methods in Greek rhetoric that were used to persuade. Much of their debate even with Christian opponents of different views turned on the nature of logic and how people could be persuaded to change attitudes and actions.

Deep interest in all the subjects taught in their education led some of these leaders to positions that have become most interesting in our own day. Both Basil of Caesarea and Augustine defended a strong emphasis on God as the Creator of all. Their best views rejected any dualisms that depicted the world as totally evil and brought into being by a powerful depraved deity. They paid close attention to the science of their era as well as the various cosmological theories. In small but pregnant texts they pointed out ways in which creation was not yet completely finished. The good Christian God offered new creation to sinful people. Nature also provided evidence of *continuing creation*. One example was the little mudskipper that popped out of the ground in a spontaneous act of creation. We would certainly say on the basis of our twenty-first-century knowledge that their example was poorly chosen, but the point they wanted to illustrate is a telling one. Neither Basil nor Augustine taught that God had fully finished creation long ago and was doing nothing of that sort in their time. Had some kind of scientific evolutionary theory been available, they had already provided the theological framework for working with it rather than totally denying it.

John Philoponos (died 570s), a Christian who wrote commentaries on parts of Aristotle's corpus, has often been buried in specialized studies of developments in Christological thought after the Council of Chalcedon (451). He found the formula of one person in two natures unwieldy and even suggested that tritheists might have a better view than Trinitarians. But he is most important for the ways in which his views on *science* were appropriated by Renaissance figures like Galileo and were reintroduced into twentieth-century discussion of the relationship between science and the Christian religion by Thomas Torrance. Philoponos's attempts to understand the intricacies of Christology led him to analogies that suggested the 'complementarity' that only twentieth-century physics could make clear. The science he knew was not capable of following the leads about explaining all reality that he had seen in the person and the natures of Jesus Christ. He had a strong doctrine of creation and thus was one of the first commentators to attack Aristotle's positions favoring the eternity of the earth and of time. For Philoponos neither the existence of the earth nor time were absolute; both were created things that did not exist before God made them and only continued to exist at God's pleasure.

The major principle of Christian *translation* of scripture into the vernacular, the heart language of each culture, was again damaged in this era, particularly among the tribes of Arabia. At the end of this period Muhammad was acquainted with Christians; evidently some of their ancestors had lived in Arabia centuries before his birth. But once more, as with the Punic peoples of North Africa, we have no knowledge of Arab Christians translating their sacred books into Arabic before the seventh-century Muslim conquest. Membership in a Christian Arab community probably involved the use of Syriac in order to understand scripture. The nonchalance about contextualization in the local culture may be treated more graciously by remembering that the oral retelling of stories was basic to Arab culture. Such nonchalance, however, is still inexcusable. Muhammad and his followers did not make that mistake. The prophet's stories and principles were written down in Arabic and were well adapted to the culture in which he lived. There is no certainty that Arabs would have heard the gospel of Jesus in their own tongue more clearly and more forcefully than they heard the story of Allah. But Christian Arabs would have been better equipped to make their case. Other regions found the translation of the Bible into their vernacular to be a necessity. Armenian, Coptic, Georgian, Gothic, Latin and Syriac versions appeared early on and were in wide circulation by the end of this era.

In an interesting contrast with much of the Graeco-Roman society in which Christians lived, many Christian *women* thrived. Apparently the ratios between men and women were reversed, more women in Christian groups, more men in the Graeco-Roman communities of worship. One reason may have been the welcome offered to women in Christian communities, but perhaps a deeper cause was the Christian abhorrence of abortion. Usually referred to as 'infanticide', it was nearly always considered murder. Wives not under the threat of such medicinal or clumsy surgical intrusions might expect healthier lives. Yet bearing too many children in some cases surely threatened their health. This status of women itself led to the growth of Christian congregations, both through the birth of children and through the attraction of pagan men to Christian young women.

One of the Roman institutions that Christians adapted was official *councils*. They used that social forum to decide issues of life and faith. Local councils like the one in Jerusalem in the first century had met to settle whether gentiles had to become Jewish. The regional council in the second century discussed Montanist prophecy and practice. But it was not until the fourth and fifth centuries that large councils of Christian leaders assembled. They sought to determine what proper confessions and virtues were. Ecumenical councils, called with imperial power and support, had to wait for Constantine's acceptance of Christian faith.

Constantine was the first Roman emperor to lend his support to the building of massive Christian churches. Preferment and growth meant that remarkable *edifices* appeared throughout the empire. At some places in the eastern Mediterranean Christians had become numerous and wealthy enough to have constructed such edifices before Constantine stepped in. Both Jerusalem and Antioch had metropolitan churches that only later were replaced by larger structures. Although many of the new buildings followed a basilica form, as one can see in the restored structure at modern Trier, various designs were adopted. A cruciform ground plan became a favorite one, but octagonal forms also existed. Numerous ruins, reflecting those blueprints and some others, can still be viewed today.

Because most of the earliest churches in Ireland and those places touched by roaming Irish monks in northern Europe were built of wood, they have long since disappeared. Occasionally, however, stone foundations and graveyards are found that indicate Christian worship and burial customs were changing the culture of those regions. In Great Britain, graves were eventually dug east–west so that on the day of resurrection the person would rise from the west and face east toward the coming of the Lord. This was a new arrangement for burial.

By the fourth century the niches in the catacombs and their decoration had become more elaborate. Being interred in the catacombs became a link with previous saints and martyrs, not primarily the only available and affordable resting place for those whose singular legal status was as a burial society.

During this period Christian *art and architecture* flourished. The emperor Justinian planned the most imposing *church building* yet erected, the Hagia Sophia in Constantinople. Because it still stands today as a Muslim museum in Istanbul, it need not be described from contemporary reports only. The structure is impressive, both for the height of its dome and the size of the enclosure. The Muslims conquerors did not destroy all the beautiful mosaics that depict not only Jesus Christ but also a series of Christian leaders including the emperor and his wife. Twenty-first-century Muslims keep them in good repair.

Sacred enclosed space and pictures of important biblical scenes had an effect on the Christians of this period. As they became more powerful, they built the best structures in various cities. In the first half of the fourth century they took over temple sites within the cities proper and shrines erected on the high places.

The use of non-Christian temples and sacred space, worked out in the fourth and fifth centuries especially in the eastern Mediterranean, became a principle of missionary expansion under Pope Gregory the Great (c. 540–604). He instructed those working in northern Europe and particularly in Great Britain to remove the altars from pagan temples but to keep and repair the temples themselves. The temples were on carefully selected sites and were viewed by the indigenous people as places of power. Thus to move Christian services and artifacts into them not only demonstrated the victorious strength of Christ but also honored parts of the indigenous culture that posed no danger. Burial traditions might change, but the buildings themselves needed merely to be renovated.

Christian *art* flourished. The mosaics in one church at Ravenna, Italy are spectacular in both the quality of the pieces and the design of the whole. One of its depictions of Jesus represents him as a clean-shaven youth rather than a bearded young man.

Mosaics and frescoes of Jesus from this period have at times been interpreted as employing the features of Roman authorities, particularly emperors, to indicate his lordship. That might be an illustration of how much some upper class Christians wanted to claim the place of being the one legally established religion. Their Lord deserved the trappings of an emperor. More careful study of those representations, however, has shown that in an overwhelming number of cases Jesus is depicted as a great healer. That suggests a different explanation. Even wealthy Christians with access to the best artists and artisans preferred to see Jesus as one who saved them from disease and physical ailments and for heaven rather than as a worthy competitor alongside a Roman emperor. They adapted figures of healers instead of those of political authorities.

Pilgrimage to the Holy Land is documented as early as the late second century, when Melito of Sardis journeyed there to check out what scriptural books were used in the synagogues of Palestine (Israel). We have the diary of a traveler from Gaul written in about 333 and the *Pilgrimage of Egeria* from about 400. Egeria's journal also gives us remarkable information about the way in which Christians worshipped in Jerusalem. These volumes not only make us aware of the deep piety behind a trip to the Holy Land, but also the emergence of institutions that developed around pilgrimage. Sites mentioned in the Gospels were identified from local memory and for local economic gain. Special buildings were erected and statuary was made; other monuments were constructed so that the pilgrim could sense the presence of the Savior. Gregory of Nyssa in the fourth century found the plethora of remembrances beyond his taste, indeed a sham that often led Christians astray. His judgment may be too harsh, but his writing does give evidence of how much money moved into Palestine (Israel) from Western Europe with pilgrims.

During the persecution under Diocletian at the beginning of the fourth century we hear of prominent Christians at Antioch in Syria (Antakya, Turkey) who served as army generals. In the fifth century Augustine of Hippo in North Africa spelled out the arguments for a *just war* theory, not to obliterate armed conflict, but to keep battles within justifiable bounds. At the end of this period we must recognize a continuum in which some Christians were pacifists and some were willing to fight in armies for rather ill-defined goals.

One of the most interesting *social institutions* developed by Christians was *monasticism* with its deepened senses of isolation and community. It appeared during the early fourth century in both Egypt and Syria, perhaps first in towns or on their outskirts and later further back in deserts and other sparsely populated places. The rise of monasticism doubtless had some connection with the increasing puritanical sense that the lives of ordinary Christians did not meet the standards set by Christ. It was both contextual and counter-cultural. Some have emphasized its world-denying characteristics and its flight from urban to desolate locations. No doubt certain people who found the daily interruptions of ordinary life too much to bear joined monasteries and convents. They sought to create the time needed for prayer and contemplation of scripture. Much literature about the desert fathers, including Anthony of Egypt, emphasizes both the 'detached' existence and the shifting orthodoxy of their faith.

Yet that picture is distorted in several ways. First, many of the earliest monastic heroes could not find places far enough away from the populace to keep from being followed. Some sealed themselves up in small caves, or in the warmer climates took to mounting pillars. But people enthralled with their holiness went to them, provided them with food and removed their excrement. Some of the pillar saints like Symeon (*c.* 390–459) and Symeon the Younger (died *c.* 596), each located not far from the metropolis of Antioch, came near death in cold weather only to be pulled down from their pillars and protected from the elements. Their bodies at times had the dirt scraped away, mixed with wax and sold as amulets. Their influence was remarkable. Symeon the Elder stopped a Byzantine emperor's march to punish a city that had embarrassed him by knocking down his statues. The emperor not only gave up his plan of bloodthirsty revenge but also went to the pillar in sackcloth and ashes asking for forgiveness. Monastic holy men held recognizable power.

Monks soon found that living in structures near each other, either sharing an occasional meal and worship or organizing themselves into strictly disciplined life together, offered assistance to the committed ascetic. Nuns agreed. These monastic communities grew up in many places and formed bases for strengthening the life of ordinary Christians and others. Shenoute (died *c.* 450) of the White Monastery in Atripe, in southern Egypt, chose an isolated location. But the roving attacks of the Blemmyes west of the Nile forced a considerable number of farm refugees toward his location on the other side. Because his monastery had developed solid farming techniques, they were able to save those in desperate flight and teach them ways of raising crops that would profit them when the danger had passed.

In the fourth century Basil of Caesarea in Cappadocia (Kayseri, Turkey) became fascinated by the stories of monks in Egypt, Palestine (Israel), and Syria. He left his academic studies in Athens and visited numerous sites, perhaps some also in modern Iraq and Iran, then made his way back to his homeland. As bishop of Caesarea, he eventually erected a group of Christian *buildings* outside the Roman city on land owned by his family. These included a bishop's residence, a church, a place to house a monastic community, and a small hospice. This last feature at first provided lodging for visiting pilgrims on their way to the Holy Land. But its shelter and food were soon shared by the hungry.

It later offered care for lepers too. So it must have been large enough for some kind of partitioning. During a miserable famine in the 370s, the hospice took in the starving, thousands of them. The emperor Valens, who was no friend of Basil, evidently helped fund some of the provisions; wealthy families in the area also assisted. This compound of church buildings proved to be so central to the life of the city that by the sixth century old Roman Caesarea had fallen into ruin. The new city was built around Basil's center.

Tales such as these stand against any sense that monasticism was always a flight from life. In the conversion of Ireland and northern Europe, monks usually led the way. They would set up their communities among people who at that time had no cities at all but lived in villages defined by membership in clans. Near the end of the period Celtic monasticism was spurned by Latin missionaries connected to the papacy in Rome and other monastic centers, particularly in France. But monastic communities became the backbone of evangelistic work in those areas and remained the stable centers for Christian groups throughout the Middle East. John Moschus (*c. 550–619*) in his book *The Meadow* tells the stories of two monks making their way from Jerusalem north into what is now eastern Turkey. There they were befriended, fed and housed in various monasteries that provided a degree of stability in the region. Monasteries often became either by plan or necessity the backbone of Christian community in various areas of the world, all the way from the British Isles and their Celtic communities to China with its East Syrian (Nestorian) monasteries.

This period saw occasional mixed monasteries, *women* and men living in the same larger compounds with inner partitions. But often the men lived in monasteries and the women in convents. Macrina the Younger (*c. 327–79/80*), the sister of Basil of Caesarea, led a small group of nuns in Pontus (north central Turkey), where her family had property. Some of her followers were women who had been orphaned or made destitute. Her convent cared for such outcasts. But others of higher station seem to have also been a part of her work.

Olympias (*c. 365–410*), a deaconess in Constantinople, refused remarriage as the law implied and placed the equivalent of fifty million of today's U.S. dollars at the disposal of the church. After the gift she was still wealthy. Women of similar means were behind Jerome's fifth-century monastic efforts just outside Jerusalem. Some of these early feminists saw no merit in being under yet another husband and chose a life of Christian celibacy. Their wealth was used to build and endow monasteries and convents as well as fund church programs. The life of asceticism thus provided a small but freeing escape from upper class family life where bearing children and managing the household were still formidable tasks.

Christians' relationships to *political power* betray some of their most dangerous attitudes. Legal preference and establishment brought in its own evils. Christians in power soon lost the memory of injustice that their persecution had entailed. Having had relatively little experience in dealing with political privilege, they too often showed themselves to be ruthless.

The 325 *Council* of Nicaea, called to decide the main outline of the faith, was in important ways Constantine's child. He provided travel and housed the bishops while they were there. He moved in and out of the chambers where they deliberated and exerted his considerable influence. Although he himself knew little about practice or doctrine, he meddled. A model was created that gave political power a strong advantage in theological, conciliar decisions. It encouraged councils to consider themselves as ecumenical and worldwide rather than regional as they had been in the past – even though numerous Christian communities were not represented at Nicaea, particularly those not under Roman rule. Five of the great ecumenical councils, designated as seven by the Eastern Orthodox, occurred in this period. Nicaea (325), Constantinople (381), Ephesus (431), Chalcedon (451) and Constantinople (553) enacted the decisions primarily of Greek and Latin Christian communities. Churches east of Antioch in Armenia, Georgia, Persia, India and on the Silk Road were not part of the Roman Empire and thus did not receive governmental funding for their participation. Occasionally a representative from the East seems to have gotten through, like the enigmatic John of Persia and a representative from Armenia, but not often.

Persecution, although coming in waves followed by still waters, had kept much of the dissension among different Christian groups at bay. Believers normally had a greater enemy outside. Christians had previously followed some different practices and held a variety of doctrines, but they did not have the political clout to imprison or annihilate their opponents. With political power came the possibility of enforcing the will of the established on the dissenting. Fanatic Christians killed Hypatia (in 415), a philosopher in Alexandria, and had a hand in burning the grand library there. Raving monks from the deserts of Egypt sometimes were brought to councils, particularly the Robber Synod at Ephesus in 449, where they beat and killed opponents.

Bishops found that they could appeal to political forces to compel acceptance of their views. By the fourth century a number of them came from families of wealth and influence; as young men they had been educated for lives of political service in the Roman bureaucracy. They were accustomed to position and power. Their riches at times were devoted to the erection of new church buildings and care for the poor. The concept of servant leadership, however, was foreign to much of their experience.

Preference in the Roman Empire had other consequences. The church in Persia (Iran) had not found it easy to live in a country where Zoroastrians formed the established religion, but it had still grown. When Persian political leaders saw that Christianity was the strongest religion of the Roman Empire, Persian Christians became internal threats. Surely they were traitors. They dressed similarly to their Persian neighbors and followed many of their customs. They spoke the native tongue, but they clearly had other contacts and loyalties. The tortures that had led to martyrdom in the Western Empire were vicious, but the Syriac texts that describe the persecutions in Persia still make one squirm. Burned with heated iron, carefully flayed alive, crushed by elephants, the martyrs' witness there was especially impressive. Commitment to Christ left many people lame if not dead.

The legal and for that matter economic establishment of Christians gave them powers neither covered by their New Testament nor encouraged by their Christ. The line was crossed between persuasion and coercion. It was a serious misstep that would lead not only to crusade and inquisition but also to gunboat mission. Relief from persecution is pleasant, but establishment kills the memory of martyrs' pain and faith. Eventually their stories seem quaint and unnecessary.

Leaders from upper class society did not always live out of their born superiority. The finest pope of this era, Gregory the Great, had received a rigorous Roman education that prepared him for civil service. He became prefect of Rome in 573 but by 575 he had resigned those duties to found a Benedictine monastery in his own home. For over six years starting in 579 he acted as the papal representative to the Eastern court in Constantinople. Later as pope, he signed his letters 'Your servant', and meant it. These experiences that offered him wisdom and cross-cultural experience help explain his view of missionary activity in Britain among the Anglo-Saxons. He sent about forty Benedictine monks from his monastery in Rome to evangelize Kent. King Ethelbert had married a Christian from Gaul, Bertha, and agreed to her wish for Christian missionaries.

Pope Gregory's admonition to these monks clearly outlines what would now be called 'contextualization'. He urged the Benedictines to remove idols from Anglo-Saxon temples but not to destroy the buildings themselves. When the people wanted to continue festivals that included slaughtering oxen for the gods, he encouraged them to kill the beasts, eat their flesh and give thanks to the only true God. Allowing such 'outward joys' would be more likely to lead them to true 'inner joy'. Pagan abuses would surely continue, but the missionaries should remember that climbing a mountain requires small, slow steps. That surely represents advice to be heeded in any era.

A CHRISTIAN CORE

Christians in this period demonstrated forcefully that spirituality and service were the heart of their life together. They were the engines of evangelism and the power behind pastoral care.

Prayer continued to be basic to all Christian life, but particularly important in monastic communities. Humble prostration before God, begging for release from the consequences of sin, and empowerment for daily tasks can be found nearly everywhere that mature Christians assembled.

Perhaps the most significant meditations on the mystical life from this period carry the name of Dionysius the Aeropagite, the name of a man the apostle Paul converted in Athens. The writer, probably a Syrian in the late fifth or early sixth century, found ways to take particularly the mysticism from Gregory of Nyssa (331/40 to *c*. 395) and deepen the synthesis of Neoplatonism's sense of the soul's ascent to God with Christian passion for the same questions. Pseudo-Dionysius' writings range across a wide spectrum. His discussion of God's nature and characteristics absolved God from being the source of evil by denying the ultimate reality of evil. God's emanations could be found in church leaders and the sacraments. Indeed meditation would improve the lives of lay folk. Any soul might ascend to God if contemplation and prayer were pursued to the point of numbing the senses and advancing beyond worldly reason. Those two could transport anyone to ecstatic experience of God, even union and deification. In this world it was possible to participate in the life of the Trinity. This vision of the soul's ultimate journey was so powerful that the genuineness of the pieces as words from the apostolic era was not significantly questioned until the nineteenth century.

Liturgies were formalized with care. In the eastern Mediterranean, Basil of Caesarea organized a liturgical service that continues even today in Eastern Orthodoxy on specific Sundays. In the West at the end of the period, Pope Gregory the Great reformed the common liturgy not least on the basis of his Benedictine monastic experience.

Various important theologians wrote on the character of priests and *pastoral care*. Gregory of Nazianzus (*c.* 329–90), in apologizing for his flight from forced ordination and service as an assistant to his father the bishop, set out a sense of what priests should be in terms of both spirituality and service. 'The scope of [their] art is to give wings to the soul.' In other orations he insisted that the task also included feeding, clothing and sheltering the poor and taking care of lepers. His was such a successful description that both John Chrysostom (*c.* 347–407) and Gregory the Great (*c.* 540–604) employed it for their own meditations on what ministry entailed. Humility in the face of care for the soul, a life of deep prayer and meditation, and openness to the needs of all those in the congregation are deftly handled by all three writers.

Monks became defenders of their sense of orthodoxy. Athanasius (*c.* 300–73) wrote a life of Anthony (*c.* 251–356) that gives us a glimpse of monasticism in the late third century. During his twenties, Anthony put his sister in a convent and entered the monastic life because scriptural texts read aloud in worship – in Coptic, since he knew no Greek – seemed to call him to deeper commitment. When he decided to go away from the villages further into the desert, he passed monks who were still in the towns but on their edges. Anthony found no peace in being totally away from others as a hermit. He had on occasion to withdraw but at other times he served almost as a spiritual director or guide for anyone who came to him. He depended upon others for food and thus had some contact with the outside even in his periods of isolation. Athanasius insisted that Anthony was a stalwart defender of Nicene orthodoxy against the Arians, but it is far more likely that this simple Coptic figure should be noted for his meditative experiences and his intermittent but close care for others.

This period gives witness to the flowering of monastic life. The variety was extensive. The Nag Hammadi community in upper Egypt is the site of the remarkable library of fifty-one volumes in Coptic of mostly unvarnished Gnostic speculations. One good guess about why they were put in a jar and buried in a cave some distance from the monastery is that someone in authority would have destroyed them.

These texts offer insight not only into second- and third-century Gnosticism but also into fourth-century Coptic monasticism.

Pachomius (c. 292–346) in Egypt seems to have been the leader who organized monks into communities of prayer and work. He was at first a hermit, but a vision told him to build a monastery where he was gathering wood. By his death he oversaw nine monasteries and two nunneries with about three thousand people. Hilarion (c. 291–371) of Gaza in Palestine (Israel) wanted to follow in Anthony's footsteps. When he returned from Egypt to his home he lived the solitary life for twenty-two years before he agreed to found with others a desert monastery. Jerome (c. 347–419/20) began monasteries in Bethlehem supported by upper class Roman widows and virgins. Convents there were led by women like Paula and Melania the Elder.

Probably the most interesting theological work done among monks is that of John Cassian (c. 365–c. 433), who after more than a decade in Palestine (Israel) and Egypt set up a monastery in Marseilles. He and a circle of acquaintances around him called monks to a disciplined life. They spelled out an understanding of Christian faith that emphasized grace but also insisted that a modicum of human free will was necessary for salvation and growth in virtue. Western councils, particularly the Second Council of Orange in 512, found any emphasis on an unbound will, that might respond to grace without first being empowered by it, to be subtle heresy. Augustine of Hippo (354–430), a monastic theologian/bishop, insisted that human will was totally enslaved. The Synod of Orange followed his lead, while Eastern Orthodoxy continued on a path made clear by John Chrysostom (c. 347–407), bishop of Constantinople and one of Cassian's teachers.

What are often considered to be the central tenets of Christian faith emerged in classical shape during this period. The *doctrines* of Trinity and Christology were developed both within unified worshipping congregations and within conflict with those perceived to be heretics. The queries were basic: Could God be both one and three? Was Jesus divine, human or both? Theologians of this era explicitly incorporated various Hellenistic philosophical positions that offered analogues for, though certainly not full explanations of, these mysteries.

From the beginning Christians believed in *one God*. Their home community, the Jews, fought the worship of any other god. Yet the appearance of Jesus in all his healing power and perceived wisdom led to confessions that he himself was God, statements ensconced in Holy Writ and daily worship.

The famous council at Nicaea in 325 worked to settle the *Trinitarian* controversies by operating within the older rules of faith found throughout the Mediterranean during the second and third centuries. The arguments inside the Christian community, however, had moved toward positions that apparently could not be resolved on the basis of scriptural quotations and depth of worship alone. All sides believed that there was only one God, but Arius (*c.* 260–336) and his followers worried that the clear subordination of the Son of God to the Father might be abandoned. Certain eastern Mediterranean church leaders including Origen (*c.* 185–*c.* 251) had developed some misgivings about overemphasizing Jesus. Origen could speak of Jesus as God but he did not want the Son's second place in comparison with God the Father to be forgotten. In his *Treatise on Prayer* he warned Christians not to offer prayer in Jesus' name, but he did so himself in other writings.

Both early and later Arians found a phrase in the biblical book of Colossians to be important: *Jesus Christ* was 'the first born of all creation'. He was not made as all other created things, but he was made before time began and then assisted the Father God in the tasks of 'creation'. The Son did not always exist; he was 'first born'. The only way to protect the singular place of God the Father was to demand that the Son be lesser in at least some significant respects.

The supporters of Nicaea found one of their banners, that in Jesus Christ 'the fullness of the Godhead dwelt bodily', in that same scriptural book, Colossians. How could anyone deny that Jesus Christ was fully God if scripture said that he was? Phrases used together in the first century by the writer of Colossians now were split apart to ground quite different positions. Each party marshaled biblical verses that supported its doctrines.

The majority of the bishops at Nicaea thus found it necessary to employ Hellenistic philosophical language in order to make certain that those they viewed as 'heretics' could not wiggle away. *Homoousios*, a Greek word that meant 'of the same nature or essence', was injected into the creed. It frustrated any attempt to say that the Son of God was indeed similar to the Father but that he did not share the Father's nature.

The emperor Constantine thought he needed a united religion to support his reign, but after his death these doctrinal battles raged on for at least fifty years. Each of the following emperors withdrew support from some Christian party, extended privileges to another, and tried to force those in disfavor into submission. Churches were closed, bishops banished, religious life generally disrupted. Only the emperor Julian developed a different policy. In order to clear the way for his revival of Hellenistic polytheistic communities, he withheld imperial favor from all Christian parties and brought back all exiled Christian leaders in the hope that their hatred of each other would mortally wound their communities.

When the Council of Constantinople met to talk about these issues in 381, its participants agreed that Nicene Trinitarian faith was central to Christian belief. Various theological issues were discussed, but the main proposals insisted that Jesus Christ was both divine and human and that Christ's divinity was the same as that of the Father. The Neo-Arian philosophical theologians, who strongly opposed Nicene views, had created remarkably subtle positions. In their defense of belief in one God, they taught that Jesus was indeed 'the first born of creation' but not a created being like other humans. His was a secondary divinity, but he surely was a divinity. Aetius (c. 300–70) and Eunomius (c. 325–c. 395), the best known of these theologians, insisted that time was not involved in any question of when the Son came into existence. Furthermore, they adopted a view of language from Plato that words stood for real things, indeed that the proper words participated in the nature of the thing represented. Thus if scripture calls the Son 'the only begotten' and various Christian theologians as well as philosophers from other communities have named the one high god 'unbegotten', then the Son and the Father must be of different natures. 'Begotten' and 'unbegotten' are clearly contradictories. Aetius, a clever logician, wrote out lists of syllogisms centered on conundrums or logical contradictions that had to be cleared up. Eunomius, his secretary, was a remarkable preacher and teacher who popularized their views and also wrote scholarly treatises arguing their case.

Alongside these teachers stood congregations of Christians who at times had developed more compassionate understanding of their views and those of their opponents. Arian scholia on scripture, little comments in the margins of Bible manuscripts, show that the common Arian worshippers could readily confess the 'passion of the impassible', the suffering of God, as a hymnic phrase. Talk in Greek philosophical theology of the high god who had to be totally impassible might be logically weighty. But for these folks holy scripture insisted that God the Father grieved over his sinful people. Thus a suffering Christ need not be only human.

These churches apparently also had a different kind of *worship*. Fifth-century church historians notice that in some Arian congregations baptism had become a single immersion in the name of Jesus Christ. The Nicene churches had for decades baptized their converts three times in the name of the Father, the Son and the Holy Spirit. According to many Nicene theologians that baptismal practice was the rock on which their Trinitarian confession of faith stood. Surely, they said, no one was baptized into a secondary or a tertiary god. Threefold baptism demonstrated the same divine nature of Father, Son and Spirit.

One of the important proponents of Nicene theology, Gregory of Nazianzus, took on groups of popular believers and learned theologians. He pointed out that Aristotle had a better sense of language than Plato. Words relate to the things they represent by human convention, not by an essential connection. It is hard to tell whether the word 'dog' by itself or the word 'dog' in 'dogfish' has a corner on the essence of 'dog'. He warned that speaking of the high God, the Father, primarily in terms of his being 'unbegotten' created the rather stilted situation of making a negative the main descriptive term. There were positive words used in Holy Writ to describe the Father and the Son. That must be true even though Christians are most often faced with how little in this world they can ever know about God. Such ignorance should not frighten them; when they look at the whole of nature outside them and the intricacy of the human nature inside them, they are continually reminded of how little they know with certainty about anything, let alone God.

Both Basil of Caesarea (330–79) and Gregory of Nyssa wrote extensive treatises against Eunomius that called his views of God and Christ into question. Friends of Gregory of Nazianzus, they successfully refuted the later Arian claims. Gregory of Nyssa employed Greek medical and philosophical learning for the task, thereby indicating how much Christianized Hellenistic views had become a part of Christian faith.

But all three of these Cappadocians argued on a more popular level as well. Gregory of Nazianzus insisted that their position was the strongest because it could account for more scripture than the later Arian positions. By referring some biblical statements to the divine Son and some to the human Jesus, hundreds of biblical passages related to Jesus Christ could be included. The Arians tended to attribute the more human statements to the divine Son in order to show that his divinity was of a secondary nature, unlike the Father's. Then they treated the statements about the Son's full divinity as filled with homonyms, words that had the same sound but a different meaning. In truth, they did not take these latter passages seriously. The Cappadocians also warned that later Arian theologians claimed too much knowledge of God's nature while they personally lacked spiritual maturity and humility.

Although fought out in the arena of educated gentlemen, the vitriolic language and the assassination of character from both sides was shameful. The high-born Cappadocians insisted that low-born goldsmiths and craftsmen like Aetius and Eunomius could not be proper leaders. The logically clever Aetius and Eunomius insisted that the great orthodox leaders were bumbling figures, incapable of understanding hard intellectual puzzles.

These intricate points will appear to many twenty-first-century readers like angels-on-the-head-of-a-pin arguments, much ado about little or nothing purveyed by pointy-headed experts. But Gregory of Nyssa was astonished that in barber shops and meat markets common folk were vigorously discussing whether the Son was of the same nature as the Father. Gregory of Nazianzus was concerned that the salons of upper class, rich women had become places in which these kinds of conversations occurred. In his view theology should be kept out of public discussion where pagans would misunderstand the issues, let alone the private gathering places of women. Pagan religious leaders knew to keep their mysteries secret except to initiates and to treat them with reverence. One remarkable Syriac treatise notes that some boisterous monks did not treat these discussions with total seriousness. They illustrated their positions on the Trinity by passing gas at the proper intervals: three equal bursts for Nicene sameness of nature and three descendingly unequal bursts for the 'heretical' position.

The orthodox Trinitarian formula became three persons in one nature. In the West, Tertullian or perhaps the earliest translators of the Latin Bible had first expressed such uses of the Latin *persona* and *natura*. In this period Augustine's work on the Trinity employed a myriad of scriptural texts and worked out the content and limits of this doctrine. He offered an exposition of what has been called a psychological view of the three in one that was modeled on how humans think. Memory, understanding, and love of self or God are not the same but they are seldom greatly separated from one another.

As these discussions of Trinity developed, the *Christological* issues were never far from view. If three persons in one nature became the standard for Trinity, two natures in one person emerged as the most accepted understanding of Jesus Christ. Yet the same term *persona* in Latin was used for the triune features of the Trinity and the singular feature in

Christology. The genius of Celtic theology appears in Columbanus (*c.* 543–615), who suggested the formula *unum substantia, trinum subsistentia* – 'one in substance, triune in subsistence'. That delicately avoided the 'conceptual seepage' that in some ways contaminated the conception of 'person'. Columbanus seems to have known Greek and was trying to find a way to bring over the Greek *mia physis, treis hypostaseis* – 'one nature, three hypostases' – developed by Basil and the two Gregories, the Cappadocians.

By letting the term *persona*, express the oneness of the divine and human in Jesus Christ, not the threeness in the Trinity, Columbanus stood against the possibility of viewing the divine nature of God's Son as already a 'person' within the Trinity. Such a position wisely countered the possibility that the humanity of God's Son somehow had to be impersonal.

The paradoxical character of both Trinitarian and Christological thought left many theologians in a quandary. Even when some of them found the Trinitarian formulae of the fourth century adequate because God was such a sublime mystery, others choked on what they found to be the odd confessions about Jesus. How could Jesus Christ be both divine and human and yet a single person? As with discussions of the Trinity, scripture and theological inferences formed the essential questions. If Jesus said that the Father was greater than he was but also said that he and the Father were one, strict theologians with training in logic felt that the two statements could not be taken as of equal truth. 'Greater than' and 'one' are contradictory. So the Neo-Arians insisted that 'one' must be a homonym and that 'greater than' described the reality.

Such positions had more than Trinitarian implications. Was Jesus Christ divine, but only in a secondary sense? The emerging orthodoxy argued that salvation was at stake. How could a secondary God save humanity completely? Humans had made too much of a mess out of their lives not to need supreme help. The liturgical acts of baptism and Eucharist turn on the true, full nature of God being involved in the person of Jesus Christ.

If Trinitarian debates laid the groundwork for a confession that Jesus Christ was true God, the Christological debates slogged through questions about *Jesus' humanity*. Apollinaris of Laodicea (*c.* 315–92) fought valiantly on the side of the Nicenes in defending God's Son as fully God, but he found no way to include full humanity within the person of Jesus Christ. If Jesus had a full human intellect and will, there would have been deep conflict within Jesus Christ himself. Everyone knew that humans had ugly thoughts and often deeds to match them. Therefore, within the Son of God the true and complete divine nature had to take the place of the human intellect and will. In that way there was no potential for the rat's nest of sin.

For years the great defender of Nicene orthodoxy, Athanasius of Alexandria, had praised Apollinaris as faithful and brave. But in his later days he saw that he had to condemn the Laodicean's teaching about Christ. The Cappadocians – Basil, Gregory of Nazianzus and Gregory of Nyssa – eventually viewed Apollinaris's position as faulty. Jesus must be fully human. Gregory of Nazianzus insisted, relying on a phrase from Origen, that what is not taken up into the person of Christ cannot be saved. How could human sin be dealt with properly if the human intellect and will were left out of Jesus? Are not those two features of human personality responsible for wrong attitudes and actions, perhaps more than the flesh alone? Human mind and volition needed the healing of the divine.

Others found that the real problem lay elsewhere. If there were full divinity and full humanity in the Christ, how could he ever be one person? A series of theologians centered in Antioch of Syria (Antakya, Turkey) insisted on the full decision-making power of the human Jesus. Along with the Cappadocians, particularly Gregory of Nazianzus, they assembled long lists of biblical texts about the humanity of Christ. Who was praying in Gethesemane when Jesus asked if his Father might find a way other than the painful death of the cross? Who in that garden insisted that God's will be done and not his own? Surely that deeply troubling experience was not merely a drama for the benefit of scripture readers.

The difficulty for the so-called Antiochenes – Diodore of Tarsus (died c. 390), and later Theodore of Mopsuestia (c. 350–428), Theodoret of Cyrus (393–c. 460) and others was how to work out the oneness of Christ. During the fifth-century Greek debate between Nestorius of Constantinople (c. 381–451) and Cyril of Alexandria (c. 375–444) positions hardened and Nestorius was condemned as a heretic at the Council of Chalcedon in 451. After years of debate and decisions going both ways the Council of Constantinople in 553 found that Theodore of Mopsuestia and Ibas of Edessa (died 457) taught heretical views of Christ.

Those worried about the importance of a full, decision-making human nature in Jesus insisted that within the Antiochene view the unity of Christ's person was shattered. Nestorius had been cantankerous and attacked the growing confession that Jesus' mother Mary was the mother of God. He preferred to call her the mother of Christ so that she did not seem in any way to be the mother of God the Father. But his simple clarification, condescendingly delivered, angered believers in Constantinople and gave Cyril of Alexandria his chance. Cyril hated the growing power of the Constantinopolitan see and worked to have Nestorius unseated. No amount of pastoral concern tempered his action. Nestorius was dismissed from his post by the Council of Ephesus in 431; a council in 449 was prepared to condemn him formally, but monks from outside Alexandria arrived with clubs and killed some people at the meeting. It became known as the Robber Synod. But in 451 the tide carried Nestorius away. His best known writing, *The Book of Heracleides*, composed in exile during the same year that council met in Chalcedon, can be interpreted as his own agreement with most all of the Christological confession accepted at Chalcedon. His reputation was refurbished in the twentieth century.

Cyril of Alexandria was the winner with his emphasis on the dominant divinity of Christ and the secure oneness of Christ's person. But some accidents of history weakened his position. After Apollinaris of Laodicea's view of one divine nature in Christ was condemned, his supporters transmitted his writings under the name of Athanasius. Unknowingly Cyril defended Apollinarian positions already declared heretical, ones that he accepted as Athanasian, and thus compromised some of his own solutions. His insistence on using the phrase 'one divine nature' opened his position up to the weakness recognized in Apollinaris's writings. But his further explications show that he had no fear of Christ's humanity as the Laodicean did and that he was most interested in emphasizing the involvement of divinity in the person of Christ. In his view that conservative position stressing the need of God's involvement for salvation to be achieved could be eliminated only at the peril of losing classical Christian tradition.

The upshot was tragic. Emerging Chalcedonians, confessing Jesus Christ to be truly God and truly man in one person, exercised their politically established position by driving those of other views out of their positions as bishops. In short, Christians of the East who eventually adopted Syriac as their Christian language often recognized the Antiochene theologians, translated into Syriac, as their greatest teachers. Theodore of Mopsuestia was a grand biblical exegete. Babai the Great (died *c.* 628), an East Syrian monastic theologian, employed sophisticated Syriac formulae to create categories in which the unity of Christ's person was clearly expressed while demanding the fullness of both the human and divine subjects.

Some Greek-speaking churches, as well as Armenians and others, were overwhelmed with the need to put the Son of God's divinity in the place of prominence. The incarnation of God, the taking on of human flesh by the Son of God, was the pivotal point. God was in Christ reconciling the world to himself. Called by their opponents 'Monophysites', those who insisted on the one divine nature of God's incarnate Son, they did not always have a place for the human nature. In the twentieth century, however, representatives of these churches have met in ecumenical discussions and grieved that their theologians and congregations of this early period could not find ways to listen to each other.

The deepest tragedy of these Trinitarian and particularly the Christological issues was that orthodox, established Christians *persecuted* both Dyphysite and Monophysite Christians. They taxed them heavily and banished their bishops. When Muslims in their military and religious power swept over the Christian East and North Africa, the unconverted Berbers were not the only ones awaiting the coming of people who would take them seriously. Christians who were often attacked by other Christians also offered little resistance because whatever the Arabs brought could not be as bad as what they had.

The center of Christian practice and faith was usually kept in place through *baptism, Eucharist and confession* as well as the communities' efforts to model their way of life. In the fourth and early fifth centuries Cyril of Jerusalem (died 387), Ambrose of Milan (*c.* 339–97), and John Chrysostom (first of Antioch, then of Constantinople) delivered catechetical lectures to candidates for baptism. The outlines for these teaching exercises were formed by the great creeds of the church, particularly the two 'Nicene' creeds from the councils of 325 and 381. During their baptism new converts would recite such creeds. These bishops in their lectures saw to it that the candidates had an opportunity to grasp the deep meaning of these confessions.

Some adults would postpone their *baptism*, sometimes until near death, at other times until their studies were complete. Several bishops in the fourth and fifth centuries, including the great Augustine, grew up in Christian families but were not baptized until they had reached some age of accountability. But by the fifth century Augustine based his teaching about the original sin of all humans on the church's practice of baptizing infants. Baptism was for the remission of sins; thus baptizing infants must mean that they were sinful. Indeed they were conceived in sin by parents who followed evil sexual urges. Augustine's development of this doctrine helped him attack Pelagius (350 to *c.* 425), probably a British monk, who was deeply interested in reforming the church along ethical lines that depended upon humans' responsibility for their actions. Pelagius had picked up Augustine's earlier writings against Manichaean determinism in order to support his own sense of the necessity for a freedom of the human will. At the same time he strongly emphasized the grace that empowered human action. Some local councils in the eastern Mediterranean found no fault with his teaching. His disciple Celestius, however, moved far from Pelagius. He insisted that the grace of creation, which gave humans free will, was totally sufficient for salvation. Grace did not have to initiate conversion for a person to repent and change.

Augustine went to the root of the issue and insisted that wrongful attitude could be seen in babies; so often they cried to get their own way. Humans were in such a corrupted state that only the death and resurrection of Christ and the operation of grace in bringing a person to repentance could bring salvation. He prevailed, and original sinfulness became a strong Christian doctrine sanctioned by Western church councils. It was so important in the sixth century that the emperor Justinian made infant baptism a part of state law. As a result the ancient custom of baptisms on Easter eve or only at other important times of the Christian year broke down under the pressure to baptize infants quickly before they suffered the high probability of early death

The Donatist controversy that had appeared early in Augustine's career had also turned on the practice of baptism, but in a different way. Donatists were not as much interested in the doctrinal orthodoxy of the one baptizing as in his moral character. Baptism would be invalid if the bishop or his representative had not lived a strict, ethical life. Donatus (died 355) himself insisted on that position. Anyone baptized by an immoral bishop must be rebaptized. A council in Arles, Gaul (France) during 314 rejected that view. Later Augustine argued that the holy effects of baptism depended on the actions of a holy God not on the holiness or the lack of holiness in the one baptizing. No person was ever sinless and thus totally worthy of baptizing another. That put Augustine at odds with the earlier North African sage Cyprian (*c.* 200–58), who argued for rebaptism when the bishop or his representative proved to have fallen during persecution. Augustine insisted that Cyprian was right to emphasize Christian unity but that he had not pushed far enough through the sacramental issues to see them dependent on God alone. In the process Augustine wisely insisted that ecclesiastical decisions should be based on scripture, the long view through the history of the church, a shorter view dependent upon recent ecumenical councils, and well-formed arguments supporting a position. That way he could claim Cyprian while disagreeing with him.

The basis of Donatist anger, however, lay not so much in the administration of baptism as in the question of whether people who gave up scriptures to the persecuting authorities during the persecution of Diocletian were really 'traitors', *traditors*, who had sinned drastically. When the important North African see at Carthage became empty in 312, the battle broke out with increasing violence. The radical purists led by Donatus rejected Caecilianus, appealed to bishops in Numidia and eventually set up their own churches. Donatus was a counter-bishop of Carthage for forty years, supported by crowds of mostly peasants, many of whom spoke only Punic. They hated a soft moral sense of Christian life and felt oppressed by what they considered to be the veneer Christian culture of the North African elite. They opposed Roman intrusion in their affairs and reacted violently against police actions intended to stop their riots. Some of them committed suicide at the graves of persecuted martyrs rather than live in their evil world. Others, called 'Circumcellians' because they wandered around with their deadly clubs, attacked the Latin-speaking church at nearly every turn, wreaking havoc. Their violence, rooted in both economic oppression and cultural dismissal, uprooted any sense of order.

The movement was still strong in rural areas during the time of Augustine. That led him not only to emphasize the unity of the church but also to ask the political authorities to put down such dangerous uprisings. An established church with access to political power should use it for the good of social order.

Architectural features of Christian churches during this period show how important both baptism and Eucharist were to those communities. Baptisteries have been excavated that form important features of church buildings. They are sometimes connected to the main sanctuary; elsewhere they stand away from that structure although they are clearly a part of the worship complex. Many are deep enough for the immersion of adults; some would cover only part of the lower legs. Pictures of baptism in mosaics and other forms show adults in water of both depths. Pouring water while the candidate is standing in a baptistery is also depicted.

The most important *Eucharistic* features of church buildings seem to be the placing of an altar in the front of the edifice away from the people and near the seats for the bishops and elders. The liturgies for the Eucharist begin to show how much the important action is being done by the ordained leadership and that the reception of the elements by the people seems necessary but secondary.

The Eucharist, because of the riches available in the communities, was in this period no longer the meeting of a few around a small table but a dazzling performance of mystery with gold or silver utensils of fine workmanship employed by men in fine robes. The poor and the oppressed were far down the line in the pecking order. The better off would not feel comfortable partaking of bread and wine with such rabble. Yet these lesser folk were not left without helps designed at least in part with them in mind. The church knew that images could sink a truth deep into the mind in ways that no argument could ever manage. Even the best educated should have the opportunity to see the glory of Old Testament stories, the life of Jesus and the deeds of the apostles. But particularly for those with no reading ability and perhaps no under-standing of the language of the liturgy, depictions of the basic Christian stories could teach well. Third-century Christian worship – which included various images and took place in houses remodeled for selected rituals like baptism and the Eucharist – suited a persecuted minority. But now Christian communities created remarkable architecture, art and artifacts that still inspire awe. Such works pose the question that can be raised in any age: does the use of wealth in outfitting houses of worship represent a total denial of the God Christians honor or does the beauty it creates touch the heart as lesser representations cannot? We find Chris-tian wealth and worship intertwined the globe over: hewn-rock churches in Ethiopia, great Byzantine basilicas in Nubia, strikingly painted East Syrian monasteries in China.

The sense of a Christian core was often maintained in odd ways. Christians in Nubia *translated* at least parts of the Bible into Old Nubian that employed Coptic letters for the written language. Thus they honored the widespread Christian principle of putting scripture into the speech of the indigenous people. But some features of their life were not so adapted to Nubian culture. Perhaps as early as the late sixth or the early seventh century, architects and perhaps even craftsmen with expe-rience in building the church basilicas of the Byzantine Empire arrived to erect the needed church buildings. Most of the structures were built of stone or brick with vaulted roofs, set on an east–west line with the altar at the eastern end just as they were in the Byzantine Empire.

CONCLUSION

European Christendom began to take shape first in Constantine's preference for Christianity and then in its establishment by Theodosius. The
worship of ancient gods in the Roman Empire did not stop immediately,
but persecution of Christians ceased; a welcome respite. Soon, however,
significant Christian leaders tortured their own 'heretics' as well as
believers in other religions. Another sad result of Christianity's establishment as the dominant Roman religion was that the Persian government viciously persecuted Persian Christians as disloyal citizens who
sided with the Romans.

Church councils, dominated by Greek and Latin leaders and supported
by government funds, helped shape what became the classical Trinitarian
and Christological doctrines. The Bible took the form it has today. Christians who were minorities outside the empire sometimes came to similar
conclusions about the faith but always with their own cultural twist.

Some people chose to become monks (first in Egypt and Syria, then
elsewhere). At first they lived in the cities but later they moved to desert
areas, sometimes as individual hermits and at other times as organized
communities. The monastic life was indeed a reaction to failing commitment among the mass of Christians, but monks did not flee from the world
never to serve it. They founded hospices that became hospitals. They
opened their compounds to refugees, occasionally in staggering numbers.
Various monastic rules about work and worship led to disciplined spirituality and widespread mission, particularly in northern Europe.

Christian traders and monks reached China along the Silk Road; they
found ways to affirm aspects of Buddhism, Confucianism and Taoism,
especially those religions' senses of family life, at the same time that they
told the story of Jesus through word and deed. In terms of the world
that the Roman Empire knew, including its sea trade relationships with
India and perhaps southwestern China, as well as Ethiopia and Nubia,
Christian communities could qualify as a world religion.

3 ENDANGERED AT THE CENTER, MOVING NORTH-WEST AND EAST, 630–1100

No one expected the power of Muhammad and the followers of Allah. Trade routes through Arabia (Saudi Arabia) had brought wealth into the area centuries before Muhammad's birth. But the region appeared to be without strong identity and lacking energy to define itself. Christians and Jews lived in communities in that part of the Middle East, but they too were not particularly lively. Without slighting the importance or the authenticity of Muhammad's own visions, it can be stated that the other two monotheistic religions were known to him. The Qur'an notes his appreciation of Jews and Christians as people of the book. His struggle against polytheists and idolaters among the Arabs, and his stand against the killing of infant girls became aspects of his teaching which Jews and Christians could admire. Yet the prophet found the Jews of Medina to be thorns in the flesh. They would not adopt his revelation. The Christians he knew may have taught a kind of Gnostic view of Christ which we find in the Qur'an: truly born of a virgin, truly a prophet, but one whose death on the cross did not occur and whose resurrection makes little sense. Whatever the borrowings, Muhammad's prophetic utterances serve as the foundation for the second largest religion on the globe, one that is growing in almost every region of the world. This third monotheistic religion that emerged from the Middle East is now the third largest religion in the United States, growing with such speed that in the twenty-first century it will become the second largest. Worldwide it is a significant faith followed by perhaps 1.2 billion believers.

Born into a home that soon failed, Muhammad was an orphan who eked out a meager existence. His birth is usually dated by Westerners in

AD 570 and located in Mecca, but there are inscriptions in southern Arabia that support a 540 date. He eventually married a widow whose wealth and influence in the trading community was substantial. At about forty years of age he received revelations of Allah from the angel Gabriel. His ability to recognize and formulate them into the remarkable Arabic that Muslims honor continued during his adult years. At first he had only a small circle of followers in Mecca. His religious views and their definition of society were so radical that numerous Arab leaders wanted him banned. Trade was good, and pagan polytheistic views served the communities' purposes. Muhammad was forced from the city and went in 622 to Medina, where he gained adherents. By 630 he had wreaked havoc on Meccan trade, taken the city and made it the sacred center of Islam.

Not only wealth from trading but also the quality of Arabian horses and armament stood ready for use. The central fact, however, is still clear. Until Muhammad appeared with his Arabic revelation, one that had the possibility of empowering not only the Arabs but also those they would soon conquer, the region was a place to pass through. He pulled together an Arabic culture and rooted it in the revelation of Allah.

The second half of the seventh century saw Muslims muster their strength and move out with remarkable speed into the surrounding lands. Expansion into Nubia (Sudan) was successfully blocked by Christian armies, both through ferocious fighting and because the country had little of value to offer to the invading Muslims. But a treaty at Baqt in 652 forced the Nubians to provide slaves every year, perhaps in trade for other things. By 661 much of Palestine (Israel), Syria (Syria and Iraq) and Persia (Iran) as well as Egypt and North Africa were in Muslim hands. Byzantine Christian armies proved to be no match; neither were the Persian Zoroastrian troops. Military superiority came from speed and precision based on tactics that Muhammad had developed in his desert raids on Meccan caravans. In the eighth century Muslim expansion engulfed Spain and much of south-western France to within one hundred miles of Paris. Only the defeat at Poitiers in 732 stopped the onslaught. Constantinople was besieged twice (672–8, 717–18). Central Asia felt the power of this new force well beyond Balkh, north to Tashkent and south to the Arabian Sea. By 751 Muslim soldiers had won a victory against the Chinese at the Talas river in what is now Turkmenistan.

Because of the twentieth-century expansion of Muslims round the world, we know that Christians' existence has been and probably will go on being continuously entwined with that of Muslims. The followers of

Allah have reinterpreted the prophetic tradition of Jews and Christians, claiming that Muhammad was the final prophet of a line that includes Abraham, Moses and Jesus. In the Qur'an, the Lord and Savior of Christians is a Muslim prophet. During the medieval period European Christians, as members of an established religion and almost unaware of themselves as such, often defined their faith as a Western religion. Some understood their struggles with Muslims as centered on the correction of a new Christian heresy. Later what they viewed as the defilement of Jerusalem and the endangerment of pilgrimage to that city took center stage. The military victory at Poitiers that stopped the Muslim surge into Europe, and the ability of Constantinople to hold out led many Western Christians to think of Muslims only when forced to acknowledge them. Disciples of Muhammad were powerful in Spain and in sections of Greece, but they could wrongly be forgotten by many Western Christians as more a nuisance than an immediate threat to Europe.

The battering of Christian political and cultural power in the ancient eastern Mediterranean centers of Christian influence was a hard blow, softened only because Christian communities, though decreasing in size, stubbornly held on. Christians in the West were often determined to extend their place as the major religion under any emperor. Emperor Justinian (483–565) had been the last to expand the Byzantine borders to near their largest extent. Now the East had its own agenda. Western Christians had to look within their own lands to find some way of recovering a *Holy Roman Empire*. Thus they had little interest in compelling eighth-century Franks to rein in their ambitions of laying claim to a 'European' kingdom. Because Pepin III was a kind of Christian, his intent to invade and control his neighbors could be taken as a sign that the Holy Roman Empire, now transferred West, could be expanded into non-Frankish territory.

Pepin's son Charlemagne, ruler from 768–814, extended the boundaries through economic and political power. He overran his neighbors and forced them to accept his sovereignty. His empire never resembled the power of law and local administration that Rome gave to its conquered peoples. But Charlemagne assembled a court of committed Christian intellectuals who were given the task of creating a Christian culture for his empire. These brilliant theologians were international: Alcuin from England, Paul the Deacon from Italy and Theodulf from Spain. These and their companions could bring into being the Christian aspects of an empire only if recently subdued pagan tribes were introduced to

Christian community and the previously converted, including the Franks themselves, were encouraged to deepen their practice and faith. Thus these leading Christian figures trained priests to preach the gospel among the pagans and centered much of their own work on writing Christian books to help the converted better understand what that 'good news' was. Some examples of their efforts are still available and represent remarkable achievements of argument, art and refinement.

In 800 the Roman pope came to Charlemagne's court both to acknowledge that the Frank had established his Christian empire and to find ways in which the Holy See could extend its own influence. Charlemagne understood that he could gain much in such an official alliance, but he put the crown on his own head rather than let the pope make him emperor. This event became a paradigm for conflict between political and religious power that has not abated to this day. The papacy had made claims for its unique position as early as the second century and, as the one power still intact, had provided political stability through its religious leadership since the fall of Rome in 410. It was not about to give up its sense of itself or its mission because one savvy Frank seized the moment.

There were doubtless other Christian leaders who praised Charlemagne's vision of a Christian empire and his success in achieving it. Weren't Christian numbers growing? Weren't they becoming the majority among a group of European tribes east of the Frankish homeland? But even within his court, Charlemagne's advisor Alcuin had penned a series of letters in which he questioned the efficacy of conversion by the sword. How could anyone know whether such forced baptisms would lead to a Christian way of life? How long would it take to overcome the memory that linked Christian mission and expansion with humiliating defeat in armed conflict? No doubt Charlemagne and his chieftains could look back on Old Testament conquests as justifications for their bloody battles. And in that period there was no way to predict that this kind of conversion would become a ruthless pattern, seen not only in Prussia during the thirteenth century but also in the Spanish *conquistadores* in Mexico during the sixteenth century. Whatever the marvels of Charlemagne's Holy Roman Empire, and they were considerable, the spread of Christian faith and life was like butter on toast, mostly on the top. One penetrating claim made by some historians of modern Europe is that there is little evidence for genuine Christian faith and life in these conquered regions even now. Europe could hardly be lost to Christian influence in the modern era because it was never fully won.

During this period, particularly in *Western Europe,* monks following the rule of St. Benedict (*c.* 480–540) were the primary missionaries. Benedict himself had not founded an order, but his rule for organizing monastic life grew in importance. It contained no theory of life in a monastery, indeed it set out a series of practices that when followed would lead a community to better understanding of their beliefs by acting in particular ways. Virtue would grow and faith be refined through repeating a series of practical things: prayer, study of scripture, care of each other and those souls from outside that appeared at the door. Christ could be found in the stranger, even in the pagan neighbor.

The rule was known in England in the seventh century and remarkably useful in the evangelization of German and Frankish tribes. Wynfrith (680–754), better known as St. Boniface, the apostle to Germany, was at first a failure in Frisia. But he went to Rome, got papal blessing and returned to the region. He converted Bavarians, Thuringians and Hessians, reformed existing monasteries and set up others as centers of faith and mission, all based on Benedict's rule. His courage and persistence became matters of legend when he cut down the grand oak of Thor at Geismar and was harmed neither by that god nor by that deity's worshippers. As archbishop of Mainz, he founded the famous monastery at Fulda and crowned Pepin king of the Franks. Near the end of his life he returned to Frisia and was killed by pagans as he tried to confirm Frisians recently baptized. The strong stance against pagan religion and much of their tribal cultures had led to certain successes but also to fierce resistance.

A series of lesser-known monks, many working under Benedict's rule, went deep into the forests of Europe and built central houses for their communities. Particularly during the eighth century the Benedictines worked out careful plans for the evangelization of large portions of what are now major European countries. When small groups of monks met fierce resistance, even to the point of death because they destroyed the sacred trees, the story would be written down and a note made that those tribes should be contacted again when a decade had passed. There was never any consideration that any people were impossible to convert. Only the timing was off.

Just as this showed the formidable strength of the missionary monks, the repeated need for reform of the Benedictine orders indicated their weakness. In the tenth century the unknown name of Cluny rose to prominence as the seat of major reform. The guidance found in the rule had been relaxed. Monks in poverty had accepted the largess of the rich and had themselves become privileged. Their lives of prayer had attracted the attention of those who wanted the righteous to remember them and their forebears before God. Mission waned; the acquisition of land increased. Many of the faithful flocked to the reformed monasteries so that large new quarters had to be built. But the seepage of worldly wealth and power into these secluded holy sites proved to be a bitter problem that has continued to plague monasticism.

Christians had spread into *Scandanavia*. When Ólafur Tryggvason began his reign in Norway (995), as a fervent Christian, he used his power to convert pagans. Missionaries had been sent to Iceland before, but Stefnir Porgilsson went to burn temples and tear down idols. Not suprisingly he was forced to leave. King Ólafur's chaplain, Pangbrandur, followed with a band of priests. They displayed Christian rituals and vestments that attracted attention, but, as Vikings, they tended to kill anyone who sought to harm them. Pangbrandur preached Christ at the Althing, the island's ruling council, and made some converts.

It remained, however, for Gissur and Hjalti, two Icelandic chieftains, to try another method. King Ólafur, furious that Iceland had refused his Christian views, swore that he would execute all Icelanders in Norway. Because a prominent group of Icelandic chieftains' sons were in Norway the threat was serious. Gissur and Hjalit went back home, spoke to the Althing, but were told that Christians and pagans would never consent to living under one law. A Christian peacemaker, Hallur, asked the pagan leader, Porgeir, well known for his wisdom, to decide which law it would be. Porgeir wrapped himself up in a cloak (or a horsehide) for twenty-four hours, evidently in accepted oracular practice. When he emerged he noted that two laws would bring terrible strife. So the pagans would be baptized and then all would live under Christian laws. But undesired babies could be exposed, horsemeat eaten and pagan sacrifices celebrated in private. Those customs were soon declared illegal. Political pressure was certainly a cause of the conversion, but pagan wisdom and Christian patience prevailed.

Christian movement along the Silk Road into *China* (and perhaps into Korea and Japan) put Christian communities in political situations in which they had no hope of being the preferred religion. They were small; their demands tended to appeal to only a few. Those traveling to the East, especially from Persia (Iran), did not know establishment as a normal way of life. They were a minority facing Zoroastrians, who as an entrenched state religion, often persecuted them. Thus the 635 favorable contact of Alopen with people in the Chinese court at Chang'an (Xi'an) was unexpected. The emperor, curious about other religions, found the stories of Christian faith to be interesting; he asked for a translation of their books to put in his great library. He allowed his picture to be painted on the walls of the structure that Christians inhabited, a decision that to those involved in this mission must have seemed to be a remarkable coup. But their success was short-lived. That emperor was a man of education who wanted to learn as much as possible from outsiders. His successors were not totally xenophobic, but they did not want to encourage religions that might displace 'Chinese' religions. When Buddhist monasteries were repressed because they represented a 'foreign' religion, Christian monasteries – fewer and weaker – found the repression almost mortally wounding.

CHRISTIANS AND PEOPLE OF OTHER FAITHS

Christians in continental Europe and *Great Britain* were still involved in intense missionary activity. King Ethelbert of Kent, married to a Christian woman of strong influence, graciously received the mission sent by Pope Gregory the Great at the end of the sixth century. When King Edwin of Northumbria, who followed the rites of *traditional religion*, suggested that Ethelbert give him one of his daughters in marriage, Ethelbert responded that no Christian woman in his family would be allowed to live with someone who knew nothing about proper worship of the true God. Edwin had been involved in a series of disputes with other rulers in the region; he had killed one in revenge for the killing of his nephew. Thus he had pressing reasons for this alliance with Ethelbert. Edwin sent his answer through Ethelbert's messenger that if Christanity were 'more holy and acceptable to God' he would convert. Bishop Paulinus from Kent traveled to Edwin's court and debated with his pagan priests about the value of the respective religions for two years. Finally in 627 Edwin and his household were baptized. Doubtless religious political and military interests all played their part in the decision.

During this period some non-Western Christian communities continued despite many difficulties. *Ethiopia* had a line of kings who were able to resist *Muslim* pressures. For much of the time Christian strength shifted backward and forward between the mountains in the Shoa region and control of Aksum in the south. In spite of the importance of various monastic foundations that city, with its claim to house the ark of the covenant, always insisted that it was the most holy place recognized by Ethiopian Christians, indeed the New Jerusalem. Even the remarkable carved rock churches at Lalibela, created in the thirteenth century, could not completely move the symbolic center from Aksum.

Muslims formed a community greatly different from Christian community. Their invasion of Christian lands was more threatening and much longer lasting than the Germanic invasions of Italy in the fifth century. Christian attitudes toward Muslim successes were ambiguous. Some Christians expressed grief and anger because they had been part of a preferred political and economic establishment and now were only one among the minority religious communities in lands dominated by Muslims. There is, however, no overwhelming early evidence that Muslims relentlessly pressured Christians to convert. The covenant, *dhimma*, with other people of the book was usually understood as allowing them a place to continue their lives much as they had done before. Steady persecution and the destruction of church buildings came later. We may speculate that on the local level, political or military leaders who themselves were fanatic Muslims could have made things very difficult. Doubtless there were common folk who thought anyone who did not worship Allah to be odd, perhaps even dangerous. But some of the well-educated Christians, like John of Damascus (*c. 650/75–c.* 749), for a time served in the Islamic governmental bureaucracies throughout the Middle East. Those who remembered reading about Roman pagan persecution found themselves well served in this new regime. Given the abuse that they had faced from the Chalcedonian Christian Orthodox, many non-Chalcedonian Christians hoped for and often received better treatment from the Muslims.

The bulk of the Christians conquered in the *Middle East* had not accepted the decision at Chalcedon that Jesus Christ was fully divine and fully human in one person. Those whom the Chalcedonians called Monophysites insisted that the Christ was divine. That was the important issue. His humanity was there but rather weak and not terribly interesting. Some of their leaders like Severus of Antioch (*c.* 465–538), however, had conceived of a robust humanity, but that was not the common position. Those whom Chalcedonians called Nestorians (East Syrians) so insisted on the full intelligence and will of Jesus' humanity as well as the full divinity that some viewed them as teaching that Jesus Christ was two sons. Their detractors did not find their explanation of the union between divinity and humanity sufficient.

The importance of these different Christological positions among the Christians with whom Muslims lived is interesting. It worked alongside the earliest contacts that Muhammad had with Christians. The Qur'an shows significant goodwill toward those who follow Christ but its comments on Jesus the prophet look much like some early Gnostic gospels that well may have been used in Arab Christian communities. Muslim conversations with Monophysites may have at times so weakened the understanding of incarnation that it became more a philosophical problem than a religious one. The East Syrian designation of Mary as the mother of Christ, rather than the mother of God, which eventually resulted in Jesus being referred to as the Son of Mary, would have done little at a popular level to contest the identity of Jesus declared in the Qur'an: a wise prophet who taught and did good but certainly was neither crucified nor God walking the earth. Being born miraculously of a virgin gave witness to his prophetic status but not his divine incarnation.

During the period covered by this chapter, Christian theologians developed a series of responses to Muslim communities. That from John of Damascus is perhaps the best known because part of it appears in one of his powerful works, *Fount of Knowledge*, a work the great thirteenth-century Western Catholic, Thomas Aquinas, appropriated. But it also fits the Damascene's Christological context in which Muslims developed their views of Jesus in relationship to Gnostic, Monophysite and Nestorian communities. For John all three of these 'Christian' positions were heretical. Perhaps for such reasons he insisted in his list of heresies that the followers of Muhammad represented one of the latest Christian mistaken views; Muslims did not represent another religion but a wrongly formed Christian understanding. John wrote his response in Greek at the monastery of St. Sabas near Jerusalem among monks who hardly knew that language anymore. Their common tongue already was Arabic.

Other earlier Christian writers had stronger views of who the Muslims were. In the 630s Maximus the Confessor had seen the Arabs as barbarous people, 'wild and untamed beasts'. The only good to come from the invasions involved watching such events demonstrate once again that Christians must turn to God as their only refuge. The patriarch of Jerusalem, Sophronius (died 639) is perhaps the first to view the fall of Christian civilization to the Arab onslaught in apocalyptic terms: God's punishment of his sinful people. Sophronius recognized little if anything that the Muslims did as occurring because of their own religious fervor. God through the Muslims was calling Christians to repentance. By the turn of the eighth century a number of Christian apocalypses had appeared, not only rebuking Christians for their sins that brought on these catastrophes, but also insisting that eventually Christian armies would conquer and subdue the Arab rulers. Furthermore, the literature that remains includes various hagiographical stories of the saints in previous times of trouble which could offer legitimacy to those who struggled to keep the faith in the present. These often fictional tales about the conversion of Muslims to Christ offered hope.

Another type of literature appears with *The Passion of St. Michael*, a work probably written in Arabic during the ninth century. In a style meant to praise a saint and inspire Christians, this piece tells a seventh-century tale about a monk from the St. Sabas monastery outside Jerusalem. The caliph's wife became attracted to him. When he did not return her affections she had him scourged, bound and taken to the caliph. While there the monk was invited to enter into a debate about the merits of Muslim and Christian faith. 'Abd al-Malik enjoyed such debates because he was not only a strong Muslim but also one who had read extensively in both the Hebrew Bible and the Christian New Testament. This caliph had a Jew join the discussions. Then he started a conversation by insisting that Christian monastic practices, denying both marriage and proper eating, were amiss. The apostle Paul had led Christians down a false path. Michael responded that Paul brought salvation to gentiles, but Muhammad steered Saracens the wrong way. He was a deceiver, not a prophet. The caliph countered that the Prophet fought idolatry; Michael answered that Muslims conquered by the sword and promised heavenly rewards that were actually earthly distractions. Indeed most people in Palestine were still Christians, including many of the learned physicians and scribes who served the caliph. Michael passed the ordeals of hot coals and poisons, but he was still beheaded because he threatened to convert Muslims.

These kinds of Christian–Muslim discussions also took place in the Byzantine court. In the eighth century a Byzantine captive, Wā'sil ad-Dimashqī, had a similar debate with the emperor Leo III and the Constantinopolitan patriarch. Many of the same issues were raised, but the Muslim was dismissed alive. That decision may just as well signify that he did not strongly demean Christian faith as that Leo III was more gracious than 'Abd al-Malik.

At the beginning of the Muslim conquests both Jews and non-Greek-speaking Christians found the events to be filled with promise. An East

Syrian leader, Išô'yaw, in the mid seventh century claimed that the Arabs ruled by God's gift. They respected Christian faith and honored both priests and saints. They even supported churches and monasteries. Išô'yaw seemed oblivious to the fact that Muslim support of his churches might be viewed as assisting Christian 'heretics' in order to weaken the 'orthodox'. A Monophysite Armenian bishop, Sebêos, in 661 insisted that Muhammad knew Moses's law, taught it to the Arabs and helped them move away from idols. God led the Arabs to fulfill promises made to Abraham and to defeat the Byzantine troops. Muslims could take their place alongside Jews and Christians as representatives of monotheism. Such statements show us both how oppressed these leaders of Christian 'heresies' had felt themselves to be under the Byzantine Christian political authorities and how freed they sensed they were under Muslim rule.

The development of *iconoclasm*, the smashing of the painted images that the Eastern Orthodox venerated, has a root deep in the Christian community. Well before the Arab conquest Epiphanius of Salamis (c. 315–403) had found a tapestry of Christ hanging inside a village church in Palestine (Israel). He tore it down in utter disgust for the 'idolatry' it represented. For him and others the Old Testament proscription of images also included making any representations of the incarnate Son of God. But the outbreak of the iconoclastic controversy, which lasted about 120 years, only began in earnest during 726, just three years after the Muslim caliph Yezid prohibited icons within his realm. The Byzantine emperor, Leo III, who had grown up in Asia Minor (Turkey), where Christian fervor against icons was strongest, thought that both Jews and Muslims had understood the dangers of such idolatry, dangers that Christians also should recognize. He fought Muslims but he still saw that they were correct about icons.

An anonymous treatise *On the Triune Nature of God*, written in Arabic during 755 and thus the oldest Christian Arabic piece known to us, seems to be intended for instructing Arabic-speaking Christians about their faith and providing them with arguments to meet Muslim objections. The author used both the Old Testament and the Qur'an as scripture that supported his views and was most interested in the pastoral needs of Christians under Islamic hegemony.

During the ninth century this discussion between Muslims and Christians had been deeply influenced by massive conversions of Christians to Allah and his prophet. Although at the beginning of the century under twenty percent of the population in Iraq was Muslim, by the end the total was about fifty percent. It rose to nearly seventy percent in the next century. Muslims in Iran, however, had reached that level of dominance by the end of the ninth century.

Reasons for the conversions were varied. Being ill at ease because of attitudes or comments moved some; occasional physical persecution affected others. Worry about the economic burden of the extra tax, the *jizyah*, and the attraction of the trade advantages Muslims had in the larger world concerned others. Ambition to succeed in a society that was so clearly Islamic moved still others. Yet it must never be denied that the religious power of Muhammad's vision, the ways in which it provided a framework for absorbing the blows of life and helping people through their daily tasks, also had a strong effect. Faithful Muslims witnessed effectively to the mettle of their beliefs by faithfully observing their practices.

We might expect that this slow crushing conversion would have led most Christian literature to take the view that Muslims were horrid barbarians and that their prophet was a liar. But Christian approaches remained complex; in fact, some of them showed important knowledge of the Qur'an and greater respect for the Muslim adversaries. Timothy I of Baghdad (died *c.* 832), who wrote in Syriac and Arabic, spelled out his impressions of a discussion he had with the Baghdad caliph Al Mahdi. He entered the palace under the emir's *majlis*, a promise from the Qur'an that he would not only be safe but would be encouraged to make his strongest arguments for Christian faith over against Muslim conviction. In the palace he highly praised aspects of the new religion but warned about other features. Muhammad was neither the Holy Spirit nor a prophet like Moses, but he deserved praise from all reasonable people because he walked in the ways of the Old Testament prophets. Muhammad fought polytheists and idolaters as he proclaimed the one God; he also forced people away from bad deeds and moved them to good ones. His Qur'an even teaches about the Trinity. This last claim is a misreading of the Qur'anic text. Timothy's apology also has at least one dreadful aspect. He appealed to the views shared by Muslims and Christians when he noted that they both properly hated Jews. But the defense of Christian faith with a mild rejection of Muslim understanding and strong praise of Muhammad is one high point in the dialogue.

The apology of Abraham of Tiberius from the ninth century probably appeared in Arabic. The topics are much the same as those in previous Christian–Muslim debates, but this Christian monk has a book from which he borrowed many of his arguments. Abraham's use of proper Arabic words for Muslim leaders and concepts and his frequent employment of the Qur'an as the source for his arguments distinguish his approach from earlier confrontations. This time the emir insisted, based on the Qur'an, that Christ was neither a Jew nor a Nazarene. He was a Muslim, not a polytheist. Abraham showed the deference that the Qur'an expected from religious minorities, but he made a bold claim that seems not to appear again in Christian discussion with Muslims until recent times. Muhammad is not a prophet, but only a king who pleased God and fulfilled God's promise to Abraham's son Ishmael. God acted in Muhammad but primarily in terms of his covenant with Abraham.

A visitor in the court asked why Christ debased himself by paying the government tax. Abraham said paying does not rest in shame but in loving kindness and good use of resources. Jesus in humility called others to be humble. It was his miracles that demonstrated his claim to being the Word of God and his Spirit.

A further apology from the famous Theodore Abū Qurrah (died c. 830) has a section that reflects Christian disdain for Muslim practices. They ate camel's meat but not that of pigs, enjoyed grapes but avoided wine squeezed from them, approved of sodomy, forbade divorce but did not punish a spouse who took a lover. The latter charges concerned serious moral issues; the former seem to be cultural quibbles.

An odd little homily written in Greek by Gregory Dekapolites (died c. 842), a deacon in the Great Church at Constantinople, is interestingly mixed in its view of Muslims. The story involves a Muslim prince who accepted Christ, became a monk and later died as a martyr. After his conversion he was told to preach Christ and curse both Muslim faith and Muhammad; no respect should be given to Muslims at all. But the recognition of the prince as a great man by this Christian priest is based on that Muslim's vision of what was happening in the Christian Eucharist. As the priest consecrated the bread and the wine, the Muslim saw a baby being slaughtered, its body and blood offered to Christian believers. He was utterly furious at such barbarity, but the priest praised him because even honored Greek theologians never were able to see such a picture of the real presence of Christ. The reaction of the priest to the Muslim's mystical experience showed no distaste for the slaughtering of the child. From the priest's perspective, this Muslim had witnessed what committed Christians knew was happening. He must be remarkable because he saw what the faithful saints had not seen.

Many of these Christian treatises react generally to Islamic positions and thus portray most clearly what the Christian author of the work believes. In an extraordinary exchange, however, of what purport to be pieces written during the ninth century by the Muslim al-Hāshimī and the Christian al-Kindī, we have literature primarily focused on the other author as well as the issues at stake. Al Hāshimī composed a long letter that indicated he knew not only Christian scripture but also how Christians lived, what doctrines separated the Melkites (Orthodox), Jacobites (Monophysites) and Nestorians (Dyphysites; East Syrians) as well as the contents of some Christian–Muslim debates, including the apology of Timothy I. He sought to persuade Al-Kindī to convert. His effort, he noted, would be far different from that of the ignorant rabble who, relying on Islamic political power, employed false and vituperative rhetoric in order to coerce Christians. He would be reasonable and genteel. His epistle first recounts the basic teachings of Muhammad that al-Kindī knew, but he lays them out with great care. The revelation of Allah was the only true religion and thus the call of the prophet, Muhammad, must be offered to all. As the Qur'an said, compulsion was forbidden and there was freedom of worship. Yet other religions were untrue, and thus his friend was in mortal danger if he persisted in his Christian faith. Al-Hāshimī wanted to avoid harsh debate with one who belonged to the people of the book, but he intended to demonstrate the superiority of Islamic teachings rationally and simply.

The primary doctrine is the oneness of God. Christian belief in the Trinity could not be forgiven. Of course, not all Christian insight was wrong, for even Christian monks foretold the coming of Muhammad. Muslim worship was simple; Muslim law was clear but also subtle and supple. At the end of this life, Muslims will enjoy paradise while Christians will suffer in hell. Earthly benefits were also overwhelming. A Muslim could marry as many women as he chose; only four wives were legal at any time, but divorce allowed for more than four. There was no limit on concubines. Furthermore, the Muslims had won; Allah had been vindicated.

Al-Kindī's response was too large to be viewed as a return epistle. It was both an apology for Christian understandings and a polemic against Islamic views. The tone was one of supreme confidence, dismissive arrogance or perhaps a touch of both. Al-Kindī recognized Al-Hāshimī's offer of immunity from harm, but saw himself as fearless because of Christian superiority. For him the Trinitarian God was clearly portrayed in scripture but could be demonstrated as true from both philosophy and logic, and Jesus' divinity was evident from similar sources.

Muhammad was not in the line of Abraham and was certainly not a prophet. His views did not agree with Christian prophecy. He also could not heal his follower who lost a finger in the way that Jesus put the ear back on the high priest's servant. Muhammad's major interest was acquiring wealth; he looted caravans and even had people assassinated. Neither was the Qur'an a revelation; it was primarily a group of texts taken over from unfaithful Christian monks who taught Muhammad the good things declared in Christian scripture. But Jews injected wrong doctrines into the Qur'an because it had not been carefully protected by Muhammad's circle against interpolation. Muslim law was inferior not only to the Christian law Jesus gave about loving your enemies but also to the reasonable law of an eye for an eye taught by Jews. Its primary aspect was Satanic; it set out rules of oppression. Muslim military victory depended on God's punishing the iniquity of Christians, not on God's favoring the Muslims.

These two apologists had paid attention to each other, Al-Hāshimī more gently to his friend with a hope for conversion than Al-Kindī in his anxiety about growing Islamic success in conversion. Within a concern that political and social pressures not invalidate the arguments, Al-hāshimī's carefully set out the bold claim that worship of Allah was the only true religion, but it still failed to move his friend. Christians might have expected some gracious Muslim to offer such a position but perhaps its delicate framing made it even more infuriating. At least Al-Kindī did not receive it well.

One final treatise represents yet another angle for viewing Christian–Muslim relations. Al-Tabarī, formerly a Christian, became a Muslim. He emphasized that his was a change of conviction and answered, without direct reference to any specific work, almost all the points that Al-Kindī had made. Muhammad and Jesus shared many similar characteristics. Muhammad invoked God, agreed with the prophets of old, had strong ethical character and taught just laws. At night his dreams brought prophetic insights; indeed he foretold events in the future. The Qur'an was infallible. More than sixty passages from the books of Moses through the Christian Gospels spoke to the appearance of Muhammad. Christians should have known that the same demonstrations that had led them to accept Jesus and Moses should have led them to accept Muhammad, the Prophet.

When we turn from the Middle East to *Spain*, conquered by Muslims in 711, the Christians at first seemed to have been only a little inconvenienced. Thus Christian sources from the eighth century seldom take notice of Muslims, particularly as a religious force. But growing concern about Jewish economic and political influence suggested that some Christians were becoming increasingly aware that their disenfranchised position would not allow them to treat Jews forcefully and badly as they had sometimes done in the past. In the ninth century a greater sense of an Islamic threat appeared among certain Christian leaders. In 851 the monk Isaac walked into Córdoba, denounced Muhammad in front of the emir's palace and was decapitated. In the next few years nearly fifty other monks demanded that fate, but their deaths brought no great outcry in the Christian community. Living alongside Muslims had become easy enough. Upsetting the *status quo* made little sense. Indeed in 857 a certain Eulogius felt he had to defend these 'martyrs' against the charges raised by Christians quite assimilated into life under the Muslims. The monks who died 'suffered at the hands of men who venerated both God and a law'. For the acculturated Christians, Muslim law differed from theirs, but they and the Muslims worshipped the same God. Eulogius strongly disagreed. Muhammad was a 'demoniac full of lies', a false prophet, a man of devious character, who did not accept Jesus as the Son of God. His teaching about Jesus was like that of the heretical Christian Arians of the fourth century. Yet at the same time the reason for writing this piece was to convince an audience of assimilated Christians that they were right to see that Muslims did worship the Christian God, but wrong not to recognize that Muhammad was reprehensible in many ways.

The writer of another book, the *Tultusceptrum*, knew the Qur'an better and relied more upon it. This book did not relate Islamic history well, but it recognized that Muhammad had received a revelation from God. Twisting the Qur'anic attack on Christians as those who corrupted Jesus' message, it warned softly that Muhammad was but a child who misappropriated the word he heard.

Christian communities in *China* may have reached their zenith in the eighth century. The Chang'an (Xi'an) stele, uncovered in the seventeenth century, was set up in 781. It intended to point out the power and prestige of Christians in the Chinese capital and elsewhere. But that claim must not be taken in any exaggerated sense. Christians had tried, probably since the sixth century, to make their Persian origins less visible.

They wanted to be known as a faith that originated in Syria, 'The Illustrious Religion', or 'the ever true and unchanging Way [Tao]'. Of course greater Syria was the original home. But the claim also moved the Persian connection out of common sight and did not force Christians to explain how they were different from the Arabs who ruled Persia and had defeated Chinese armies only thirty years previously. The reference to Syria mentioned a land that Chinese traders had known for hundreds of years. Chinese porcelain was found in the excavation of Syrian Antioch during the 1930s. Indeed the best description of the emperor Diocletian's Antiochene palace, built around the turn of the fourth century, appears in a Han dynasty Chinese text. Certainly these Christians in China might continue to be perceived as foreigners. But as 'Syrians' their forebears had a lengthy history of useful trade relationships with China

These East Syrians adopted various Chinese words and concepts to make themselves less visible as a foreign religion and more successful among the indigenous peoples. The theological summary of their faith in the Chang'an (Xi'an) stele noted that in creation the one ineffable God, the Trinity, organized the forces of chaos, inspired all the venerable sages and 'brought to life the two forces of nature', a reference to *Yin and Yang*. This synopsis retained central doctrines like the Trinity, but also showed that Christians found truth in the best teachers of other religions, and adopted a deeply Chinese conception like Yin and Yang. Two of the Dunhuang documents, found in western China at the turn of the twentieth century, may date from this period. They deal with creation. They appear to be strongly *Taoist* in orientation, sprinkled with enough Christian truths to give them a partial flavor. The *Jesus Messiah Sutra*, probably written about 150 years before the stele, began with praise for Chinese societal structures, ones perhaps best seen in *Confucian* teachings but also found among *Buddhists* and Taoists. It prepared to tell the story of Jesus by clearly indicating that Chinese family life and daily relationships with others had many features that a Christian could gladly accept.

In the capital the small group of Christians who created the stele mingled with other Persian expatriates including the exiled court, mostly *Zoroastrians*, as well as *Manichaeans*. After the Arab conquest of Persia and victory at the river Talas in western China during 751, Persian refugees must have been expected to be anti-Arab. That would have cleared them politically. Yet all these 'exiles' counted together were only a tiny conclave in the world's greatest city, perhaps forced by the over-whelming majority of Confucians, Buddhists and Taoists to listen a bit more closely to each other.

Texts on the beautiful Chang'an (Xi'an) stone were chiseled in both Syriac and Chinese. Their author, Ching-Ching (with the Christian name Adam), was a master of both languages. Here the Chinese inscriptions are clear and uncluttered. They are quite different from the *Jesus Messiah Sutra*, which was perhaps written by Alopen, the missionary who struggled with the language. An interesting narrative on the stele itself tells of the founding of East Syrian monasteries in about 635 under the influence of Alopen and the command of the Emperor T'ai-tsung. A period of persecution by Buddhists arose in 698 and reached the capital in 712, but a Christian abbot, Lo-han, and a bishop, Chi-lieh, came from the West and strengthened the faithful. Around 742 the emperor, Hsuan-tsung, had at least one major Christian shrine rebuilt – perhaps the Chang'an (Xi'an) monastery – put pictures of five famous emperor sages inside and offered a large gift of silk. Other emperors followed his lead up to 781, so that when the stele was set up, the Christian community was quite optimistic about the strong and widespread influence they would have in the future. The stele mentions over seventy major leaders who served churches or monasteries from the end of the Silk Road up to Chang'an (Xi'an) itself.

Ching-Ching, the author of the writings on the stele, may have been responsible for translating at least thirty Christian books into Chinese, some of which were portions of the Bible. His ability as a linguist was considerable. Well known outside East Syrian circles in the capital of Chang'an (Xi'an) for his skill in translating foreign documents into stellar Chinese, he offered his talents to others. Some *Buddhist* mission-aries from India went to him for assistance in rendering their sutras. One of these was the famous Prajna, who knew no Chinese. He and Ching-Ching worked together on the translation of seven volumes, at least one of which probably had been written originally in Sanskrit. During this same period two important Japanese Buddhists, Kobo Daishi (Kukai) and Dengyo Daishi (Saicho), also lived in the Buddhist monastery in Chang'an (Xi'an), a building located not far from the East Syrian monastery. The conversations must have been rich, the influences both ways impossible for us to grasp fully.

The erection of the stele was attributed to the priest Yazdbuzid, whose father, Milis, had been a priest in Balkh. Thus the connection with

Christians along the Silk Road was important to these Chinese Christians. Balkh was one of twenty-four sees of the East Syrians that historians suspect were served by metropolitans – church officials of significant influence – before 1000. Chang'an (Xi'an) itself was another. Many of them were located in Syria (Iraq), but others stood on the Silk Road or on trails that led off it: Merv, Samarkand, Yarkand, Almalik, Hami and Dunhuang, to name a few. This route stretched from India eastward as one of the roads that Buddhists had traveled into China. Thus Christians along the Silk Road would have encountered, through contact with settled people or traveling traders, most of the major Eastern religions. They surely met Buddhists in these regions. Later, Muslims expanded east not only through Persia (Iran) but also up along the northern routes east through the lands of various Mongolian tribes. At each of these metropolitan sites of the East Syrians there would have been exchanges with tribal peoples who had their own indigenous religions that served their purposes. Sadly, we do not have much information about what such discussions might have been like.

The history of Christians in *India* during this period lies buried in ashes. Those in Kerala had lived among their *Hindu* neighbors for hundreds of years before the emergence of Muslims in their region. Yet because of the ignorant insularity of Portuguese Christians who sailed to the western Indian coast at the turn of the sixteenth century, numerous written documents on various kinds of media, including copper plates, were destroyed as heretical writings. Thus what would have been a considerable treasure of Indian Christian treatises is no more. Only small stories in oral tradition and at times recorded elsewhere remain available.

Letters from two East Syrian leaders, Ishoyahb III (bishop from 647/8 or 650/1 to 657/8) and Timothy I (bishop from 789 to 823) show that Indian Christians, at least on the western coast, thought of themselves as under the authority of the East Syrian Church. At the beginning of this era, the direct access to such church authorities was through Rew'Ardashir, a metropolitan see in south-western Persia (Iran). But sometime before the turn of the ninth century the Indian church developed its own metropolitan centers outside the authority of Rew'Ardashir. One of Timothy's epistles mentions that many missionary monks had traveled to India and China by sea as well as by land. Another speaks of potential intermarriage between East Syrian Christians from Syria (Iraq) and Persia (Iran). Still another warns about irregularities in the ordination of leaders.

A legend about Sapor and Prot appears quite late in sixteenth-century materials, but may describe an infusion of Armenian Christians into the Indian communities some time during the ninth or tenth century. The two brothers came to Quilon, built a church and converted a number of people through their miracles. Some artifacts may fit the time of these legends. An extant copper plate records the gift of land to Christians in Quilon by the Indian king Ayyan of Venad. Two Persian Christian crosses found in Mylapore and Kottayam may also come from this expansion.

A fourteenth-century Arabic book written by Abu-Salih, *Description of Churches and Monasteries of Egypt and Some Neighboring Countries*, gives some details about the shrine to Thomas at Mylapore. It also talks about a second community with churches dedicated to the Virgin Mary and St. George in Kulam (Quilon), and a third group of churches in 'Fashur'. All these Christians are identified as Nestorians (East Syrians). 'Fashur' or Fansur well may be the contemporary city of Barus on the western coast of Sumatra.

Portuguese accounts from the sixteenth-century in *The Book of Barbosa* mention a church at Cape Comorin that Armenians had founded. Armenians still led worship there, and a group of old graves surrounded the building. Another record from the Portuguese mentions that where the Beypur river emptied into the sea a group of believers said they belonged to the Thomas caste and were related to the Christians of St. Thomas.

Therefore, although much has been destroyed, we know that East Syrian Christians still existed in India when the Portuguese arrived. They had survived in many ways through contacts with Syrian and Persian Christians and perhaps through some mission efforts by Armenians.

In *Europe* at least one major mission project deserves recognition. Cyril-Constantine (826–69) and his brother Methodius were asked by Michael III to take the gospel to Slavic peoples in Moravia, Slovakia and parts of modern Hungary where Western Catholic missionaries were at work. Probably for both religious and political reasons, Michael wanted Eastern Orthodoxy established in the region. Cyril-Constantine was an accomplished scholar, librarian at Constantinople. But he saw this request as a way to use all his talents. His interests in such efforts were already evidenced not only in debates with Muslims about the nature of the Christian Trinity but also in a mission to the Khazars. He and his brother went to the Slavic peoples and created the Glagolitic alphabet –

not the Cyrillic one sometimes attributed to them. They translated the Gospels and the Orthodox liturgy into the written language they had created so that the Slavs could hear and eventually some read about Christian faith in their own tongue. Their approach, which continued the ancient model of translation of the gospel into a people's heart language, was adopted in many of Eastern Orthodoxy's mission efforts. For centuries it formed a marked contrast with Roman Catholicism's decision to make Latin the Christian language.

CHRISTIANS AND THEIR CULTURES

Women as a rule had difficulty rising to positions of authority in Christian communities. But a few in each era worked themselves into unexpected roles. Hilda of Whitby (614–80) came from a noble family in England. Her father, Hereic, had been defeated by a rival so that he and his family fled to Northumbria, where his uncle, Edwin, ruled. When Hereic was poisoned, Edwin took responsibility for Hilda. On his conversion to Christ in 627, Hilda, as part of the family, converted also. She lived within the family until the age of thirty-three, when she decided to become a nun like her sister. She moved to East Anglia, where her mother's family resided, and stayed there for a year. She intended to go on to the Chelles nunnery near Paris, but the Celtic missionary Aidan (died 651), a preacher from Iona who would become the abbot at Lindesfarne, urged her to come north. He had no difficulty recognizing her gifts for leadership. She lived in a small community on the river Wear for a year and then was appointed abbess of Streaneshalch, later named Whitby.

The place was a double *monastery*: monks led the community worship and nuns spent their time in separate meditation. Hilda was the chief administrator and thus oversaw the local people who labored as farmers, shepherds, smiths, carpenters – anything needed. The monks and nuns in this monastery did not work, but the lands owned by the community, when properly managed, provided good livelihood for all. Hilda allowed no private property. She set up a remarkable library that included most biblical books, and had copies of its holdings reproduced. Five of her well disciplined and educated monks became bishops. Perhaps her most significant find was a herdsman, Caedmon, who wrote and sang poetry. She urged him to become a monk and then gave him time for his gift. He is still regarded as 'the father of English poetry'.

At Hilda's monastery in 664 the Synod of Whitby was held, in which Celtic practice and theology were submerged under Roman views about Easter's date, the proper liturgy and the acceptable tonsure. A friend of people on both sides of the rancorous debate, Hilda was an important figure in the eventual decision.

Boniface (*c.* 675–754) in his letters about the Germans noted that women trying to make pilgrim journeys to Rome often faced threats of slavery or death. Bringing converts to a level of maturity was extremely arduous. The German upper classes loved frivolous finery. Their pagan culture was deep and difficult to uproot. They followed quite different practices from the Christians, especially in regard to polygamy, incest and divorce. Boniface was horrified that some German Christians, who themselves no longer offered sacrifices to the pagan deities, would sell their slaves to pagans to be killed in worship of those bloodthirsty gods. Charlemagne (*c.* 742–814) forced conversion on pain of death, but he and his leaders noticed how difficult it was for German warriors to take the Christian ideal of poverty with any seriousness. Love of enemies, concepts of sin and repentance in one's own and the tribe's life proved almost beyond their ability to conceive let alone practice. He even found that the building of roads for trade and the movement of troops was problematic because trees were still regarded as sacred and water spirits in the rivers would be disturbed by the construction of bridges.

The connection between *Persian* and *Indian* Christians continued during this period. The exact date of the move into India by Thomas of Cana, Syria and a group of Persian migrants ranges from the fourth to the eighth century. That is because the information is lodged in eighteenth-century writings; earlier records had been destroyed by the Portuguese. When the tale is placed in 754 it includes a significant social comment. In the south-western state of Kerala, the caste system had no Vaishya or trader group. The four hundred Christians from Persia were primarily merchants. They were heartily welcomed by the Brahmins of Kerala because the local culture needed traders to enhance business.

The cultural power of Greek Orthodox *liturgy, art and architecture* emerges most clearly during this period in the story about the conversion of the Russ. A rustic pagan people, not unlike the Vikings in their ability to sail the rivers of Europe and plunder at will, the Russ had come into contact with Jews, Bulgarian Muslims, German Catholics and Greek Orthodox. Prince Vladimir of Kiev welcomed representatives of each religion who debated the value of their respective practices and beliefs. When Vladimir sent his own emissaries, they found 'no glory' among the Germans and 'unhappiness' among the Bulgars, but they were so taken up by the atmosphere of Hagia Sophia in Constantinople that they did not know 'whether [they] were in heaven or on earth'. Vladimir's decision in 988 that the Russ should be baptized as Christians was influenced both by his grandmother's Christian faith and the Boyars' sense that she was 'wiser than all other men'. But the worship in the greatest and most adorned church building in Christendom had overwhelmed his delegation.

Within the Byzantine sphere of influence, *Bulgaria*'s khan Boris accepted Christian missionaries in 866. The Greek mission there was founded by Cyril-Constantine (826–69) and Methodius (*c.* 815–85). They always took the local language and culture seriously and created both scripture and liturgy in Old Slavonic that could serve a number of these Eastern European peoples. But the Bulgarians began to balk at the Byzantine influence. Perhaps through contact with Paulicians in Armenia, a sect appeared called the Bogomils who were dualists like the Manichaeans. The physical world was totally evil, created by the Devil. Christ could not be incarnate in evil flesh. Mary was not an honored mother of God. At the final judgment, Christ would come to free the angelic souls of humans from their physical bondage. In doing that he would overturn the rule of Satan and his accomplices, the rich. They would perish whether their ill-gotten gain came from secular or religions sources.

This was surely a Christian heresy in terms of central beliefs. But in many ways it represented a social protest against corruption within the church, particularly the Byzantine church. Bogomils were not a large group and did not call for the use of force against Byzantines. But they insisted that church buildings were houses of the Devil and that the home of Satan was Hagia Sophia in Constantinople, the greatest, most lavishly decorated church in Christendom. Their ideology created a space for Bulgarian nationalism. Because they sent missionaries further West they probably had some impact on the rise of Cathars or Albigensians in France. In both cases the context was church wealth and abuse of power.

The Muslim conquest that began in *Arabia* (Saudi Arabia) swept through *Palestine* (Israel), *Syria* and *Egypt*. It absorbed Christians and their professions. For the first few centuries the Arabs found that Christians had bureaucratic skills and experience that were quite helpful. They frequently used their financial expertise in service of the new regimes.

Syrian and Egyptian clerks normally were Christians; the majority of the doctors in Syria belonged to the church. Particularly during the Umayyad Caliphate (661–750), Christians held offices of honor in the court. In the reign of Mu'awiya (661–80) the police force in the sacred city of Medina was made up of Christians from Ayla. Even as late as 991 the vizier of Baghdad was Nasr ben Harum, a Christian.

The Muslim rule that made the continuing fellowship of Middle Eastern Christians with the West more difficult had significant cultural effects. The adaptation of these Eastern Christians to *Arabic* and the culture in which it was imbedded was swift and did not necessarily involve conversion to Islam. An important portion of the Greek-speaking elite used their wealth to escape into lands still held by Christian political authorities. Most of the Christians in an area like Palestine (Israel) were Syriac speakers who themselves had never been quite certain that Greek culture and learning were necessary for Christian life. Even the important St. Sabas monastery by the end of the eighth century had few Greek speakers or writers within its confines. When the brilliant theologian Theodore Abū Qurrah died about 820, almost all Melkite (Orthodox) theologians wrote in either Syriac or Arabic. By then Christians of the Holy Land were once again primarily Semites in culture and speech and thus cut off from Christians in the West whose theology was dominated by Latin and Greek. As those Western Christians contextualized their life and faith into their cultures and languages, a chasm began to open up that would threaten Christianity with permanent divisions.

Christians in Muslim lands eventually felt the weight of their rulers. Even in this period their taxes became oppressive. The time of their collection was a time of fear. Before the end of the seventh century, the Greek-speaking Christian administrators who were so helpful to Muslim governments early in the conquests were being replaced as Arabic became the language of state. Christian images, so basic to houses of worship when Christians were in power, aggravated Muslims. They were defaced or destroyed, sometimes their buildings with them. By about 720 Christians could not pray loudly in their worship or ring bells. They were allowed neither to ride saddled horses nor to wear clothing that resembled that of Arab soldiers. No Arab would be executed for killing a Christian, although he might have to pay a large fine. These cultural and religious changes put great pressure on ordinary Christians. The sum total of Middle Eastern church buildings in use by 750 was only half those necessary in 600.

None of this can be denied. But at the beginning of the tenth century, after almost three centuries under Islamic rule, Nicholas I, patriarch of Constantinople, wrote to Caliph al-Muktafī that despite such clear differences between Christians and Muslims they should continue to be in discussion with each other as brothers. There was no reason to think of each group as being totally alien to the other. In a letter to the emir of Crete, Nicholas granted that there was a dividing wall between them in terms of worship, but said there must be friendship among those who seek the good. Both Christians and Muslims admired wisdom, intelligence, stable conduct, love for all people, indeed any attribute that made human nature better.

At the upper levels of learned writers, Muslims and Christians shared such interesting points of view. Christians in the Middle East had many manuscripts of *Aristotle*. The East Syrians, as they were forced further and further east in Syria toward Persia because Greek Orthodox Christians found them heretical, moved their schools with them. Those schools not only had the writings of their fourth- and fifth-century Christian theologians, such as Theodore of Mopsuestia's commentaries on scripture translated into Syriac; their libraries also contained manuscripts of selected Greek philosophers like Aristotle, some still in Greek and others already rendered into Syriac. Before the end of the first Islamic century a number of those latter works had begun to appear in Arabic. Muslim interest in Aristotle also meant that some Christian commentaries on Aristotle became guides for Muslim philosophers. Avicenna (980–1037) was an Arab sage and physician who worked in Persian Muslim courts. He employed writings on Aristotle by the sixth-century Christian John Philoponos in his attempt to understand the ancient Greek philosopher on points where theological views might come to play in each religion.

The life of learning eventually flowed back in the other direction. Greek wisdom had waned around the northern edges of the Mediterranean and in the interior of Europe. Charlemagne had assembled a remarkable court of philosophers and theologians, but a darkness eventually dimmed European insight into the scholarship of antiquity. Thus it was Muslim erudition, which had absorbed the Jacobite and East Syrian cache of Greek culture, that became a significant source of this scholarship's rebirth in greater Europe. As one example, Adelbard of Bath, England, an early twelfth-century figure, traveled in North Africa and Asia Minor (Turkey), where he met Muslim scholars. He returned to Bath with a copy of Euclid's *Geometry* in both its Greek original and an

Arabic translation. When he wrote about a Christian understanding of the world's creation, he emphasized his faith's conception of God as the ultimate Creator. But he also stressed that the Arabs had taught any person willing to think carefully that nature could itself offer lessons about any conception of creation and the Creator. He was willing to learn from nature as well as from the Qur'an and other Muslim sources; he used them all in deepening his theology.

A CHRISTIAN CORE

One of the great figures of *European* Christian *spirituality*, Maximus the Confessor (580–662) was born in the East, probably in Constantinople. He was forced west by Persian invasions and eventually settled in a Byzantine monastic community at Carthage. Some of his writings focused on ambiguities in scripture and in the writings of previous spiritual writers like Gregory of Nazianzus (*c.* 329–90) and the Pseudo-Dionysian works (*c.* 500). He developed a set of one hundred maxims for living as a Christian, all of them centered on the balance in God's work between the incarnation of Jesus Christ and the sharing of God's nature by humans, called 'deification'. The latter entailed the restoration of the image of God in humans through Christ taking on humans' destruction of their original condition. The core of God's act in Christ was not the bringing of some 'objective' religious knowledge. It was in creating the conditions for and offering the power to live the virtuous life through the imparting of mystical understanding. Various disciplines of contemplation and charity, each attempting to control worldly desire, could lead to union with God. Maximus's commentaries on the Lord's Prayer and the liturgy helped make clear their purposes in the meditative life.

In terms of specific *doctrines* Maximus stood against Monophysite and Monothelite views of Christ, i.e. that he had only one divine nature and one divine will. In those views neither human nature nor will was a part of his person. The battle over these questions was so strong that Maximus was eventually brought to Constantinople, where his tongue was cut out and his right hand severed. Exiled to the Caucasus mountains, he soon died from his wounds. The positions he took were in line with the Council of Chalcedon (451) and were confirmed in the Sixth Ecumenical Council of 680. Once again we see the sad consequences of Christians defining their teachings with such passion that they caused the death of one of their spiritual giants.

In the Middle East the character of majority Christian communities changed as their political power disappeared. The Melkites (Orthodox) could not regularly exert pressure on the Jacobites (Monophysites) and the so-called Nestorians (East Syrians) to get back in line. Now they and any other Christian group were minorities – or at least communities with much less political power. Disagreements continued, but no Christian 'orthodoxy' could be imposed on Christian 'heretics'.

The Orthodox defense of *icons* was a central issue during this period. The Seventh Ecumenical Council (787) settled the question for many, but the battle had begun in 726 and was not completed until 843. John of Damascus (*c.* 650/675–749), probably the greatest theologian of his time who wrote in the midst of Islam, mounted strong arguments in favor of icons; Theodore of Studios (759–826), a monastic reformer, best represented those views in the later stages of the debate. It might seem odd attempting to understand the ban on idolatry in the Old Testament as supporting defenders of icons. The earlier fathers of the church almost unanimously fought against the depictions of gods which they found in paganism. But the ground the iconodules (those who praised the images) laid out has often been viewed as persuasive. Of course they distinguished between the veneration of icons and the worship of God. No one should worship an image as one did God. Intriguingly, however, they made the definitive question one of Christology. Was the Son of God, the second person of the Trinity, truly incarnate in the flesh, living as a man with a full human nature? If he were human, he could be pictured without breaking the prohibition of making graven images of God. The iconodules charged that the iconoclasts were denying that Jesus Christ came in the flesh. In a similar way these opponents were insisting on the evil essence of all things material, whereas God in creation said that they were good. The iconodules charged the iconoclasts with viewing salvation as freedom from the flesh rather than the taking on of a resurrection body like Jesus' and like the one described by Paul. What might have appeared to be a rancorous debate about a style of worship turned out in the eyes of the iconodules to be tantamount to denying the core of Christian belief. The character of Eastern Orthodoxy perhaps is best revealed in the decision to keep the icons. Deep popular piety and intricate theological argument melded. The unlettered could read God's care in the images. More significantly in the Orthodox view, in an icon earth and heaven met, and that meeting was accessible to all.

Mass *baptisms*, employed by Vladimir in 988 for the Russ and by the Franks when they conquered new tribes in Western Europe, have presented problems. At least this one went through the natural decision processes of the Russ; it was not enforced from outside. Such baptisms have been a continuing experience, marked first by the three thousand on Pentecost in Jerusalem. Cultures that have strong group identity have found such baptisms easier to assimilate. Pastoral care, always so important in Christian communities, then becomes the overriding issue.

When we ask about the center of Christian faith, the need for the reform of a secularized church that was run primarily by lay political rulers pops up once more. Even the monasteries that had been so important in the conversion of Central Europe's indigenous tribes required clearer focus. A series of *monastic reform movements* appeared at the beginning of the tenth century, the most famous one at Cluny in France. During 909 William of Aquitaine, a duke who mourned a murder he had committed, gave the entire village to abbot Berno with the renunciation of any rights for his heirs to the property or to the selection of the abbot. That freedom allowed Berno to bring back the rule of St. Benedict as Cluny's guide. Some outstanding abbots over the next two hundred years made Cluny a center of reform, itself marked by an increase in monastic concern with liturgical prayer. From that life of devotion, Cluniac monks were encouraged to work for reforms through their exemplary lives and their powers of persuasion. They fought simony (the purchasing of church offices) and clerical marriage, but rather than working for the ouster of sinful priests, they were most intent upon guiding lay church leaders toward embodying virtues. Cluny abbots had open doors to most European courts. In 1095 Pope Urban II, a previous grand prior of Cluny, returned to consecrate the altar of the Cluny church, by 1132 the largest in Europe until the building of St. Peter's in the sixteenth century.

One of the truly remarkable pieces of medieval Christian literature is the *Heliand* (*Savior*), a tale of the gospel written by a poetic monk who attempted to let the gospel 'sing' in the culture of the Saxons. Evidently King Louis the Pious (778–840) ordered the bard to write it for the benefit of new Saxon converts. The facets of culture that were important to the Saxons became the carriers of the news about Jesus and his kingdom. Jesus appears as a liege lord and his apostles as loyal vassals. Heaven is a lush meadow. They make their way to that land in their sleek boats. Both humility and love for their enemies emerge

as themes to counter much of the Saxons' warlike culture. Yet in form
the piece wisely resembles other indigenous Anglo-Saxon poetry of the
time.

One of the main Christian sources for the *Heliand* is Tatian's *Diates-saron*, a harmony of the four biblical Gospels, which eventually had been
rejected by the Syrian communities it was supposed to serve. Why a copy
was available in Central Europe is difficult to say. But it would not be
the last time that a Christian work found to be deficient by an earlier
generation would arise again as a significant help.

In *Africa* the Christian community in Ethiopia had developed a way
of life that did not strike some others as genuine. Because the first king
converted in that land, a man named Ezana, ruled over a people either
of Semitic origins or acculturated into Semitic customs, Ethiopian Christians lived in an unusual relationship with Hebraic traditions. Their language is a Semitic tongue. Their earliest manuscripts date from the
thirteenth century; thus we can describe Ethiopian Christians of this
period only cautiously. They claimed to possess the Jewish ark of the
covenant. The Jewish sabbath was important in their history and at the
end of this era became a contested feature of the church. Various practices and doctrines of Jewish origin, particularly circumcision, dietary
laws and ritual cleansings, marked their life. Both their liturgical music
and their division of seating arrangements in their churches – priests,
males and females – gave their worship a shape not quite like that of
Western Christians.

Why these features dominated their life can be answered in a number
of ways. The community claimed that it went back to contact between
the Queen of Sheba and Solomon and the conversion of Queen
Candace's treasurer by Philip the Evangelist. The Falasha, a group in
north-west Ethiopia, although apparently Jewish through neither blood,
language nor full Hebrew traditional ties, had described themselves as
'the house of Israel'. They did have the late Jewish *Book of Enoch* in
their language, a writing that nearly disappeared except for a few scraps
in other languages. Thus the Jewish influence on Ethiopian Christians
seems to have traveled a twisting path that changed the character of that
influence on the journey.

Strong African influences that undergirded some of the same features
must also be given their due. Circumcision of both males and females
appears elsewhere in Africa without any contact with Jews. Dietary
laws and ritual cleansings also need not be explained only by Jewish

background. Even the Coptic Christians of Egypt may have introduced Ethiopian believers to or confirmed some of their apparently Jewish characteristics. These Ethiopians appear to have accepted an amalgam of African indigenous religious practices, various Jewish customs brought into their culture through the southern diaspora, and views held by Coptic Christians. Alexandrian Christian authorities employed monks to Christianize other aspects of their culture.

Christians in Nubia (Sudan) survived the first Arabian invasions by fielding savage armies, agreeing to a treaty and keeping even Arab merchants from moving deeper into the country beyond the first cataract of the Nile. But in the Baqt treaty of 651 the Nubians agreed to keep in good repair the mosque at Old Dongola. And in the ninth century Arab traders not only penetrated the borders but eventually settled in the country because trade between Christian Ethiopia and Muslim Egypt was quite lucrative.

The development of Christian communities in Nubia is marked by their isolation on one hand and their trade and political connections on the other. After nearly a thousand years of experience with a divine king who ruled through pagan religious and political power, and then a period of odd religious toleration from the Ballana kings, Christians created a strong separation between church and state. In the ninth century no ruler was accorded divine status; no burial sites for Christian kings are even known. The Nubian kings who resided at Old Dongola lived as if they were potentates who owned all lands and considered all people their slaves. When challenged, however, that proved to be untrue. Peasants sold their lands much as they wished.

These kings are depicted in the paintings at Faras as wearing robes resembling those worn by Byzantine emperors and as accompanied by important government figures whose titles are sometimes Greek ones. Local bishops are also attired in finery, but it does not seem to be that close to the vestments of Constantinopolitan patriarchs.

There has been some evidence of *Chinese* Christians borrowing from other religions to the point that the charge of improper syncretism has arisen. But one of the Dunhuang treatises insists that however deep the adoption of Chinese religions was, it did not replace 'the core of Christian faith' with something else. The remarkable song of Christian praise 'The Hymn of the Saved to the Trinity' closely resembles the 'Gloria in excelsis Deo' in Syriac, but is a slight expansion in content rendered into beautiful Chinese. It contains verses of four lines that rhyme in the second and fourth lines with each line composed of seven Chinese characters. It is quite orthodox and composed by someone of considerable talent. There are three clear references to Father, Son and Holy Spirit, each worded a bit differently. At the same time two Buddhist concepts, the root of good in each human and the saving raft, are also mentioned. This is a Chinese Christian hymn.

The text of the Chang'an (Xi'an) stele also follows a well-established outline of Christian faith in its description of what the community believes: God as Trinity, creation, humanity, sin, incarnation, salvation, a twenty-seven-book canon, ministry, baptism and Eucharist. Chinese Christians fasted regularly, met for worship seven times a day and once in seven days they observed 'a sacrifice without the animal'.

This description depicts a monastic community. The monks have kept their beards but shaved the crowns of their heads. As Christians did in Persia, they beat wooden boards rather than striking bells. These Chinese Christians kept neither male nor female slaves and did not make distinctions between high-born and common folk; indeed they tended to give away their wealth. The stele makes clear that East Syrian Christians in China may be accused of a syncretism too deep to be ignored but that they cannot be said to have lost their moorings in the practice of Christian virtues.

A list of saints, mostly monks and bishops, is included at the end of the stele inscription. One in particular demonstrates how well some of these Christians lived their faith, yet in somewhat ambiguous ways. The chief commander of one of China's regional armies that won victories in the 750s and 760s, Yazdbuzid, a Christian from Balkh in Bactria, eventually retired from his duties. He turned to the calling of his father and became a Christian priest in a rural district outside Chang'an (Xi'an). The riches he received from the emperor for his military service he gave to the church. That wealth paid for the repair of monasteries and the building and beautifying of churches. His fortune created the great stele and had it erected. He insisted that the full Lenten and Easter week services were kept. But four lines represent him as more than a powerful rich patron: 'The hungry came and they were fed. The cold came and they were clothed. The sick were healed and raised up. The dead were buried and laid to rest.'

In *Europe* Boniface (*c.* 675–754) became known as the apostle to the Germans. He worked strongly not only in evangelism but also in the reform of the existing churches. He was certain that clergy should live strictly by the Benedictine rule so that their lives would be formed around worship, meditation and service.

In the West the Carolingian renaissance also was concerned with the clergy, particularly monks who lived after the manner of Boniface. Chrodegang of Metz (died 766) came from a wealthy family and knew personally how secular riches and customs could affect the clergy of churches built and endowed by noble families. He insisted on personal piety and went back to the Benedictine rule. Similar canons became the manuals for secular clergy at most of the cathedrals of Europe up to the Reformation. Usually, when strict compliance was mandated, Christian leadership flourished in worship and service. But laxity crept in and reform was a constant concern.

In Western Europe, Benedictine monasticism ruled from the eighth to the twelfth century. Benedict (480–540) founded no order but his rule became dominant early in this period, but it was not the most important guideline in Rome until the tenth century. Primarily it called for the reform of ministry by establishing a counter to the moral decline of non-monastic, secular priests. Benedict of Aniane (c. 750–821) was an early force during the reigns of Pepin and Charlemagne. The heritage of reform was so strong that the next era saw recurring attempts to root out the effects of lax obedience to the call for ascetic poverty, chastity and obedience. No full description of any Christian core could be constructed without attention to Benedictine practices and definitions.

In Europe, Anselm of Canterbury (c. 1033–1109), a monk among the Franks before he became a bishop in England, was one of the finest theologians of the period. Immersed in the prayer and devotion of medieval monasticism, he also had a love for the common people and a curiosity about their conditions. In his view all theology was faith seeking understanding because any theologian must lead a life of prayer and meditation before anything like understanding could appear. The most famous of his treatises were written primarily for the monks who had some contact with the folk outside the monastery. They are too long and intricate for direct consumption by those who could neither read nor had the interest to follow the arguments. His apparent proof for the existence of God in the *Proslogium* suggested that the supreme being must be the greatest figure imaginable. Since it would be greater to exist than not to exist, God must exist or someone greater than he could be imagined. Peasants would have found the logic dense – it is more intricate than the statement here. In the twentieth century the philosopher Charles

Hartshorne still found merit in that proof, but surely only a few common medieval folk could have sensed its weight. But the framing of the argument within the treatise itself both firmly and poetically insists that only through joy and love could a level of illumination be reached in which such an argument for the existence of God could emerge. Within Christian community, joy and love were basic to the life of any believer.

The core of the *Cur Deus Homo*, however, probably could have been taught to the illiterate who had felt the sting of Frankish law. Punishment was meted out on the basis not only of the extent of the crime but mostly in reference to the status of the people involved. If one peasant killed another, both the court and the law grasped that retributive payment would be small and involve only the criminal. If, however, a peasant killed the son of a prince, everything that the peasant and his family had, including their lives, was owed to the prince. There was no way in which they could ever really pay the debt. Anselm used this law to tell the story of Jesus dying for human's sins. Jesus Christ had to be a full human being because a human had to pay the human debt. But the unpaid debt to God was massive; sinful humankind did not have the necessary funds. So Jesus also had to be the divine Son of God in order to possess the wealth needed. Boiling down his consequent argument could lead to sermons that even the underclass could understand. Given to monks as the foundation for their preaching and explanation, this argument became a source of significant penetration of the gospel among Frankish people.

Anselm tells us in various places in his writings that he had visited the markets and talked with the people in order to find out how and what they thought. They did not know the Bible, so it was unwise to begin evangelizing or re-evangelizing them by quoting it. What was necessary was living goodness before them and trying to find bridges of understanding whose foundations were sunk deeply in their everyday conversations. From his musings we can observe both a great theologian at work preparing for the popularization of the gospel and an attentive preacher who tried to see and hear what those around him understood.

During the eleventh and twelfth century among *Arabic-speaking Christians* in Andalusian Spain, various works appeared from these Mozarabs who had grown up in the midst of Muslim culture. They knew the Qur'an and much of the law that directed Muslim life, particularly the Hadîth, but they also were aware of Arabic Christian writings from the Middle East and various Latin Christian writings on the Trinity. Some of this literature has come down to us primarily in the manuscripts of later Muslim refutations. Their Muslim neighbors took them seriously. In a wonderful fashion they open a window on Christian communities that had educated scholars who made their way through Muslim religious claims from within the Islamic culture in which they were nurtured. At the same time they stood for the doctrine of the Trinity and incarnation and even reflected some of the recent developments among Latin theologians. These authors had a deep respect for Muslim revelation from God, but they did not sacrifice their own deeply Christian revelations of Trinity and incarnation.

The saddest tale of intra-Christian relationships during this period is the excommunication of the Orthodox patriarch, Michael Cerularius, in 1054 by Cardinal Humbert, the leader of a small delegation from Pope Leo IX. Humbert was one of the appointees to the Cardinalate, the close advisors of the papacy. Leo IX had recently selected many Western cardinals, so Catholicism looked almost entirely like a Western religion. Humbert traveled to Constantinople to negotiate with the patriarch because Norman attacks on southern Italy had endangered property of the Holy Roman Empire, the Vatican and the Byzantine Empire. Agreement between Pope Leo IX and Patriarch Cerularius would surely assist the battle against the Normans. But the pope wanted the few Greek churches in Italy to follow Roman patterns. The patriarch responded by insisting that Latin churches in Constantinople follow Greek patterns. Other disagreements about Bulgarian mission also proved to be sore points.

When Humbert arrived in Constantinople he wanted the patriarch to fall into line as a bishop under the papacy. A series of doctrines and practices struck him as heretical: the lack of the *filioque* clause (that the Spirit proceeded from both the Father and the Son) which the West had added to the Eastern Nicene Creed, the use of unleavened rather than leavened bread in the Eucharist, and other liturgical matters. When Cerularius did not budge from his tradition, Humbert wrote out a bull of excommunication and placed it on the altar of Hagia Sophia, the central church in Constantinople. This affront, grounded in Humbert's sincere belief that anything not Roman was heretical and his arrogant anger at any disagreement, was followed by Cerularius's excommunication of the Roman legation.

Humbert had no sense of different traditions or adaptations to cultures. Cerularius stood on the singular truth of Orthodox tradition. Each insisted that 'the core of Christian life' had to be embodied in his way.

The continuation of such views has made it difficult (but not impossible) for traditional Catholic and Orthodox missionaries to recognize as fully authentic various contextualization projects that affirmed significant aspects of other cultures. That has been especially true of anything that the missionaries understood as part of the Christian core. The center, whether practice or doctrine, had to remain just as it was in Rome or in Constantinople. Tragically, this clash between Humbert and Cerularius created a fault line among Christians that still causes earthquakes. When Pope John Paul II visited Greece in 2001, some Greek bishops refused to receive him because of this 1054 débâcle.

By contrast Margaret of Scotland (c. 1045–93) found other ways to work reform that took Roman Christianity as its goal. Raised in Hungary and well educated by Benedictines, she and her family made their way to England in 1058. As endangered Saxon nobles after the Norman victory in 1066, they attempted to sail toward Europe but were blown to Wearmouth. There they met Malcolm Canmore on one of his raids. In an unexpected move, he took the family into his court in Dunfermline. Margaret had planned to become a nun but Malcolm, a widower, married her.

She had six sons and two daughters with Malcolm and proved to be a good mother and wife. Her refinement and education made her seem a bit odd in the rough surroundings of the Scottish court, but Malcolm loved her dearly. He neither learned to read nor gave up his warring ways, but he valued books because she did. He watched with amusement as she gave away much of her own wealth, even at times her outer clothes. When she got into his money chests he joked that he would have her put in jail, but instead continued to support her alms.

Margaret was upset by the state of Christian practice and faith not only among the people but also among the Celtic monks called Culdees. Because they had no contact with Rome or the seventh-century Whitby decision to follow Rome, they still worshipped according to a Celtic rite that seemed 'barbarous' to her Latin spiritual director, Turgot. Their sabbath was on Saturday, making Sunday a workday. They did not kneel but stood in church. Neither the Lenten fast nor the celebration of Easter was their custom. In discussions with her in which Turgot translated – she could not master Gaelic as she had Latin and French – these Celtic monks agreed to the reforms. They had resisted taking communion because they were sinful, but she cajoled them even on that point. But when she met Celtic hermits, she did not attempt to sway them toward her Latin customs. When they would not accept money she gave it to people in the region whom they selected. Furthermore, after the end of the Norwegian raids, she and her husband went to Iona, found it in disarray and rebuilt the monastery. She also erected hospices for pilgrims traveling to sites of St. Andrew.

Her practice of giving alms for the poor got her a hearing from the Celtic monks. They found her reforms bearable and followed them. And she responded with help for their sacred sites and pilgrimages.

Celtic theology was not always weak and in need of reform. One of its gifts to the whole church has been its concern for and communion with *nature*. Particularly among the Celtic saints, a high regard for God's creation, for God's earth and its creatures, emerged. In one example of various tales about St. Cuthbert (died 687), the saint has otters drying his feet after he has been in the ocean. In another story an osprey brings him and his companions a fish. He accepts it, cuts it in half and gives one half back to the osprey. The continuing point of these narratives emphasizes cooperation with nature rather than a dominion over it that leads to its wounding or destruction.

CONCLUSION

The rise of Muhammad and his followers displaced Christians in the Middle East and elsewhere. At first disciples of Christ were honored by Muslims as people of the book, but within two centuries the tolerance of the Muslims had begun to wane. Their responses to Christianity ranged from severe attacks on the moral character of Jesus to praise of his war on idolatry and his support of the helpless. Christians expressed similar views of Muslims.

European Christendom recovered under Frankish kings, particularly Charlemagne. The evangelization begun by Benedictine monks was 'solidified' under Frankish political power. Whole tribes converted because their conquerors demanded it. How deep the change was is questionable. Mission among Scandinavians included a similar mix of political power and cultural affirmation.

Orthodox Christian missionaries created written languages for Slavic tribes so that they could read the Bible in their own tongues. The Russ chose the Christian faith because Prince Vladimir's grandmother, 'wisest of men', lived by it; they may have selected its Orthodox form because the church, Hagia Sophia, in Constantinople seemed to draw them up into heaven.

The sad split between the Catholic West and the Orthodox East at the end of this period was due not only to differences in doctrine, but also to widely divergent cultures and the temperaments of flawed men. Only in the twentieth century did serious progress in healing the breech begin.

Chinese Christians, centered in monastic communities, probably reached their zenith during this period. Their faith was similar to that of Christians in Europe. They translated a Trinitarian hymn in Syriac into beautiful Chinese poetry. Their best leaders well understood how important taking care of the needy actually was. But during persecutions of Buddhists as believers in a foreign religion, Christians, as foreigners, also suffered.

4 CRUSADES TO THE NEAR EXTINCTION OF ASIAN CHRISTIANS, 1100–1500

Although Christians have failed in many times and places, their worst débâcle, arguably with the single exception of the European Holocaust, was the *Crusades*. These movements of European Christians into the Middle East, most often through armed incursions, encompassed nearly two hundred years of conflict with Muslims, from 1096 until the final expulsion of Christians in 1291. The depth of the tragedy, however, is most clear in the way that both Jews and Muslims in the twenty-first century still view Christian motives and actions through the lens of crusades. Christian mission is thus seen as oppressive from beginning to end, backed by established economic and political power in the United States and elsewhere. Tragically, Western conservative Christians still seem imprisoned in such language. They can still refer to their evangelistic campaigns as 'crusades' with no sense of the chilling overtones.

Some historians have numbered the Crusades as four, distinguished by different leaders and results. The first, called by Pope Urban II in 1095, primarily involved armies from France and southern Italy. Probably the most successful militarily, these expeditions took Antioch of Syria in 1098 and Jerusalem in 1099. For twenty years Western troops held those areas and expanded both along the coast of Syria–Palestine and further east all the way to Edessa. They built castles and set up feudal kingdoms whose boundaries were difficult to sustain. The second, supported by the great spiritual leader Bernard of Clairvaux, set out in 1147 with both French and imperial soldiers. It attempted to retake Edessa, lost in 1144, but proved rather ineffective. The third, in 1189–91, involving imperial, English and French armies was a reaction to the great success of Saladin in 1187. He had recaptured Jerusalem in that year and overrun a large part of the Latin kingdoms. Nearly 100,000 troops under Richard the Lionheart sought to cut off the 'pagan' Muslim hand that held the Holy Sepulcher. Only one in twelve of those troops returned to Europe. The fourth crusade had severe repercussions for the relationships between Greek and Latin Christians. The Venetian fleet took the European soldiers on their venture and demanded that Venice's trading competitor, Zagreb, on the eastern Adriatic coast be sacked as payment. But once that looting was completed, the Venetians insisted, in 1204, that Constantinople also be pillaged to compensate them further. This strange invasion battered two Christian cities and strengthened a Latin kingdom in Constantinople, but it had almost no effect on the Holy Land. Further adventures in the thirteenth century had little success. Jerusalem was recovered for fifteen years but retaken in 1244. By 1291 the last Latin kingdom disappeared under the thankful praise and pledge of Muslims that such folk should never again set foot on their land. Europe itself had tired of the carnage and turned to preaching the Christian gospel to Muslims in the Holy Land and to Mongols in the East.

The reasons given for these incursions often include Muslim interdiction of pilgrim travel to Jerusalem. Such journeys were built into medieval Western consciousness. The closing of pilgrim routes to the sacred sites in the Holy Land had created its own horror in European minds. The earliest 'crusades' were called 'pilgrimages'; only later did the name 'crusade' appear. Thus religious motivations emerged as a main root for the conflicts that turned into conflagrations.

These wars also reflected economic and social realities. Italian traders from Venice and Florence were making hoards of money trading for Eastern goods that became accessible to Europeans at ports on the eastern edge of the Mediterranean. The feudal structure of Western European society also left a series of noble young men without positions to which they felt born. The ability to get many of them out of Europe to fight somewhere else for a cause sanctioned by Christian clerics, monks and popes suited the entire culture's sense of honor. These leaders going to Jerusalem were able to exert the military skills in which they had been educated and had the promise of booty to support their dreams. On top of that they took with them some disciplined soldiers and a rabble who also would have disrupted life if left in their European homes.

The Crusades have little for which they may be commended. Early French and German armies moved overland through Eastern Europe eradicating the Jews who had been settled for centuries in various cities. If these 'pilgrims' were going to the Holy Land to wrest it from the damnable Muslims, they could surely assist European life by ridding it of the Jews whose ancestors had killed Jesus in the first place. The moral degradation expanded its range during the so-called fourth crusade when the crusaders sacked the 'Christian' city Constantinople because the Eastern Orthodox were heretics and did not deserve what they had. The effect was to weaken the one Christian stronghold in the East, Constantinople, that had held out against the Muslim conquest since the seventh century.

One of the later crusades was composed primarily of children who went in their innocence under God's protection in order to melt Muslim hearts. Supporters mused that it could fulfill the real needs of Christians for connection with their Holy Land. These misguided youths either died of malnutrition and disease or were sold into slavery by the shipping interests who took them to Egypt. Even the apparently pacifist approach represented no mature judgment of dedicated adults, only the persuasive words of unbalanced prophets leading children astray.

As in the midst of most disasters that surround wars, some benefits occurred. The learned among the Crusaders soon found that Muslim education in all areas, including military strategy, was often much better than their own. These incursions shattered the isolation of Europe because even those who could not read could return home with stories of different ways of fighting, dressing, eating, building houses, etc. The term 'Dark Ages' that some historians have used to describe the preceding period in Europe has been greatly overstated. But the resurgence of learning in the West depended substantially on the ability of Western travelers to find new developments among the Muslims and bring back in stolen manuscripts even aspects of their own classical Greek heritage that were then a staple of Islamic thought.

Whatever might be said about good consequences from the Crusades, the overall effect has plagued Christians for more than seven centuries since the last incursion. Ousting Jews through persecution and death became a broad undercurrent of European Christian society. Mistrust grew between Eastern Orthodox and Western Catholics that only began to abate in the twentieth century. And the continuing misunderstanding of Muslims and Christians, then written in blood, now can be laid to the Crusades. Muslims during these invasions continued to see jihad as a holy war even though a group of their intellectuals demanded a larger and more peaceful context for the concept. It need not require armed conflict. Western Catholic canon lawyers worked diligently to flesh out the Augustinian understanding of a just war. They knew that the Crusades had not followed rules of justice, but they claimed that just wars should. Yet at their best these two intellectual undertakings did not solve the difficulties. Although the Muslim effort created a space in which fierce loyalty to Allah could be lived without bloodshed, it left intact a powerful call to die in battle for the one God revealed to Muhammad. The Christian development depended on a sense that just war theory could reign in the worst abuses. The theory was never intended to eradicate armed conflict; the outcome was primarily an attempt to sanitize war. It never cleans up easily.

CHRISTIANS AND PEOPLE OF OTHER FAITHS

The Crusades dominated the way in which European Christians approached both Jews and Muslims. Yet a different, more gentle approach to *Muslims* tiptoed through some of the written works we have from the period of the Crusades and beyond.

An important apology for Christian faith over against Muslims, delivered in the *majlis* (the protected discussions) during the early eleventh century, is attributed to Elias of Nisibis, a famous Arabic Christian writer. The piece has a peculiar twist for this kind of literature. An East Syrian (Nestorian) theologian, Elias claimed that Christians like those in his group as well as Melkites and Jacobites confessed that God is one just as the Qur'an claimed. Indeed the Qur'an itself described Christians as such believers. The polytheists were those who tried to imitate Christians but were not genuine believers: Marcionites, Daisānites, Manichaeans and Tritheists. Muslim practice agreed with the restrictions of the Qur'an but at the same time it included marrying Christian women and eating meat butchered by Christians. Christians did honor Muslims and lived well among them because the Muslims and their Qur'an both honored and protected the Christians among them.

This is an interesting riposte in at least two ways. First, few Christians seem to have claimed that Nestorians, Melkites (Syrian Orthodox) and Jacobites (West Syrians), whose Christologies so often seemed at odds, shared something more important than their differences: their oneness in defense of monotheism. Second, few pointed out to Muslims that the four other groups – Marcionites, Daisānites, Manichaeans and tritheists – could be described as imitators of Christians but who in reality were polytheists.

Yet another *majlis* encounter in an emir's court, probably in the twelfth century, shows that occasionally a strong attack on Muhammad as more concerned with his own interests than those of God could be made in this protected setting. The monk George defended worship of the cross as directed to the prototype where Jesus hung, not the symbol itself. No idolatry was involved. In what probably appears to a modern reader as a humorous aside, George suggested a second ordeal when that of fire, which he requested, had been refused. He proposed that each participant in the debate, the emir included, take a bath to see which one was the dirtiest. Perhaps he did think that cleanliness was next to godliness.

In the Middle East during the twelfth century a Christian theologian named Paul of Antioch wrote a letter to some of his Muslim friends. In his travels to the West he had been asked by various Christians to indicate how they should understand and approach Muslims. Paul made no personal attack on Muhammad as an untruthful deceiver who waged horrible wars. In his view Muhammad raised the religious consciousness of ignorant Arabs and thus had an honorable mission. But his message was not universal; it was addressed to pagan Arabs. Paul favorably quoted the Qur'an to support his views, but insisted that Christians had a superior revelation and thus had no need to become Muslims. Christ appeared in the Qur'an and was in important ways celebrated there. Indeed the central Christian doctrines of Trinity, incarnation, and union with God did not contradict Muslim conviction about the oneness of God.

By the thirteenth and fourteenth centuries a series of Muslim theologians had responded to Paul's letter. Ibn Taymīyah's large response attacked Paul's main points, particularly the claim that Muslims did not represent a universal religion. The Qur'an, Jewish scripture, and reason by itself all confirmed Muslim teachings. For Taymīyah the Qur'an was the fullest of all the holy books. Indeed there was a wholeness in all prophetic religions. Muhammad as the last prophet was the final word. Christian gospel stories about Jesus' resurrection and the work of his disciples were late interpolations into Christian scripture. Baptism into the Father, the Son and the Holy Spirit in Matthew 28, verse 19 could not mean what Christians said it did.

The Majorcan Raymond Llull (1235–1315), after a conversion that led him to leave family and wealth, spent ten years in conversations with Jews and particularly Muslims because he wanted them to become

Christians. He convinced rulers and the rich to set up colleges for the preparation of missionaries to Muslims, always insisting that the learning of Arabic and the study of Muslim literature comprised the first step. He himself traveled to North Africa on mission trips. In Tunis during 1291 he vigorously engaged the Muslim literati and confronted them with what he claimed were the errors in their doctrine of God. Just after the turn of the century he made an attempt to preach in Syria, but was rebuffed. Tradition says he died in Bugie about one hundred miles from Algiers after a final attempt to preach Christ to Muslims. Whether or not he opposed the Crusades is unclear, but he did find apologetic argument about the truth of Muslim philosophy and religion the better approach. He believed that all people should be of one language and faith. He studiously avoided basing his arguments on Christian scripture. His starting point was the shared monotheism of Jews, Christians and Muslims. This he linked both to various Neoplatonic conceptions and to his own mystical visions.

The founding of the Franciscans in 1209 and the Dominicans in 1220–1 had strengthened this more understanding response to Muslims. Both orders are noted for their renewal of Christian life as well as missionary work in Europe, but they were influential elsewhere. After being turned back from trips to Syria and Morocco in 1212–14, Francis of Assisi in 1219 traveled unprotected to Egypt in order to preach to Muslims. His discussions with Malik-al Kamil led to the possibility of Franciscans moving into the Holy Land. This important mission, centered on persuasion and care for people who held other beliefs, was important to Franciscans. Francis's 1221 rule, chapter 16 is entitled 'Those Who Are Going among the Saracens and Other Nonbelievers'.

St. Dominic had a similar view for his order. Some of them worked among the Turkic Cumans who lived between the Black and Caspian Seas (north-western Turkey, Georgia, Armenia, Azerbaijan and parts of southern Russia). Others moved alongside Crusaders in Syria and Palestine (Israel), where they called the Western invaders to account for their ethics. They intentionally worked among the various kinds of Middle Eastern Christians to promote acceptance and attempted to convert Muslims in what was a very difficult climate. William of Tripoli (c. 1220–73) was born to European parents who had settled in the Latin kingdom centered in Tripoli. He grew up fluent in both Latin and Arabic. As a Dominican he preached the good news to Muslims and claimed, probably inflating the number, to have won a thousand. Going against the pope, he rejected military conquest and philosophical debate as improper approaches. In an interesting book in which he attempted to picture those considered by the West to be heretics and unbelievers, he depicted Islamic life equitably by using many quotations from the Qur'an. For him there were similarities between the teachings of Christians and Muslims that were important and could open up a different kind of contact. He optimistically read the Mongol conquest of the Abbasid Caliphate in 1258 as the beginning of a time when the shared vulnerability of Middle Eastern Christians and Muslims could lead to conversions of Muslims.

Near the end of this period Christian writings about Muslims fell into three types: (1) literary narratives whose 'argument' was presented almost entirely in stories and images; (2) polemics written by the well-educated built up through intricate logical inferences; and (3) some small treatises that directly attacked Muhammad's character through story and argument.

In the first category, Jerome of Prague during the fifteenth century translated into Latin a Greek text found in the Holy Land. It tells the tale of Christian traders in Arabia who, accused of murdering a Saracen and threatened with torture or death, miraculously escaped the ordeal. When they raised the Muslim from the dead, he criticized Muhammad as a magician and Islamic revelation as a fairy tale, and proclaimed that Christian revelation represented the only true religion. All Muslims were headed for hell. Certainly this was strong critique, but it attacked neither Muhammad's sexual activity nor his ambition as other anti-Muslim polemic had. The conceded high morality of the Saracens formed the basis of an attack on the lives of immoral Bohemian Christians.

Jacob van Maerlant's thirteenth-century historical chronicle, written in poetry and mining many anti-Muslim sources, probably fits the second category. He seems to be one of the first to use the learned form of chronicle to talk about Muslims. Jacob attempted to put his stories in their historical context. But in that way he depicted Muhammad as a devil dominated by lust and lies, theft and killing. In this chronicle Muhammad even claimed to be the Jewish Messiah and thus was clearly a false prophet. His miracles were tricks. The Qur'an contained no new insight; it depended upon both the Old and New Testaments.

In the early fifteenth century Andrea da Barberino, a native of Florence in Italy, wrote a series of romances that represent the third category. When he described travels to the East in these works, he could refer to Muslims as those who lived by rules similar to chivalric customs he knew, but he could also describe them as cruelly mutilating their prisoners. When Muslims did not follow the morality he assumed, he found them wanting. His description of the mosque at Mecca was a fantasy, nothing like the simple Ka'ba, but it does appear to have depended upon Eastern accounts of architecture that are authentic: alternating use of white and black stone and showing some use of round features. Yet his description of Muhammad's tomb in the mosque surely reflected the common Western Catholic custom of burying holy leaders in churches.

The real value of his novellas, however, was the detail about Muslim communities that he provided. Saracen men loved their beards and long hair. Being shaven was to them a disgrace. Wine was forbidden, but a drink of water with spices and crushed grapes served as a substitute. Polygamy was known among them; Westerners suspected that sodomy was also one of their illicit habits. Guerrino, one of Andrea's leading characters, was so fully assimilated into Muslim culture that he served as the captain of Persian troops. He despised their religion as false and wicked. But in many ways he had accepted his fellow soldiers in Persia as valued people. Some of their culture was worthy of adoption, indeed better than what he had learned at home.

From 1242 to 1342 Dominican and particularly Franciscan missionaries made the difficult overland journey east to the *Mongol Empire*. Their papal commission was to work out protection for Christians living along the Silk Road among these Eastern peoples, and to evangelize the heathens. Ten different expeditions are known to us, the most famous being the second trip of the Polos (1271–95), who were accompanied by missionaries. The first to leave, however, was John Plano de Carpini. He was surprised at how many East Syrian Christians lived in the Great Khan's court. Some of them said that the khan himself might convert, but in a reply to the pope Carpini made it clear that the ruler was content with his own belief 'in the power of eternal heaven'. He had killed Magyars and other Christians because they had put his envoys to death. He did not understand why the pope's envoys wanted him to convert or how the pope could know who finds the most favor in God's eyes. The khan and his people must have pleased God not least because he ruled an empire that stretched from sunrise to sunset.

When William of Rubruck, another Franciscan, arrived about ten years later, a new Khan had emerged. There were not nearly as many East Syrian Christians as he expected, but there were important ones among the Khan's ruling elite. They had only one church, whereas there were two Muslim mosques and twelve 'pagan' (Buddhist?) temples. At the court of the Great Khan, William took part in a debate over truth in religion among *Buddhists, Muslims, Manichaeans,* East Syrians and himself. The khan demanded that the debate be tolerant and then left the leaders to their discussions. William seemed to win a point with the Buddhists when he forced one of their priests into silence. The Buddhist's insistence on many gods as the final truth seemed to imply that having more than one khan might represent a better political system.

Later William had a private audience with the khan. The Mongol leader indicated that he believed in one God but clearly in different ways than William did. To the khan, just as we have a hand and many fingers, so one God can reveal his wishes in many religions. The khan's Mongolian *shamanistic religion* was not merely good; it was much better than Christian faith. Followers of Christ have scriptures that they do not follow. Mongols have diviners, do what those holy ones tell them to do, and thus live in peace.

In mid thirteenth-century *Ethiopia* the establishment of new monasteries provided the base in the pagan highlands for what in the next century would become a concentrated plan to Christianize the region. Some of these Christian buildings were erected on sites sacred to pagan worshippers. At first these small communities were composed of strict ascetics much like those of early Christian Egypt. But within a few decades they were buzzing centers of mission to the pagan peoples. In the fourteenth century, however, Emperor Amda Seyon insisted on a tolerant religious policy toward *Muslims* and the *Falasha* who considered themselves to be the house of Israel. Ethiopian Christians had depended heavily upon their king, but Amda Seyon found the pressure for conversion exerted by some monks to be unsettling. In his view each group should live in peace according to its own religion. The monks disagreed, sometimes politely, sometimes with direct refusals of his sovereign gifts – which led to their being whipped.

Christians in the *Ottoman Empire*, which existed from the late thirteenth century into the twentieth, at first experienced their new rulers in ways that their ancestors in the faith had known the earliest *Muslim* dominance. As is the case with all invasions, some groups were killed and others lost their positions. Those who were skilled and educated, however, were at times incorporated into government, particularly representatives of Christian Balkan princes whose people served with honor. Christians had kept their practices and beliefs alive in the midst of

Muslim conquest, although some had converted through changed conviction, cultural and economic pressures, and intermarriage. As the Turkomans gained ascendancy, they had varied relations with Christians. Some of their mystical orders took over Christian holy sites. As at selected shrines in Palestine under the Arab Muslims, at these sites Turkoman Muslims worshipped alongside Christians.

The Turkomans viewed Christians as people of the book who could enjoy the protection of their rights. The system required that they pay a head tax rather than serve in the armies of the empire. That tax brought in enough revenue to make forced mass conversion seem a poor economic plan. Resistance to Ottoman rule was the major cause of enslavement and loss of one's holdings; thus Christians in each area continued to convert to Islam. Notably the Bogomils of Bosnia, moved to that area in earlier times to defend the western frontiers of the Byzantine Empire, had been declared heretics and persecuted. They found the Turkoman conquest to be liberating and reason enough for conversion.

When Constantinople fell in 1453 to Turkish forces, the *millet* system quickly emerged. In this relationship the leader of a minority religious group was given autonomous authority over that group. Appointed by the sultan, that leader owed the sultan an allegiance that created his power. Gennadius Scolarious was made Greek patriarch, given both civil and ecclesiastical power and promised protection from any union with Catholics. The West at the Council of Lyons had imposed union on the Orthodox representative – though an influential group vigorously resisted – and promised troops for the defense of Constantinople who never came. Neither the Ottomans nor the Orthodox wanted Western ties. The empire included most of the Balkans, whose Orthodox leaders were placed under the Greek patriarch. Thus Ottoman conquest protected Orthodox Christians in ways they deeply appreciated.

Under the *Pax Mongolica* of Genghis Khan (c. 1162–1227) and Tamerlane (1336–1405), Christians east of Edessa all the way to China were still regionally strong. The two Mongol leaders were warlords who led mounted troops on successful conquests both south and, particularly, west. Tamerlane, the more destructive of the two, slaughtered Christians and Muslims alike. Only because there were Muslims with their own political and military connections did the followers of Muhammad outlast Tamerlane's reign.

Under Genghis Khan, Christians such as three sisters from the Kerait people proved to be influential. One of these sisters was the daughter-in-law of the Great Khan. There were enough Christians among the various Mongol tribes that at certain points the possibility of Christian influence in that empire was strong. Mongolian law showed some signs of Christian principles. But in each instance the movement of people in the western regions toward Islam and similar shifts toward Buddhism in the east left too little space for Christians to flourish. Two forces sealed Christians' demise: pestilence and war. Fourteenth-century grave inscriptions along the Silk Road witness the spread of the black death. Stone after stone marks the plight of a Christian struck down with the illness. Many other people were infected too, but weakened communities became too fragile to survive. War also ravaged the area. The struggles to maintain control of the Mongolian Empire took its toll on Christians and others alike, but the rise of converted Turks, particularly the Seljuks, presented a Muslim force almost completely intolerant of non-Muslims. Thousands of Christians were massacred; many of the cities in which they were the strongest almost disappeared. In one instance nearly a million people died. It was Ottoman Turks who stormed the walls of Constantinople and ravaged that Christian citadel.

In the eastern regions *Tibetan Buddhism* became the most accepted religion and without the sword conquered former Christian strongholds. As in earlier times Buddhists thought that the best of Christian life was to be found in their attempt to follow the Tao. That became the portal through which Christians entered Buddhism.

In *Europe* the *Renaissance* represented a flowering of humanism that could be strongly Christian or strongly Graeco-Roman in its religious concerns. This rebirth of learning involved intense attention being paid to Graeco-Roman texts that often reflected their pagan authors' beliefs. Many of the manuscripts were found in Christian monastic libraries where they had languished for centuries. Earlier they had been collected as part of the background to the authoritative church fathers of earlier centuries. But now they were catalogued and even published with a view to what ancient Rome and Greece had actually been.

Treatments of the ancient philosophies and the *Graeco-Roman pantheon*, either directly or as asides, meant that those hoary ideas and powerful deities were once again available for the best students to read about. Some of them still had appeal. Lorenzo Valla (*c.* 1406–57), a priest who was one of the transitional figures in the Renaissance, wrote a dialogue between Epicurean, Stoic and Christian representatives. He argued that the Epicurean love of the pleasure that came through the senses was the better view in spite of its unattainable goals. Niccoló Machiavelli (1469–1527), noted for his handbook of politics, *The Prince*, agreed with many figures in the Renaissance that humans could change their lives, but he insisted that humans were not good. Machiavelli expected evil from every person. The goddess Fortuna always determined half of human actions. The only way to grasp the rest was to resist her with *virtù*, not Christian virtue, but the energy, might, skill, intelligence and fortitude that make up the 'will to rule'. Know her power and fight against her.

Machiavelli's hero was Cesare Borgia because he had neither scruples nor compassion and lived by the proper *virtù*. Cesare, the illegitimate son of Pope Alexander VI (1431–1503), regained lost parts of the papal estates. He was a political master. From a vantage point like that of Machiavelli, both the Borgia and the Medici families knew the truth about life and thus should have produced both ruling princes and popes.

CHRISTIANS AND THEIR CULTURES

During this era Christians in Western *Europe* were creating such a strong culture that it was difficult for them not to see their way of life in terms of its products. Painting and carving had reached a level of excellence that focused the attention of worshippers and moved them to deeper meditation. Various *altar pieces* for *cathedrals* drew in the roving eyes of those in attendance at services to see the central scenes depicted there.

It was the cathedrals themselves with their high ceilings and amazing vaults and stained glass that, more than anything else, put Christians in touch with their God. Chartres, perhaps the most magnificent, was begun in the eleventh century and not dedicated till 1260. Cities in Europe competed with each other to produce the grandest and the most elegant cathedral. Both the rich and the poorer craftsmen were able and ready to participate. The shared piety led to centuries of investment and construction.

Some of the attempts brought failure when arches crashed because of poor planning, materials or building skills. But so much energy was put into the erection of these buildings that no story of Christianity could avoid mentioning them. Often overpoweringly beautiful, they always raise some questions: How well did this contract work? Were the skilled craftsmen paid fairly? Did the unskilled poor have a place in this pious effort? There can be little query about the beauty, but surely some concern about the care and service to others that both positively and neg-atively marked their construction.

The Cathars were dualists who saw power in the world possessed in nearly equal weight by God and Satan. Starting obscurely in the eleventh century and eventually viewed by Roman Catholics as danger-ous heretics, they had been annihilated by the fourteenth in the only *crusade* that was focused in Europe. The 'perfect' among them were wandering preachers in France supported by people of lesser religious status (sometimes with greater social and economic status) who gave them money and did not follow the strict asceticism of the leaders. Sometimes known as the Albigensians because of their strength around the city of Albi, they refused to pay the Catholic tithes, disdained the sacraments and ridiculed the priests. Parts of their teachings were decid-edly odd. Regular 'believers' were not required to live the ascetic life of the perfect. But if on the deathbed any believers became perfects through the proper rituals, they might be starved to death by fellow Cathars to prevent them going back to the evil world. Despite such horrors, their demand for a way of life different from the corrupt church seems clear enough and no unworthy goal. Their leaders appear to have viewed the power of the church to extract money and to form people in less than Christian ways as Satanic. How could a corrupt church flourish in the world if it were not somehow connected to Satan? Too few ecclesiastical leaders approached the Cathars pastorally with patience and understanding. The connection between immoral church practices and the development of heretical doctrine to understand them escaped most Catholics. Heretical doctrines deserved death. Sinister practices could wait for reform. The Cathars, surely strange reformers, looked for a different kind of Christian community. They crossed not only the church but also the king, who wanted the land of the nobles who sheltered them. Although real concerns about wrong teachings of central Chrsitian beliefs were involved, it was the economic and politi-cal desires of the powerful that spelled their doom.

The travels of Franciscan and Dominican missionaries out of this European culture along the Silk Road to the *Mongol Empire* from 1242 to 1342 led them to make many shocked observations about East Syrian (Nestorian) Christians. According to William of Rubruck their dress, their food, their daily lives were not what these Westerners saw as proper. Particularly among the Mongols, these Christians had, to Catholic eyes, proved their heretical character. Their priests wore robes that were almost impossible to distinguish from those of Buddhist monks, rather than proper vestments like those some of the Catholics had brought with them to celebrate the Eucharist. East Syrians ate meat rather than fish on Fridays. Inside their churches were revolting images of the dead, perhaps even corpses packed in felt. Their worship services were in Syriac, a language they themselves no longer understood. They offered no confessional for their people.

Tragically in Rubruck's eyes, they had absorbed many shamanistic ways, including sorcery and divination. Their priests used swords, ashes and charms in their healing rituals. Most offensive to William were the priests' morals. They practiced polygamy, sold their offices, collected interest on debts, frequently lied and were often drunken scoundrels.

These East Syrians had become inculturated; they looked and acted like Mongols and had adopted many customs that would endear them to their people, to the native religious healers, and in specific ways to Buddhists. They knew who they were and confessed themselves to be Christians. Yet they lacked weighty Christian virtues. As important to a Franciscan, they were culturally and thus religiously so different that they could hardly be seen as fellow believers. Syncretism always occurs when a new religion meets another culture; this one seemed deeply absorbed doctrinally into its milieu. But its penetration into the Mongol culture at other levels seems commendable and not to be set aside because Western Christian missionaries could not stand the sight.

One of the unexpected aspects of the *Holy Land* Crusades was the way in which Western institutions showed themselves strong enough to transfer well into the world of *Arab culture*. At no point did Muslims in Palestine exactly welcome their invaders, but insights in the various Muslim chronicles emphasize how much easier it was for an Arab peasant farmer or small businessman to live in the areas controlled by Western knights. These lower class and economically deprived families could count on kinds of civil rights that depended on Western conceptions of law and the ways in which its legal decisions were rendered and enforced. One traveler, Ibn Jubayr, as he entered the Crusader kingdoms, noted that the fields cultivated under the hegemony of these invading knights were green and well cared for. That was in stark contrast to the disorganized and unsuccessful attempts at working the earth which he had seen in Arab-dominated regions. Thus he prayed to Allah that Muslims in the Crusader-controlled areas would not succumb to such a great temptation and convert to Christianity.

Under Crusader occupation Muslims owned their land and their claims were not threatened. The Western institutions worked. They supported the succession of political leadership without armed conflict, depended upon a kind of council that at least balanced and at times checked the will of the kings, and involved even a clear role for religious leaders in the courts. Arab political reality was far different. Civil war broke out nearly every time a ruler of the Arabs died. That was true partly because non-Arab rulers and armies were strong forces in the Middle East and the Arabs themselves did not control their own destinies during these difficult times.

Many Christians enjoyed their privileged position in Western *Europe* and made their peace with the demands of political and economic power. Surely the Crusades are one of the worst examples of Christians' misuse of power during their history. They are a specifically sad case because even a spiritual giant like Bernard of Clairvaux was so immersed in the climate of the day that giving God's blessings to these movements seemed totally appropriate.

If the Crusades were so reprehensible, particularly in terms of Christians' relations with other religions, the *Avignon papacy* and the *Great Schism* can be viewed as the worst collapse of Christian institutions into the cesspool of Western economics and politics. Boniface VII (*c.* 1294–1303), in spite of his education as a canon lawyer, had no eye for European law and the growth of European royal authority under and within it. He continued to make the claim in his bull *Unam Sanctum* that all powers on earth were created by God and thus owed God allegiance. As the vicar of Christ, the papacy voiced God's commands, but even local priests should wield the power of God over knights and even kings.

That argument had been stated before, but Boniface had not reckoned with Edward I of England and Philip IV of France. Each needed money to gain control of English property in France. Both were offended when Boniface demanded that clerics should not pay taxes to the state. Philip had a courtier take troops and attack the papal palace at Anagni. For three days Boniface was imprisoned, his life threatened. He died within a month. His successor to the papacy issued a bull against that travesty and within a month was dead, probably poisoned by the French.

Clement V (1305–13) looked at the instability in the city of Rome, the force applied to his two predecessors by Philip IV, and moved the papacy to Avignon, France. It stayed there seventy years. To defend itself the papacy first appointed so many French cardinals that any pope selected would be French. Second, the papacy reorganized itself in order not to concede to the powerful French kings anything that might harm it. Lines of authority and collection of funds were centralized to the point that some bishops and their priests, especially the French, found it difficult to care for local Christians. The international diplomacy of the papacy demanded people and money. One of the ironies of the Avignon papacy during its later years was that there were too few privies in such a small place for all the papal retinue. Avignon stank.

The pious emperor Charles IV and Catherine of Siena had pleaded particularly with Pope Gregory XI to get the papacy out of French control and reform its own mania for money. They implored him to return to the spiritual home in Rome and concentrate on caring for souls. He went back in 1377 but died in 1378. His successor, Urban IV, was a strong anti-French Italian who so infuriated the French cardinals that they elected their own pope, Clement VI. Thus the papacy that had nearly been overcome by French economic and political power and had responded by thorough centralization and a demand for international control, split into fighting factions for nearly forty years.

One remarkable result of this embarrassment was the emergence of the *conciliar movement*. Each line of papal power had too much at stake to ask for help in resolving the conflict. Thus a council appeared because of the need for reform, one organized by church leaders who knew the blot had to be removed. The emperor Sigismund (1410–37) insisted that the Pisan pope John XXIII (1410–15) call a council. The Roman pope Gregory XII agreed, then voluntarily resigned. The Council of Constance (1414–18) accepted Gregory's resignation, deposed John XXIII and the Avignon pope, Benedict XIII. Only death removed Benedict in 1423 (or 1424). The council also selected Martin V (1417–31) and thus ended the Great Schism. But the unified papacy with its large economic and political power now centralized in the Avignon organization would continue to produce intrigue. The Renaissance popes with their wars and expensive cultural projects soon proved how easily papal position could lead to anything but pastoral care of souls.

In spite of that unholy mess, many Western Catholics may have received good pastoral care. Bishops tended to live all too well from the money they collected, but they had to send funds on to Rome as well as keep in repair the various church properties that were their responsibility. Any diocese they oversaw might contain many lands and buildings that needed attention. Parish priests also had to ship funds up the organizational elevators, but they had immediate bodily mercies to support: giving food and drink to the hungry and thirsty, housing the homeless, clothing the naked, visiting the sick and prisoners, and burying the dead. A good priest who preached to a church that both princes and paupers attended could appeal to the example of Jesus Christ. Where spirituality was strong, where some of the wealthy felt the stain of their own sins and the cleansing of Christ, life for the outcasts, the ill and the oppressed could be improved. Roving friars and attentive monks enhanced the ministry of the priests. Yet the enormous disparity between royalty and peasants remained. With the needy papacy and the landed bishops much of that disparity continued within the church.

In *Eastern Orthodoxy* a view often called 'caesaropapism' had developed which saw church and state as potentially harmonized. During 1395 Anthony, the patriarch of Constantinople, insisted that there would be no church if there were no Christian emperor. That made the fall of Constantinople less than sixty years later much harder to take.

Around 1357 Sir John Mandeville wrote in French his *Travels* through Muslim lands. This work circulated among popular audiences more than any other in Europe. It followed Sir John on his journey through the Middle East to both India and China. In an unexpected way it emphasized the closeness of Christians and Muslims, not in their apparent similar worship of the one great God but in their devotion to trade and its necessary support either by diplomatic negotiations or by war. Sir John viewed Muslim lands in ways like modern Westerners employed in the recent Gulf Wars. Subdue religious concerns and protect the oil.

This period is often marked in Western church history by the *fall of Constantinople*. When the city collapsed as a center of Christian rule in the eastern Mediterranean in 1453, it marked the end of an important era. Surrounded by Turks for centuries, its years of glory well behind it, Constantinople moved toward its present condition as Istanbul, a great city in Turkey.

Just as notable but too seldom recognized was the continued existence of the *African* Christian kingdom of Nubia (Sudan), a Christian community that had begun as early as the middle of the sixth century. Recent excavations have shown the richness of its art and the extent of its ecclesiastical organization. Documentation for the consecration of the Nubian bishop Qasr Ibrim by Patriarach Gabriel of Alexandria in 1372 still exists. We know of a Christian king named Joel and a Bishop Merki in 1484. Here was an African Christian community that for about a millennium had kept itself intact and had resisted the growth of various Islamic societies around it.

In the mid fifteenth century one of the last Berber Christian strongholds in North Africa disappeared. North African Christians had been primarily associated with Latin culture; they had tended to weaken under Vandal and then fail under Arab conquests. But small pockets of North African tribes had converted to the Christian faith. Tuareg nomads were part of the reason for the expansion of Muslims into western Sub-Saharan Africa. They went south across the desert probably during periods when at least one string of oases made it a much simpler journey than it is today. We may speculate that some Christian Berber traders using similar oasis routes traveled south to Nigeria and brought with them some of the remarkable symbols with probable Christian content that have been found in the art of native Nigerians.

In the previous century the Christian communities among the Turkic peoples who surrounded the Chinese Empire had waned. Once posing a serious religious option for the great *Mongolian* leader Ghengis Khan, because one of his preferred wives was Christian, these Christian groups seemed to disappear. They had lived the pastoral, nomadic life, having beliefs and organizations that were dissimilar to those in the West. Mixed in among them were remnants of people who believed as did the East Syrian followers of Christ who seemed to Western travelers to be anything but Christians.

Syrian and Armenian Christians who absorbed the Mongolian invasions observed from afar that some of this horde were Christians. Rabban Sauma during his visit to the papacy in 1287 insisted that many among the Mongols worshipped Christ. Some were well placed. The wife of the Mongol leader Hulagu saved many Syrian Christians from execution when his troops ravaged Baghdad in 1258. But by the beginning of the fourteenth century the Christians among the Mongols were nearly gone. Muslims represented the state Mongol religion; Christians and Jews had to wear clothing that set them apart. In 1291 with the capture of the Christian Crusader city of Acre in Palestine (Israel), the Mongol ruler of Persia (Iran) named Öljeitü, who had been baptized a Christian, rejected his faith and joined the Islamic community.

Syrian and Armenian Christian reaction to Mongol rule thus became subdued, but fiery in terms of God's apocalyptic response to individual, corporate and national sin. The note of sadness increased when early relations of mutual respect were replaced by intense hatred of the Mongols for Christians. In their earlier wars Mongols had slain Jew, Christian and Muslim alike, perhaps expressing most ferocity toward the Muslim believers in the countries they had ground under the feet of their horses. But in this latest invasion Christians reacted with both fear and a kind of fatalism by insisting that they had been 'abandoned by God'. Thus the end of the era saw a serious decline of long weakened Christian communities from Armenia and Syria along the Silk Road to China.

The vitality of intellectual *Europe* was focused in the precursors and the leaders of the *Renaissance*. The search for ancient sources and the belief that humans had many good features led to a kind of scholarship that impinged greatly on Christians. The recovery of manuscripts that contained the wisdom of ancient church teachers deeply enriched the understanding of Christian practice and faith. But the research that shed light on those brilliant texts produced scholars who developed linguistic and historical methods that put other documents in jeopardy. The *Donation of Constantine*, so much a part of papal claims to rule over all political leaders because Constantine had given that right to a pope, was a fake. Lorenzo Valla (*c.* 1406–57), both a maverick priest and a humanist scholar, demonstrated this and forcefully attacked papal power. Cardinal Nicholas of Cusa (1401–64), who defended papal prerogative, and Bishop Reginald Pecock (*c.* 1393–1461), who strongly disagreed with the criticism of the church offered by John Wycliffe (*c.* 1330–84) and his followers, also found the document to be a forgery. Historical criticism in these cases emerged from and for the church.

Leonardo Da Vinci (1452–1519) was the model of a Renaissance man. Perhaps most noted for his painting the *Mona Lisa*, he created numerous works with Christian themes. As a scientist, he studied everything. His drawings show that he paid close attention to the make-up of the human body. He enjoyed watching birds fly and thought that a human might take flight with the proper equipment. At least his imagination flew freely. When Florence was under attack, he used his genius to design better defenses and planned a device that looked much like a tank. It is difficult to know for certain what his religious commitments were as a younger man. How much did he share the views of those who commissioned his work? Later in life, however, he turned fully to Christian trust and thus experienced what was either a conversion or a recommitment. There needed to be no chasm between art, science and faith.

A CHRISTIAN CORE

During this era one central point of Christian faith came back into focus. Many of the Christians worshipping in lands under Muslim control had long held that *Jesus* was incarnate in one divine nature. The West Syrians (Jacobites) of the previous period had been quite successful in their missionary efforts, both within and outside Christian communities. In Ethiopia and Nubia (Sudan), the latter a Christian kingdom up into the sixteenth century, (Cyrilline) Mia-Physite Christology – as the West Syrians called their doctrine – had won the day. A small period of political rule of the Makuria over the Nobatae (northern Nubians) had introduced the two-nature doctrine of the Byzantine Empire, but it did not last long.

Looking to Europe for expressions of the center of Christian life leads us first to *monastic reform*. The influence of Cluniac monasticism dominated the tenth and eleventh centuries, but criticism had appeared, particularly concerning the use of the wealth that the monastries had attracted. The Cistercian order emerged in 1098 when Cluniacs rejected their abbot Robert's call for them to take the *rule of St. Benedict* more seriously. Robert took twenty-one monks to Cîteaux and worked out a more austere form of life. The venture nearly failed, but Bernard (1090–1153) arrived in 1112 with thirty men, including members of his family. Within three years he was selected abbot. He preached poverty and the simple life with such force that the order grew dramatically.

The life of *prayer and work*, the former the primary aspect for the monks, drew not only the devout but also the poor. Granges led to successful farming in which lay brothers tended fields and flocks. Not since the earliest monasticism in the Middle East had the poverty-stricken been so welcome in a monastic community. These men had hours of worship, but their main task was work. That work, so well organized and supported through labor for food and shelter, made them economic engines wherever they were established. The movement expanded by sending an abbot and twelve monks to each new site, so by 1500 there were 738 houses for men and 650 houses for women spread throughout Western Christendom.

In this period the outstanding figure is Francis of Assisi (1182–1226). The claim has even been made that he was the only human ever to live a fully Christ-like life. We have few writings from him but those around him after his conversion began to collect the stories of his daily life. His early years as the privileged son of a merchant gave no hint of what was to come. Participating as an armed knight in a war between Italian cities, he succeeded in squandering almost everything he was and owned through his romantic urges. Yet his awareness of the needy, whom he had so carefully avoided, burst forth one day as he was riding. He gave his cloak to a leper and kissed the man on his misshapen face. Later when he heard God call him to repair the church, Francis thought that the task was to rebuild a small chapel. To finance the operation, he stole cloth from his father. The enraged father had him tried before the bishop in the public square. Francis took responsibility and paid the debt, but he also took off all his fine clothes and standing naked rejected his father and his father's wealth.

The rich of Assisi were astounded and ridiculed Francis's choice of homelessness, poverty, working with his own hands and serving the needy. But his radical decision and the vision behind it captivated many young people. He never returned to the material wealth and political power of his youth. Most of his waking hours were dominated by prayer. He always gave preference to the poor but found his own ways to minister to the rich. In an age of crusades encouraged by church leaders, including the mystic Bernard of Clairvaux, Francis preached a gospel of nonviolence. His love of God's creation in all its forms, particularly animals, has made him a patron saint of some modern ecologists who do not choose to be Christians.

The order carrying Francis's name tried diligently to spread his message. They begged for their food, often slept in barns and publicly preached the gospel. Women were drawn to Francis's vision, but they could not live as the male friars did. Thus Clare of Assisi (1194–1253), also an aristocrat, insisted that women in a cloister could also live the commitment of absolute poverty, both individually and corporately. Beyond these orders marked by poverty and service, a third order emerged composed primarily of faithful urban people whose responsibilities in marriage and raising children kept them from the first two orders. Directed spiritually by Franciscan friars, they observed the church's calendar of fasts and festivals and followed a regimen of devotion and penance. Their offerings underwrote many Franciscan projects. This involvement in the Franciscan movement also kept them from the call of groups like the Waldensians and the Cathars who so successfully drew common folk into communities that opposed the corruption of the church.

Dominic de Guzman (*c.* 1170–1221) responded to the spread of the Cathars in France by setting up another order of preachers. He planned from the beginning that the Dominicans should be well educated and live a life of abject poverty in order to compete with the compelling rejection of materialism that marked the Cathar leaders. Dominicans founded their own schools and enrolled their best in the emerging universities.

The *Waldensians*, led by Valdes (died between 1205 and 1218) of Lyons, had already embodied some of the visions that Francis and Dominic preached. Valdes, a wealthy merchant, was stricken by the tales of the fifth-century St. Alexis who left a rich bride to begin a life of mendicancy. Words from Jesus about helping the poor and giving away wealth moved him first to make arrangements for his wife and children, and then to give away all he had to the poor. His deeds brought him a following. He and others preached against the riches of the clergy as well as the heresy of the Cathars and made vernacular translations of scripture for the people. There was no hint of heretical practice or doctrine in the movement, but when Valdes petitioned the papacy for proper standing he was rejected. Because he had disobeyed the command not to preach unless invited to do so by clergy, his 'poor men of Lyons' were excommunicated in the same ban that declared the Cathars to be heretics. The Waldensians continued their work outside the established church and grew ever more suspicious of the clergy's morality and its ability to properly administer holy sacraments. It is likely that the papacy's mistake in turning these reformers away led to the easier acceptance of both the Franciscans and the Dominicans. The Roman church had to listen to calls for repentance regarding its abuses of wealth and power.

Many would find Thomas Aquinas (*c.* 1225–74) to be the outstanding European theologian of this era. Born in Italy and educated in France, Thomas underwent a journey into monasticism that allowed him to present the scope of the Christian gospel. A large, strong man, he went against his father's wishes when he became a Dominican monk. The stories differ. One says his brothers imprisoned him. Another indicates that in anger his father locked Thomas in a room in the large family home. When Thomas would not change his mind, his father decided to taint his character in a way that would make him unacceptable to his fellow monks. He opened the door, threw an attractive prostitute inside and relocked the massive door. To the father's dismay Thomas broke the door from its hinges, led the prostitute back to his father and returned to his room. When Thomas left home, the family understood that he was on a path he would unswervingly tread.

In France he studied with Albert the Great, who was working out a Christian theology based on Aristotelian rather than the more common Platonic philosophical principles. French intellectuals had experienced a rising interest in Aristotle. Spain and Portugal had both Jewish and Muslim communities who had various teachers developing their religious views through that ancient Greek philosopher's categories; for example, Maimonides (1135–1204) for the Jews, and Averroes (Ibn Rushd, 1126–98) for the Muslims. Aquinas's first large effort in systematic theology, *Contra Gentiles*, was itself a missionary treatise meant to help Dominicans in Spain explain their faith to Jews and Muslims. His later *Summa Theologica* was intended more for theologians whose interests were in explicating the faith to those within the Christian community. It was laid out in a type of pro and con argument that worked from apparent disagreements within the church's teaching down to the more agreed-upon positions.

Aquinas's command of all kinds of resources is phenomenal. He put together a commentary on the four Gospels that seldom gives evidence of his views through his own words but most often speaks through the quotations of previous theologians in the Christian tradition. He insisted that the Bible was the major authority in Christian teaching but that human reason could discover much of God's truth in nature and human nature. In the last phases of his life he had a deep mystical experience that led him to call his previous systematic studies 'straw'. He died condemned by the bishop of Paris for theological errors and not overwhelmed by the worth of his life's work. But he was a revered theologian who understood that God was infinitely greater than his own brilliant system.

Thirteenth- and fourteenth-century Franciscan biblical exegetes saw the collapse of Middle Eastern crusades, the European Christian kingdoms set up in the Holy Land, and the possibility of Mongols becoming Christians as reasons for deep reflections on their own faith and that of strong non-Christian communities like the Muslims. Their agitation led them to the book of Revelation in the Bible, as a guide. The figure of the Antichrist became particularly prominent, in some ways spurred on by reactions to the apocalyptic figure Joachim of Flora (*c.* 1132–1202) – his life, teachings and a commentary on Revelation. Peter Olivi (*c.* 1248–98) had deep misgivings about claims that all mysticism was closely related to various Antichrists. Furthermore the society that St. Francis formed and the pope who sanctioned it were battling corruption in the church. Clearly, God would use the Muslims to destroy that false church, maybe even to vanquish all Western secular power. Persecution of the faithful Christians might ensue, led by Muslims and a false pope, but the needed reshaping of Christian community must follow. Yet why God allowed his instrument for reform, the Muslims, to rule for six hundred years was difficult to understand. Nicolas of Lyra (c. 1270–1340), who also treated Revelation as a historical chart, suggested that the Muslims would not fade. Indeed the Antichrist had not yet appeared. Up to chapter 20, verse 17 the book of Revelation deals with history. Nicolas, not being a prophet, could not say anything about how the book of Revelation and the present age fitted together. One interesting aspect of some Franciscan exegetes was their growing sense that the Crusades had accomplished nothing.

No sketch of the period should pass by Dante Alighieri (1265–1321). This Italian studied philosophy and had a deep interest in politics, particularly the independence of a strong monarch over against the papacy. The present papacy was too rich and too powerful. Not surprisingly those views were declared heretical. Dante's fame, however, rests with his *Divina Commedia*, a compelling Italian (not Latin) poem dedicated to his beloved Beatrice. This poetry so colorfully described hell, purgatory and heaven – each populated by important figures of the past – that it remains timeless. It influenced not only art but also later poems like the *Paradise Lost* and *Paradise Regained* of John Milton (1608–74).

In Western Europe during this period a series of influential *women* appeared within the male structure of leadership among Roman Catholics. Their insight and talent was so great, their humility and other virtues so strong that they could not be suppressed. They filled every open space that medieval Catholics allowed them and became in many ways the backbone of Western European spirituality. Hildegard of Bingen in Germany (1098–1179) had seen visions early in her childhood, she had been raised by Jutta, an anchoress who lived in a cell near a Benedictine abbey. As Hildegard matured she became a part of the Benedictine community centered around Jutta; later she succeeded Jutta as abbess. The archbishop approved of her work, so that for the decade of the 1140s she had her visions recorded under the oversight of her confessor. In that time her community also moved to a place near Bingen where they built a large convent. The poetic images that she developed in her mystical works not only resemble but sometimes surpass the biblical psalms.

In the Byzantine church an older *spiritual exercise* was capped both by extended practice and subtle theological explanation. What came to be Hesychast spirituality, the devotional ways of the Quiet Ones, had developed among Orthodox monks for nearly a thousand years. In the fourteenth century they extended a deep sense of prayer by lying down, putting their chin on their chest, focusing their attention on their navel as the center of the body and repeating the Jesus Prayer: 'Lord Jesus Christ, Son of God, have mercy on me, a sinner.' They were convinced that through such careful use of the body in meditation they could more clearly understand the ways in which God dwelt within them. Their opponents insisted that they were merely belly button gazers, a misguided group of dreamers who should be reprimanded.

Gregory Palamas (*c.* 1296–1359) became their champion. He knew their practice from experiences he had at Mt. Athos in Greece. His controversy with Barlaam the Calabrian turned not so much on the practice of Hesychast prayer as it did on the underlying doctrine of God. Barlaam, a Greek educated in Western Europe, was himself a Nominalist, one who insisted that universal concepts had no reality in themselves. There was no idea of 'chairness' in which all 'chairs' participated. There were just chairs. Barlaam read the more ancient devotional literature of Eastern Orthodoxy, particularly the works of Dionysius the Pseudo-Areopagite, in a very strict way. For him the most important point was that God's nature was completely beyond human comprehension, thus God was in essence unknowable. In his view Hesychasts vainly sought knowledge of a God who indwelt them and could be known in some mystical ways. Their search was vanity itself. Palamas responded with two important points. First, although the deepest nature of God was indeed unknowable, the uncreated energies of God interpenetrated everything in the universe. Divine light in the form of those energies could be experienced by human beings. It came to humans in the form of the grace that brought them deification, participation in the divine nature. Second, the practices of the Hesychasts that emphasized the body as a tool for prayer depended upon the unity of body and soul, a Christian doctrine weakened in previous periods and now in need of strong restatement.

Ten groups of Franciscan and Dominican missionaries who traveled to the *Mongol court* between 1242 and 1342 found *East Syrian (Nestorian)* churches all along the Silk Road and at the court of the Great Khan. A number of their observations about these Eastern Christians were formed by their own Western understanding of what constituted the core of Christian faith. Their negative judgments on the faithfulness of these Christians indicated just how offended they often were. Many cases had to do with the dress and customs of these Christians whom they expected to be heretics. William of Rubruck on a trip from 1253 to 1255 reported strong Christian presence among the Uighurs, Maimans, Keraits and Merits, significant central Asian tribes. But when he depicted the Christians among the Uighurs, he was clearly appalled. The common folk seemed to believe in one God but to deny the incarnation of Christ. East Syrians at the court were somewhat different, but still in need of deep reform. They knew biblical accounts from creation to Jesus, but in some ways were Manichaean in their teachings, believers who accepted a dualism of good and evil. They also wrongly rebaptized Christians who had different views. Sadly, Buddhist priests were much better examples of disciplined moral life. For Rubruck the East Syrians had radically changed 'the core of Christian faith' to the point that in debates with other religious leaders they were a part of an opposition to truth.

There is little doubt that Rubruck's comments genuinely reflected his own evaluation of East Syrian Christians. But he saw everything through his Western eyes and at times was blind. He did not know that some important officials he met in the courts of lesser khans were actually Christians. Although he had read earlier reports of strong Christian presence, these Asians evidently looked so foreign that he could not recognize their faith.

Had his views of the heretical center of East Syrian faith been totally true, the remarkable travels of the Uighur monk Sauma, born in Beijing, and his companion the patriarch Mark, probably an Ongut, would make a pope heretical. In 1287 the Great Khan sent Sauma as his official envoy to the papacy and various courts of Europe and included Mark on the journey because an alliance seemed to be to his advantage. Thus these two Mongol Christians arrived in Rome and were required to defend their faith. Sauma was asked why he was chosen as the khan's representative. Both men answered the queries by, first, indicating that their faith was like that of early Syrian Christians who centuries before had made their way east as missionaries, and second, reporting that Christians among the Mongols were honored and could serve in such posts. After traveling in France and astounding the courts there with their looks, stories and relics, they returned to Rome. When Sauma asked Pope Nicholas IV if he might celebrate an East Syrian mass, he gained permission. People who watched the service could not understand the language but they sensed that this Eastern rite was surely Catholic.

Among *Ethiopian* Christians the fourteenth century brought an impressive renewal. The state was strong, embodied in Christian kings who threw their support to improving conditions in the church. But these kings were not always certain that conversion of others was the best plan. Abuna Ya'iqob and his successor, Salama, made significant contributions. Ya'iqob, himself a monk, reorganized and strengthened monasteries in order to make them centers of evangelism. They had success with both pagans and nominal Christians but were always inhibited because their Christian literature, in Arabic and Ethiopic (including the Bible), was not nearly sufficient to penetrate the many languages used in the country. There was even a distance between literary Ge'ez and popular Amharic languages, so the common people had little sense of what the liturgy meant and thus developed a faith that was only partially Christian and strongly reflected the traditional beliefs of the specific region. Translation projects into local languages had no high priority for church officials. In his forty years as abuna (the national Christian leader of Ethiopia), Salama oversaw a burgeoning project of translating Christian works from Arabic into Ge'ez, the Christian Ethiopian language. That effort included a thorough revision of the Ethiopic Bible. As welcome as it was, Salama's work left only the better-educated, usually priestly, families connected to Christian literature and liturgy.

A number of issues agitated the community. Almost all held to the importance of circumcision for Christian men and women, but polygamy remained a strong practice. Various monks insisted on monogamy, but both the kings and the nobles saw little reason to abandon the taking of many wives. They had the wealth to support them. Polygamy was not only an Old Testament practice; it was also strong in their indigenous heritage.

Ewostatewos, who found the keeping of the sabbath to be essential, led another Ethiopian reform and evangelistic monastic movement. The importance of the sabbath may have been linked to a traditional custom not only in the north but also in the south at Aksum. It is difficult to say, although it seems unlikely that this reform was based on totally original foundations. When others did not share his view, Ewostatewos took many monks and traveled to Egypt, apparently looking for support, which he did not receive in Cairo. He traveled on to Jerusalem, Cyprus and finally Armenia, where he died. His fellow monks returned to Ethiopia, gathered up those they had left behind and set up the monastery of Dabra Maryam.

With some other northern monasteries, these followers of Ewostatewos evangelized both Muslims and the Falasha. They formed themselves into something like a Western order and encouraged nuns by allowing abbesses to have increasing powers, even of absolution.

Councils in the early fifteenth century tried to suppress this sabbatarian movement with force, but they had little success. Ewostatewos's original followers and those after them formed themselves into monasteries. The anti-sabbatarian party had not granted them ordination, but they seemed not to want it from sabbath breakers. The monks, however, gained adherents from other places and were eventually recognized as expressing one authentic way to live as Christians.

Ethiopia also became the repository of some aspects of Western popular piety – with rather unexpected results. A twelfth-century French work, the *Miracles of Mary*, was carried east and translated into Arabic, probably in the fourteenth century. When it was rendered into Ethiopic in the fifteenth century, King Zara Ya'iqob insisted that priests should read it during the thirty-two Marian feasts. The faith of common French people thus became a part of official Ethiopian orthodoxy.

Although often isolated from other Christian communities, Ethiopia did see some important contact during the fifteenth century. First, Ethiopian monasteries in both Cairo and Jerusalem had much wider discussions with people who lived in or traveled through those places. Two Ethiopian monks attended the Council of Florence (1438–45) under the auspices of their abbot in Jerusalem. Their emperor apparently knew nothing about their participation, but when Peter, one of the monks, spoke, he said that his emperor would gladly submit to the pope but that without the emperor's express permission they could not act. Thus Ethiopian Christians were a part of the Florence reunions. Second, Ethiopian officials knew that they needed more priests for their churches and called a council in 1477 to deal with the deficiency. They hesitated to ordain their own priests and thus sent representatives to Cairo, who returned with properly sanctioned leaders. The ancient chain of ordination was not broken.

CONCLUSION

European Christendom displayed its good and bad sides. Monastic reforms such as those made by Cistercian monks made the practice of the gospel appealing once more. A series of Catholic orders began, in particular Dominicans and Franciscans, which would be important not only in European reform but also in world mission. Whole cities in Europe dedicated their lives to building cathedrals: edifices that are still impressive today and yet raise questions about the use of wealth and the power of the upper classes.

Christendom knew that the Crusades were right. Even the spiritual giant, Bernard of Clairvaux, supported them. They were pilgrimages to wrest the Holy Land from 'heathen' Muslims. Their legacy is a hatred between some Christians and Muslims that still poisons relationships between nations and in society. The near eradication of Jewry in south-eastern Europe and the sacking of two Christian cities including Constantinople only serve to confirm the view that these armed excursions were travesties.

Christians had become the dominant religious group among various tribes along the Silk Road and in Mongolia, and were strong in some areas. However, first the persistent traditional religions and then Islam became the path followed by the majority of people. When European Christians traveled through the Mongolian Empire, they considered the East Syrians (Nestorians) they met to be pagans, sometimes even less moral than Buddhists. The judgments of these Christian leaders were deeply determined by their near unquestioning acceptance of European cultural values. Yet a Mongolian bishop, Sauma, who traveled to Europe as an envoy of the khan, presided over a mass in his language and according to his rite, and the pope and Christians in Rome did not find it offensive. By the time, however, that the Mongols attacked Europe, they had few Christians among them. Christianity in Asia had nearly disappeared, yet Christians in Africa (Ethiopia and Nubia) struggled on.

5 CONQUEST, REFORMATION AND INDIGENOUS GROWTH, 1433–1600

China went to sea. Near the beginning of the fifteenth century the emperor Zhu Di, an inquisitive leader, joined forces with court advisors who were both curious about the outside world and supportive of his vision. All of them had an exorbitant sense of China's importance and planned a navy unheard of anywhere. Sailors on the coast were encouraged to strengthen their skills of navigation. The government arranged for lumber from the interior and for coastal shipbuilders to create larger vessels. It turned its considerable forces toward the construction of a fleet numbering over sixteen hundred junks, some of gargantuan proportions for the time. The main vessel was more than four hundred feet long, five times as large as the caravels used by the Portuguese, over three times as large as many nineteenth-century European ships. That junk was so carefully built that its wooden compartments could be filled with water in order to bring back exotic fish. When one scout vessel fell into the hands of a local prince, that prince was extremely fortunate when he waited to deal with the 'pirates'. Would the Chinese fleet really be large enough to fill the horizon as the scout captain had claimed? It was.

The entire armada began to explore seas to the south. Eventually some expeditions sailed westward to what are now called the Gulf of Aden near the Horn of Africa and the island of Madagascar off the East African coast. They returned with knowledge and treasures. Yet, for reasons that are not entirely clear, China's efforts stopped. The country's rulers changed. These new leaders, more attuned to the Confucian conservatism present in the palace, apparently found nothing of particular interest that would require such extensive sea voyages. Things of value from foreign lands could be acquired through overland trade that would make the danger and the expense the traders' problems. Turning Chinese energies toward internal projects was the best use of the empire's resources. When Portuguese ships reached Chinese ports near the beginning of the sixteenth century, they saw the dry-docked, rotting hulks of the Chinese navy.

We may ponder what the world would have looked like had China taken advantage of its position as the ruler of south-east Asian seas all the way to Africa. Surely the economic shape of Asia and Africa would have been decidedly different had China decided to set up colonies or at least trading posts during those thirty years of naval expansion that ended in 1433. Even a Chinese emperor and a court with an expansive vision did not think about making China a giant trading power in regions well beyond its coastline. The remarkable voyages were undertaken to tell the rest of the world that their betters lived in the Middle Kingdom.

The Chinese reversal of policy from looking outward to focusing inward becomes even more important when we consider that Portugal had started its explorations of Africa by 1415. Portuguese ships had begun to trade for gold, ivory and slaves in Upper Guinea by 1471 and Portuguese traders had set up shop on the Congo river by 1483. Bartolomeu Dias sailed around the tip of the continent in 1488; ten years later Vasco da Gama reached Calicut, India. The Portuguese and Spanish fleets provided transportation, troops and Catholic missionaries for the spread of Christian faith. By sheer accident Pedro Álvarez Cabral sailed so far west from Portugal in 1500 that his necessary turn south to go around Africa landed his expedition on the shores of Latin America (Brazil). He reached there less than a decade after Columbus's failed attempt to reach the East Indies put him in the Caribbean. The only period of Christian expansion that can compare with these global ventures, led by the potential for trade, were the nineteenth-century mission efforts of both Protestants and Catholics.

CHRISTIANS AND PEOPLE OF OTHER FAITHS

At the beginning of this period *Africa* was still a dark continent for most Europeans. But even with the expansion of Muslims north of the Sahara and the strength of indigenous African religions nearly everywhere, there were two areas of the continent in which Christian communities thrived.

Disciples in *Ethiopia* flourished during the fifteenth century. Their emperor, Zara Ya'iqob, who chose the Christian name Constantine, called a council in 1449 to meet in a monastery, Dabra Mitmaq, that he had founded. Located in the mountains in a province then mostly Christian, it became the hub of Christian activity in the country. The emperor settled on that name for the monastery because Muslims in Egypt had demolished one with the same designation. A large group of church and monastic leaders from both Egypt and Ethiopia attended the council, and decided a series of issues. The celebration of the sabbath and Sunday was ratified; sabbatarians agreed to accept ordination from those who had opposed them. Thus unity was established.

But Zara Ya'iqob did not find this breakthrough to be a sufficient achievement. He worried about the weakness of Christian faith. He wrote the *Mashafa Berhan*, a treatise that not only argued the Christian doctrine of Trinity but also designated biblical texts to be read on Saturdays and Sundays. More forcefully, he set out ways to keep people Christian. Believers would be branded; the military would plunder the houses of priests who were not diligent. His soldiers also attacked those of other religions. He wanted to be known as the exterminator of *Jews*, perhaps a reference to the Falasha who thought of themselves as the house of Israel. In his view killing a *pagan* was not sinful. His attempt to keep a thin Christian veneer in place while he thickened it was endangered by such oppressive actions. He tried to institute a yearly rite of rebaptism because so many had converted to other religions and now wished to re-enter the Christian community, but that rite became primarily one of purification little related to baptism.

In 1484 *Nubia* (Sudan) still had a Christian king in Dotawo named Joel and a bishop in Qasr Ibrim named Merki. During the 1520s Francisco Alvares, the chaplain of a Portuguese expedition that had docked in Ethiopia, spoke with a Syrian named John who had journeyed through Nubia. John had seen 150 church buildings with both crosses and paintings of the Virgin Mary. But his assessment was that the believers there were neither Jews, Christians nor Muslims. In his view they wanted to follow Christ but did not fit his own categories of what Christians were. The truth may be that they were well-contextualized Nubian Christians whose dress, customs and liturgies were too different from Syrian practices and teachings for John to recognize them as authentic. Before Alvares left Ethiopia, Nubians had come to the Ethiopian authorities requesting both priests and monks. But because ecclesiastical precedents demanded that Nubians go back to Alexandria from where their first Christian missionaries had come, the Ethiopian emperor, Lebna Dengel, gave them no leaders. Thus they were forced to return empty handed to a church that probably had no scripture in its indigenous tongue, only Coptic translations, no specialized leaders and perhaps no Christian king. Continued *Muslim* pressure was slowly squeezing the life out of Nubian Christian communities.

Portuguese journeys around Africa brought Christian missionaries into contact with peoples who had followed their indigenous religious customs. By the end of the fourteenth century the Portuguese had recaptured parts of their own homeland that had been under Muslim rule; their victory had made them bold but not fanatic. Now they sailed the Mediterranean and traded at some Islamic ports; they took control of a few but found no way to conquer any significant area of North Africa. They were primarily interested in trade and slaves, who had become a growing workforce for their tiny land. The establishment of plantations similar to those in the Mediterranean made the importation of black slave laborers a growing business.

Portuguese skill in sailing took them to various places along the long coast of West Africa. They knew that gold was being brought up through the Sahara to North Africa. Perhaps they could find the source of that trade by sailing south. During 1482 they had built a fort at Elmina along what came to be known as the Gold Coast (Ghana). The next year the Portuguese settled on an uninhabited island, São Tomé, and began a thriving trade in slaves, black Africans primarily provided by African traders. The Portuguese knew that they did not have forces large enough to overpower and enslave by themselves.

Eventually the Portuguese set up twenty-one forts on the West African coast. Such ventures were economically driven. Outflanking their mortal enemies, the North African *Muslims*, was never far from the surface. But bringing Christ to any people was part of their mandate from king and pope. By 1534 a Catholic diocese on São Tomé had emerged that was made responsible for every area south along the coast of West Africa.

The most unexpected Christian expansion in Africa came a bit further south on the Zaire river. There in 1483 the Portuguese, led by Diego Cao, made contact with natives who were part of the Congolese kingdom. Trade flourished. When the trading expedition departed, they left a Catholic priest behind. He had stayed in Soyo, the Congolese province along the coast, and in 1491 had baptized the chief of that province, Mani Soyo, and his son. These men took their conversions seriously and demonstrated the influence of the changes by burning many of the fetishes necessary for their indigenous religious practices. Within only two years, Portuguese priests had reached the inland capital, Mbanza Congo, and baptized the king, Nzinga Nkuvu. He took the Christian name João I, in honor of the Portuguese king, João II. The speed of this conversion of the Congolese from their *indigenous religions* to some form of Christian life suggests that Portuguese religion and society probably contained elements paralleled in Congolese life. Portuguese Catholics had developed a popular sense of Christian faith that included gory warfare with the Devil. God was active in daily life. Local heroes had became saints. Artifacts that would aid in worship and everyday experience were plentiful.

Such quick conversion of the Congolese, however, meant that Christian practice and faith were not deeply rooted. King Nzinga Nkuvu missed his fetishes and many wives; he eventually reverted to the indigenous religion. But his son Mvemba Nzinga, who had taken the Christian name Alfonso, did not. He enjoyed his contact with the Portuguese and rejected the decision of the elders that he should not succeed his father in 1506. With Portuguese assistance he defeated his rivals and then worked on what he considered to be improvements in Congolese life, from education to medical care. In 1512 the Portuguese king Manuel treated Alfonso as a Christian potentate and sent him all kinds of Portuguese workers and priests who were commanded to help him build a strong Christian kingdom. Both Alfonso and Manuel wanted to raise up Congolese priests, but young Congolese men sent for education in Lisbon failed to return, swallowed up by Portuguese culture. In order to counteract these failures, Alfonso sent one of his own sons to Lisbon with the hope that he would become the bishop of the Congo. He returned ordained, but, suffering from poor health, he soon slipped out of sight. Alfonso pleaded for the building of a great school at São Tomé, one to educate both boys and girls, but overwhelming Portuguese inattention to such needs and their acquisition of material goods and slaves soured the relationship.

By 1514 the oba of Benin, Ozolua, had heard of the Portuguese. He sent representatives to Lisbon with the message that he wanted Christian faith and guns. Advisors let the Portuguese king know that Benin had even more treasures than the Congo. The contact should have been another carefully planned one, with success on both sides, but the Portuguese insisted that weapons of war could not be sent until conversion was secure. They had not sent firearms to the Congo. On his side Ozolua had no interest in selling slaves. Indeed his warlike character led to his death, killed by his own soldiers who were tired of fighting. The Portuguese missionaries, interested only in first converting the royal house, left Benin disheartened because a great opportunity had been forfeited. But a Christian from the Edo tribe, who took the name Gregorio Lourenço at his baptism on the island of São Tomé, learned Portuguese and then went to Benin. He offered to the Portuguese church on the island a slave girl as a gift to God and wanted to be baptized with his family. The oba, however, prevented that. But it was from such contacts rather than any 'foreign missionary' effort, that a type of Christian community, small in number and marked by many indigenous religious views, emerged in Benin.

The seafaring prowess of the Portuguese brought them to East Africa. The international Jesuit center in Goa, India evolved after Vasco da Gama landed on the Indian coast in 1498. Goa eventually became the residence for the archbishop of the Roman Catholic diocese in East Africa. By 1550 word had reached this diocesan headquarters that Mozambique might be open to the gospel. A brilliant young Jesuit, Gonçalo da Silveira, and two others arrived in the country in 1560. Again employing the Portuguese strategy of moving directly to royal houses, they quickly baptized the king of Tongue along with four hundred of his people and finally, traveling up the Zambezi, they baptized Monomotapa (Mwene Mutapa), who turned out to be the most important figure. Silveira wanted Mozambique's resources for Portugal, particularly gold, but primarily he was a convinced, fearless missionary. *Muslim* traders, perhaps aided by some threatened *traditional believers*, eventually had Silveira killed as a sorcerer.

The emergence of Christians in *Latin America* also occurred during the expansion of Portuguese and Spanish sea power and at the expense of *traditional religions*. The background of Spanish Christian interest included a long history of economic, political and religious might unified in a single effort: to extend Spanish hegemony, and thus the dominance of Christendom, to any area its ships would touch. Queen Isabella outfitted Columbus's voyage to the East Indies in 1492 as a way to reach the rich resources of those islands without having to sail around Africa or depend upon the difficult land travel over the Silk Road. Columbus himself followed an apocalyptic faith discovered through studying the book of Revelation. That led him to see himself as a powerful actor in God's global drama. Priests were part of his company on the trading ships because Spanish culture and religion were considered the best. Unexpected arrival in the West Indies brought a quick change of plans. Silk, jade, certain spices and other Eastern valuables were nowhere to be found. But gold, alluring plants, land and slaves to work it were ready to hand.

Dominican friars arrived in the region during 1510 but their influence was limited. Pope Julius had set up three dioceses for America in 1504, but King Ferdinand insisted that he should control the church in these new lands, a right he acquired in 1508. Thus the Christian mission that reached this New World – from the European perspective – was a deeply rooted form of European Christendom, one tested in Spanish wars that had driven most of the Moors from Spain. The difficulty was that the natives of these new lands often experienced 'Christian' concern as a political and economic force that enslaved them in their own homes. The religions of the Amerindians in nearly every case were considered by the Spanish to be primitive superstitions that merited neither serious encounter nor extended formal discussions. Some European priests studied their artifacts in order to understand but most of them burned what they could and defaced what they could not. A few other Christians fought for the rights of the natives against the traders and farmers. But even those good deeds often had a paternalistic air about them.

This first phase of Spanish conquest ended around 1518 when readily accessible gold supplies dwindled. Silver continued to be mined, but the Amerindians themselves had died by the thousands of smallpox and perhaps other European diseases as well as direct attacks by the Spanish soldiers. Early on the *conquistadores* exposed the Amerindians to their imported diseases more by accident than by design. But it did not take them long to recognize that as they obtained all the gold available they could eliminate some of the natives by giving them smallpox-infested blankets in trade. There are documented stories of the Spanish soldiers going on picnics and finding whetstones to sharpen their swords. To test their new edges they would ride to an Amerindian village and see if their blades could cut a human in two. The mutilated bodies and any others who had not run away became food for the Spaniards' dogs. Population figures are difficult to obtain but in some areas of Mexico there seems to have been nearly a ninety percent decline in the indigenous tribes by the end of the sixteenth century. The enormous death rate was primarily caused by disease, but it can only partially be attributed to unavoidable accident. We can only guess how many of the Amerindians gave up on life because nearly everything that made their existence livable had been changed or destroyed. Neither the Crusades nor the Holocaust caused as much death as did Christendom's conquest of America.

The Spanish authorities allowed the *conquistadores* to take total possession of the native people after the land and all its inhabitants had been claimed as part of the Spanish realm. The second phase of the conquest turned to the land itself as the source of wealth. Plantations for imported sugar cane proved to be quite successful. Their prosperity, however, depended upon the availability of African slaves, who not only could survive the plagues of European disease but also endured the hard work of the cane fields a bit longer than the Amerindians could. Even when the slaves did not last long, the Europeans thought there was an endless supply of such workers in Africa.

These productive economic efforts led to totally unforeseen religious outcomes. The Portuguese had converted some Africans probably through the similarity of their popular piety to significant features in Africa's indigenous religions, but they still saw no difficulty in enslaving Africans for their own economic purposes. The Portuguese and Spanish entrepreneurs who settled in Latin America, however, had little regard for either *Amerindian or African religions*. Thus under their unseeing eyes were born the powerful 'voodoo' religions that still attract various people in the region. These blends of the spiritual worlds in which indigenous Indians and imported Africans lived might have been met early on with the popular Christian piety that characterized both Spain and Portugal. But the condescending ignorance of Catholic religious leaders kept them from discerning the difference between what they might have considered to be good and what they would consider evil. Too few cared.

One strong priest eventually cared deeply. Bartolomé de Las Casas (1484–1566), born in Seville, made the trip to Central America in 1502 as an *encomendero*, a kind of tax collector empowered to take things from Amerindians. His merchant father had sailed on Columbus's second voyage. The junior Las Casas was influenced by Dominican action and preaching against the Spanish mistreatment of Amerindians; he was ordained a priest in 1507. After 1514, when he was wrenched from his indecision by a powerful experience, he spent the rest of his life making the Spanish legal system serve the Amerindians of Latin

America. When he returned to Spain, Cardinal Cisneros in 1515 gave him the title 'Protector of the Indians'. On a later visit to the land of his birth, he was warmly received by the emperor Charles V and began his career of shaping imperial policy toward Amerindians.

He was bitterly opposed by Spanish colonists, particularly those *encomenderos* among whom he had formerly served. He set up a farming community in what is now Venezuela, one composed of both Spaniards and Amerindians, but it floundered. Yet he continued to work for such enterprises because he knew they were right.

Las Casas was fearless in his cause. He insisted in one writing, *The Only Method of Attracting All Peoples to the True Faith*, that evangelism should always be a peaceful venture, based both on the assumption that Christian revelation was true and that the peoples to whom missionaries preached had the intelligence to see its worth. For him, dialogue and persuasion were the bone and muscle of Christian mission. He described his own life as 'walk[ing] through the world in search of Christ's poor'. It was his plan to establish both justice and salvation.

Las Casas became so angry about the abuses he observed that in another tract, 'A Brief Account of the Destruction of the Indies', he probably exaggerated the situation. On the basis of his claims many have thought that Spain's entire policy was exploitation. It certainly was the official view when Las Casas reached the Americas. In the name of God and the king of Spain all lands and peoples had been claimed as part of Spain's realm. Yet Las Casas's successes demonstrated that there were those in Latin America and Spain as well as elsewhere in Europe who heard his arguments against such violations with open ears and moved to improve the situation. In 1537 Pope Paul III insisted that Amerindians were rational human beings whose rights did not differ from those of Europeans. By 1542, owing in no small part to Las Casas's arguments in Spanish courts, laws had been created that restricted what the Spanish authorities could do to the Indians of Latin America. His debate with Juan Ginés de Sepúlveda during 1550–1 showed once more the fury that led to his somewhat distorted reports of the Amerindians' plight. But he so vigorously questioned the legality of the Spanish invasions and successfully defended the rights of the Indians that his position has been honored ever since. He was bishop of Chiapas in Mexico from 1544 to 1547. After his death, his *Historia de las Indias* was published by friends, a work that attempted to see these indigenous peoples as far more significant than most Europeans viewed them. The naming of places in

Mexico after Las Casas suggests that he is remembered among the Amerindians who still struggle for their freedom.

José de Acosta (1540–1600), a Spanish Jesuit who worked among the Amerindians in Peru, wrote a manual, *Taking Care of the Salvation of Indians*, that both defended the mission to them and spelled out how it should be done. Arguing against their detractors, he rebuked their mistreatment by rhetorically conceding that Spanish masters might see the Amerindians as children or even simple animals. But in that case, they should be treated with tenderness. No one of good sense beats a child or a donkey. De Acosta himself insisted that Indians were intelligent and had many virtuous characteristics: at the least much patience and humility. Some of their customs were barbarous, but no more so than those Paul found practiced among the Corinthians.

According to de Acosta, when the *conquistadores* killed the Amerindians' king, whom they still mourned, those Spaniards were looking for gold, not seeking to save anyone. But many missionaries were themselves not the best and brightest; they forgot their purpose. They resisted learning the Amerindian languages and their cultures and thus proved their incompetence. The mission to the Amerindians was slow in reaching results because of the slowness of missionaries. The gifted ones who could speak with the Amerindians and experience their customs knew that nothing in their way of life should be changed that was not diametrically opposed by the gospel. Much needed correction but much could be confirmed. Much of De Acosta's advice is still sound.

In 1500 a Portuguese expedition led by Pedro Alvarez de Cabral landed in Brazil and claimed it for their king. Among the passengers on the thirteen ships were diocesan priests and fifteen Franciscans. Because the Brazilian Amerindians lived exclusively off the land by raising a few crops and killing game, a debate ensued among the Europeans about whether these peaceful folk could be considered human, but the Christian leaders spent most of their time serving as pastors among the Europeans. Martím Alfonso de Souza's expedition from Portugal in 1530 planned to set up colonies for the longer term. They brought sugar cane with them as the cash crop for European plantations. Almost immediately other ships brought numbers of African slaves to work the fields. Again the focus of most priests was on the Europeans, neither the Africans nor the Amerindians.

Intentional missionary activity among the indigenous people began in earnest with the arrival of Jesuits in 1549. The most important of these was José de Anchieta, born in the Canary Islands. Following the age-old path of absorbing the culture of those to whom he ministered, he created a dictionary and a grammar for the Tupí-Guaraní language of Brazil so that there would be a written language for the translation of scripture. He also listened carefully to *Amerindian religious themes* and music; he eventually put Christian doctrines into their tunes. Not neglecting his own European heritage, he also wrote songs, dialogues and dramatic plays in Latin, Spanish and Portuguese as well as Tupí. But Bishop Sardinha officially stopped Jesuit use of the indigenous languages by insisting that the gospel should be preached only in Portuguese. In order to overcome that prohibition, Jesuits worked to create their own province in the region, one outside the authority of any single regional bishop.

Leaders of the Protestant Reformation in *Europe* showed only a modicum of interest in other religions except *Judaism*. They were not strong in Spain or Portugal and thus had little or no experience with Muslims. Indeed the countries in which they first emerged were either landlocked or had no navies of world consequence. Their relationship with Jews, however, was too often full of distrust and vengeance. In the first part of his career Martin Luther (1483–1546) had pleaded for tolerance, even love, between Christians and Jews. He was convinced that with the eradication through his reformation of the worst vices of Christian communities Jews would be more open to the gospel. Later in life, however, when he was ill and numerous Jewish conversions had not occurred, he vigorously attacked the Jews. Nearly all of his energy that was focused on such issues burst forth in venomous tracts and offhand remarks in his commentaries. He cannot be held responsible for the Nazi genocide of the twentieth century; his concern was religious not racial. Yet he also cannot be held up as a man of virtue who on such questions went beyond the common thought of his own era. His late words focused on the Jews did little to support those who stood against the twentieth-century German catastrophe.

Luther knew about the *Turkish Muslims* and their successful warring incursions into Europe before they were stalled outside Vienna in 1529. He referred to them primarily as rank pagans who were enemies of Christ and his followers. His knowledge of them, however, seems to have been derived from tales told by soldiers and travelers. The remarks of John Calvin (1509–64) relied on similar sources. Although some had thought that the Turks were only mythical creatures, all Europe now knew that they were a serious military threat. God was so provoked against those who lived in Greece and Asia Minor that he had used the Turks for their punishment. Only the Turks' passion for what they did was worth emulating.

In *Spain* during 1568 unexpected Christian praise of *Muslims* appeared while the Islamic threat to Christians in the Middle East was strong and the Inquisition was demanding adherence to Roman Catholic views by brutally suppressing heretics. Only protection within the Spanish court evidently allowed Ginéz Pérez de Hita to write his work on *The Civil Wars of Granada*. Catholic Spain had driven out many Jews and Moors at the end of the previous century. The Muslim Moriscos' uprising in Granada was dangerous enough, however, that King Philip II asked for and received the pope's permission to conduct a crusade against them. De Hita, in the first volume of his history, described Moorish culture in vibrant detail. He was impressed and almost demanded that his readers share his views. In ways other writers had not, de Hita told the stories of Moorish suffering and suppression in terms that not only made their hatred of the Spanish sensible but also made the justice of their cause plain. He neither argued for the supremacy of Christian faith that would defend the oppression of Moriscos nor showed deep interest in its truthfulness. In his opinion King Philip would have been better off to lose all his holdings than to have repressed the Moriscos. Wars against them could not be holy.

Whether their efforts at this time be referred to as the Catholic or Counter Reformation, Roman Catholic leaders at the beginning of the sixteenth century had a clearer picture of *world religious pluralism* than did Protestants. Much Catholic energy was taken up by internal reform but another part of Catholic focus was on relations with those of other faiths. An influential group viewed Jews as killers of Christ, always to be watched and more than occasionally persecuted. Spanish Christian piety found nothing wrong with driving Jews from their long-established Spanish homes. Catholic majorities in other European lands saw little reason to reject the crushing of Jewish communities in their cities as Christian troops had done in the Crusades.

But the Spanish expulsion of Jews had an even larger counterpart. Muslims were also driven out. No other European Catholic region reacted so consequently to a sense that both Jews and Muslims were mortal enemies. Spanish Catholics were forced to think about Muslims; some knew a bit about their teachings and had been impressed with their lives. But the national interest was in uprooting these two communities from Christian Spain.

At least one other major factor pumped information into the Catholic view of other religions. Both Spain and Portugal at the end of the fifteenth century had developed fleets that sailed not only the Mediterranean but also toward the British Isles and down the coast of Africa. The Spanish and the Portuguese knew Muslims in their own homelands and from the trade they pursued; they had contacts all along the southern shores of the Mediterranean with those who believed in Allah and his prophet. They were ready, because of their love for East Indian goods that came over the Silk Road, to find a sea route without bandits and tariffs. Columbus went to the Spanish court with such plans.

During the sixteenth century the English and the Dutch were the only inveterate sailors who might have challenged Spanish and Portuguese dominance. But they came to prominence later and entered the Protestant Reformation in different forms as Anglicans and as Dutch Calvinists.

The enormous wealth promised by trade with the East Indies drove both the Iberian countries to dare major undertakings. Catholic orders, some like the Jesuits committed directly to papal direction, soon found their own mission among people of other religions to depend upon Iberian sea journeys. Ignatius Loyola (1491/5–1556), after his own deeply religious experiences with death and war as well as a kind of theological education, had founded the Jesuits by 1534. Among the initial group of seven was Francis Xavier (1506–52), one of the most important missionaries ever known to any Christian community. In 1541 he accepted an invitation from King John of Portugal which had been arranged by the pope. Francis boarded a ship headed around Africa for the East. Voyaging for the next fifteen years, he reached Japan and died not far from China. He proved his evangelical fervor for the evangelization of those without Christ. The Jesuit estimate is that he won 700,000 people in various lands despite his debilitating seasickness and the short period of time he actually was on land in Asia. The first voyage allowed a brief stop at Madagascar, and then took him to Goa on the western coast of India. For two years he traveled to the Indian cities of Pescheria, Travancor and Chochin, where he met not only *Hindus* but also East Syrian (Nestorian) Christians. His mission in India was focused primarily on those not in power: women, children and the poor castes like the Paravas (Bharathas), impoverished fisherfolk. He baptized so many of the latter that for days he went to sleep with his arms crooked from sprinkling them. Only when he fell into a deep sleep could the muscles relax.

From Goa he also sailed to Ceylon (Sri Lanka) and the Molucca Islands (eastern Indonesia). His vision of Japan developed from meeting a Japanese samurai, Yajiro, in Malacca and sailing with him back to Goa. By the time they arrived in Japan in 1549, Francis had learned some Japanese and had changed his strategies for penetrating that culture. Concentrating on the feudal princes and local religious leaders, he had considerable success. In 1552 he returned to Goa and then headed out for China.

Xavier has been correctly criticized for not taking either the full cultures or religions of those he contacted with ultimate seriousness. At first he intended to wipe the slate clean in order to preach the gospel, but his attempt to create vernacular translations in India began to shift his thinking. The change in his operations from Goa to Japan further demonstrates that he was trying to understand the lives of those whom he hoped to convert. He highly praised the Japanese and their culture. On the voyage from Goa he had studied Japanese and talked at length with his Japanese companion, but that man, more Westernized than he initially appeared to be, did not have the connections in Japan that he had claimed. Xavier was under the wrong impressions at other points when he made bad decisions. He found nothing deeply evil in the Catholic Inquisition, persecuted the Nestorian Christians he found in India, and in writing his major Christian catechisms had some difficulty identifying the best ways Christian community might be contextualized within the local cultures.

During his stay in Japan, however, Xavier's best vision of mission was embodied in the unlikely conversion of two people. The first, one of only a few *Buddhist* monks who became Christian, was himself an esteemed Buddhist scholar who had been educated in a renowned center, Ashikaga Gakko. Because of this background his contributions were twofold: (1) he was able to teach the Jesuit missionaries about Japanese culture and important aspects of Japanese Buddhist life; (2) he could explain Christian faith to those asking questions, usually elite Japanese, in terms of their culture and their faith. The second person was a nearly blind Japanese wandering minstrel. This musician's influence was most felt among the common people, where his ability to put the Christian gospel into Japanese song led many to make Christian faith theirs. This assured that evangelization was not limited by Xavier's new attempt to turn from the focus on children, women and lower classes that marked his ministry in India to the ruling parties in Japan. Conversion seldom if ever came completely from the top down.

Allesandro Valignano (1539–1606), a brilliant Jesuit organizer of the mission efforts in both Japan and China, showed himself to be a man of insight with decisive diplomatic and listening skills. He insisted that the Jesuit mission was under his control, not that of the Portuguese political or Catholic religious authorities. An Italian who did not see much insight in those leaders, Valignano took full advantage of his designation as Jesuit 'Visitor to the East'. He expected to find value in Japanese society because he had seen such in other cultures, including India. His efforts in Japan and China were based on the evaluation that the cultures and societies of those countries could form the bridge for creating Christian community that would be neither Portuguese nor Spanish. Because the religions in those countries provided guides to the moral life and family structures that were the backbones of culture and society, Valignano's principles for gathering Japanese and Chinese Christians together provide one of the most interesting inculturation projects of this period.

Matteo Ricci (1552–1610) was mentored by Valignano. Assigned to China, he put into practice the principles of his teacher. His preparation included the study of Chinese language and culture during a stay in Macao. In 1583 Ricci was able to convince Chinese officials to allow him and his colleague Michele Ruggiero to settle in a city not far from Canton. The Chinese who came to their home were fascinated by the world map that hung on their wall, so Ricci put the names of various countries and cities into Chinese. At first he attempted to represent himself as a *Buddhist* priest, but later he abandoned that style of clothing and living for the stance of a *Confucian* teacher. He thoroughly studied the ancient classics, particularly *The Four Books*, and translated them into Latin. A new Chinese governor general of the province forced him to leave, but later he was able to return to a different city near Canton. His new presentation of himself as a Confucian scholar with unusual artifacts from the West such as clocks and maps led to slow but steady invitations to go up river eventually to the capital, Beijing. He found ways in which the Chinese classics provided truths that not only were compatible with Christian teachings, but, in his view, could be fulfilled only in Christian practice and faith.

Ricci insisted upon the translation of scripture into Chinese. He ran afoul of Roman authorities during what is usually called the Rites

Controversy. The loss that he and other Jesuits suffered in this decision produced one of the lowest points in seventeenth-century Roman Catholicism. Some of the missionaries in China felt that there was no term in the Chinese language that could be used as God's name. Each potential word had such a 'pagan' history that to employ it would confuse the truth of Christian doctrine from the very start. Ricci and his friends, however, had found the Chinese word for 'King of Heaven' to be not only adequate but also the fullest concept available. They had finished the translation of some biblical books when the investigator from Rome arrived. He soon confiscated what had been done and stopped the printing of anything else.

The official Roman *translations* that eventually appeared put the Latin *Deus* into Chinese characters. In the minds of these European Roman Catholics responsible for this modification, the truth of the faith had been protected. The upshot of the affair, however, was disastrous. First, it depended upon their assumption that a Latin word for 'God' was the only proper one. This odd belief meant that a gospel presented by Jesus in Aramaic and then written in Koine Greek by the earliest church only reached its final full meaning in Latin. Thus liturgies and practices of the official Latin-speaking Roman church were the ultimate touchstone of Christian faith. Second, Chinese officials soon referred to the Christian tradition not in its ancient Syrian designation established in the eighth century as the 'luminous religion' but as the cult of the 'Deusts'. Such a designation assured that even Chinese Christians would most often be viewed as foreign 'devils' who should be both closely watched and roundly persecuted whenever xenophobic fears were further aroused. How sad that in a huge proud country, often certain that it needed nothing from any other culture, a mission theory would demand that the transliteration of foreign words became official policy.

The Thomas Christians of *India* may well have been there since a visit from the apostle Thomas. By the turn of the sixteenth century there were probably 80,000–100,000 of them concentrated in Kerala on the southwestern coast of India. Their relationships with *Muslims* were primarily antagonistic, most probably because many of the Thomas Christians were merchants who competed with Muslim traders for all kinds of goods and routes. Such contentious relations had opened a place for any kind of military assistance. If the Portuguese, who would soon appear in their ships, could help these Christians build forts to protect themselves, the Westerners would serve a welcome purpose.

In the middle of the sixteenth century, however, some Christians living in villages around Quilon had converted to Islam. Daughters who married Muslim men brought their mothers along with them. Muslims had enough influence with the rajah that they were able to get him to prevent the building of churches in the area. But the rajah recognized that he needed the European horses that came to him from the Portuguese in Goa. His military efforts required these animals, so he reversed his position. Christians could baptize and build churches; indeed he gave them land and even helped them erect a church in his capital, Kalkulam.

CHRISTIANS AND THEIR CULTURES

Much of the contention between the various Christian groups during this period can be described in terms of disputed cultural traditions. None of those issues ever stood outside theological debate, but some insight might be gained by treating them in this section. In *Germany*, Martin Luther (1483–1546) understood the importance of *translating* the Bible into the vernacular. Kidnapped by troops loyal to Frederick the Wise and spirited off to 'protection' in the Wartburg Castle, Luther spent the time there translating Jerome's Latin Vulgate Bible into German. That kept alive within the Protestant Reformation one deep Christian sense of mission: all people should hear the word of God in their native tongue, their heart language. Translation into a vernacular German dialect preferred by Luther had an even more powerful cultural outcome. Because of the various tribes that had emerged in German territory thousands of years before Luther, people in different areas could not understand each other. (This is sometimes true of strong German dialects even today.) There was no unifying German tongue that all peoples could hear and some could write. The victory of Protestant Christians and Luther's German Bible in much of the region was a high water mark in the development of the German language. Luther's Bible can be studied not only as an important religious document, but also as the printed book that created the modern German mother tongue. It is another of the strong pieces of evidence that show how Christians often did not destroy local cultures but gave them a voice they had not previously attained. Had Luther's translation appeared in a country other than Germany, outside the European Christendom that was desperately in need of reform, it would regularly be viewed as a marvelous mission project providing a successful example of the translation principle, surely one of the century's most significant accomplishments. Luther neither thought deeply about nor executed plans for world mission; two men sent to Silesia (Poland) hardly qualifies as a vision of world outreach. But he stood squarely in the middle of this most important translation principle for the missionary activity of Christians.

Luther gladly accepted much of the Christian *art* adored by medieval Roman Catholics. Faced with a strong urge among some of his own colleagues at Wittenberg like Andreas von Carstadt (*c.* 1480–1541) to tear down or deface the statuary of Christian art, Luther flew into a rage at the culprits. Previous art and architecture had their own beauty, their own truthful witness to give. On the one hand Luther thus accepted and strengthened the place of such human creations in his attempts to reform the worship of God. On the other hand it is not clear that he fully understood the power of such imagery to contradict some of the teaching against Roman Catholic piety that he also demanded.

Anabaptists, nearly always persecuted, had little peace or money to create art and architecture. They usually were small groups who met in homes or other halls much less imposing than medieval cathedrals. Partially for religious reasons, they preferred simplicity in both their dress and the decoration of their meeting places.

Throughout sixteenth-century *European* Catholicism, *celibacy* was the ordered and harmonious role for priests. It was a cultural given. Only on occasion, as in parts of Africa, did any Catholic leader of this era suggest married life as a possible option for Christian clergy. Martin Luther early in his manhood heard the call of God to become a celibate monk. His frightening ride in a thunderstorm, lightning striking close enough to knock him from his horse, provided the shock to push him in that direction. The decision infuriated his merchant father. He had not paid for his son's education in order for Martin to slip beneath the sea of monkish poverty. Luther, however, could not grasp any other way to live. But as he studied celibacy deeply and began to recognize insurmountable difficulties with monasticism, he eventually revoked his vows and married Katy. She had been a nun; both continued habits from their monastic life: prayer, study, worship. But they increasingly valued married life, not merely for its pious gift of producing children, but also because of the strength for living that it gave marriage partners. Jesus had found marriage to be proper for men and women. Paul even said that it is better to marry than to burn with passion. The celibacy defined by the Roman hierarchy now looked abominable, another way in which medieval choices overemphasized one of the possibilities.

Katy was no shrinking violet. She married a man of extraordinary talents and energy, but in their partnership she found ways to serve and to direct. Once when Martin was suffering from a miserable attack of kidney stones that might have prevented him from missing an important conference, Katy filled his stomach with ale to the point of drunkenness. Then she shoveled horse manure into the kitchen stove, put it in a sheet and wrapped him in it. Lifted into a wagon by a couple of strong helpers, Luther slept and on the journey passed the painful stones. Katy had command of such common cultural wisdom. Large consumption of beer and the application of heat to the body near the kidney continued to be one aspect of treating kidney stones in twentieth-century German medicine.

Economic and political power clashed in the battles between Protestants and Catholics. Martin Luther's reform would never have continued without the support in both those areas from Frederick the Wise. In his first yearnings Luther had little interest in anything other than reforming the practices and teachings of the Catholic Church. He wanted to work within and change things. But his fiery delivery, even more the points that he made, threatened political and economic interests. He would not give in to the decision of the Holy Roman Empire in council that his views were dangerous. But his call for the halt to indulgences – forgiveness for sins not yet committed – was both a religious and an economic matter. People with wealth paid for those indulgences. They were no insignificant factor in the church's ability to pay its leaders and to erect and adorn its sumptuous church buildings.

Put under a ban by the empire's authorities, thus an open target for anyone to kill, Luther would probably have died had Frederick the Wise not whisked him away to the Wartburg Castle. It is difficult to know how deeply Frederick was interested in the religious views of his captive. But he quickly saw in the popular response to Luther's writings how he himself might be relieved from sending so much local money to Rome for the gilding of St. Peter's cathedral. As the Reformation developed he was happy to set up a faculty of theology at Wittenberg so that the ideals might be instilled in other pastors and teachers. But political and economic independence from Italian Catholics formed much of his goal.

Luther found no reason to reject *religious establishment*. He needed protection. His sense of the unity between religious and political concerns was crucial. The peasants' revolts of the 1520s had soured him against the rabble. Traveling in slow wagons, he was able to see some of the disasters that these struggles had created. The Christian gospel certainly involved freedom, but it did not undercut order. Some of Luther's most vitriolic tracts were those against the Schwabian peasants. In them he called the divinely ordained princes to put their armies in the field and destroy the riffraff who had so terribly misunderstood his call for reform. Returning from wars in Italy, German armies killed a great many peasants. The soldiers were both experienced and far better armed.

As the Protestant Reformation in Germany met with success, Luther eventually agreed with Roman Catholic leaders that the best political solution was for the lower classes to move into regions ruled by either Catholic or Protestant figures. In his mind this was by far the simplest solution, much superior to the battling that had cost so many lives. Catholics would live under Catholic princes; Protestants would live under Protestant princes. Anabaptists would be exterminated – their sense of following the call of Christ without living in a land where Christians enjoyed established privilege seemed quite odd. Being a political minority presented too dangerous a plight.

John Calvin (1509–64) initially failed to set up his understanding of Christian society in Geneva, *Switzerland* but when he was invited back he put his theocratic ideals in place with the help of the town council. Earlier in France he himself had fled from Catholic authorities. Local officials of the Roman church had discovered the gifts of this youth and had given him an education of highest quality. He in turn had accepted various ranks of clerical status, but in the end had to refuse ordination to the priesthood because of his theological views. It is possible that he was either threatened with imprisonment or actually imprisoned. He also had Waldensians in his extended family for whose safety he pleaded with the French king in one of his early writings. But when he became the primary force in Geneva, his earlier experiences did not make him a more compassionate bearer of authority. For Calvin pure life and belief were not merely a goal; they had to be the reality. Sadly his city attracted free thinkers who looked at Christian practice and faith in different ways. Calvin and the city council had many of these people arrested and banished. During his leadership over fifty people were burned at the stake for God and his glory. Calvin always hoped that the person would repent before or in the flames. The Genevan community thought that the threat of death should warn many away from the consequences of wrong practice and faith.

Anabaptists, much like Christians in Constantinople and further east to China, suffered constant persecution, but their pain and death flowed from Protestant and Catholic Christian action, not from established figures in other religions. At times Holland offered them shelter and freedom, but almost everywhere else in Europe they were hunted down. Of their major leaders only a few reached old age. Menno Simons (1496–1561) lasted nearly thirty years longer than many but he lived underground, hunted continuously for at least twenty years and died in northern Germany rather than his native Friesland. Anabaptist understanding that some of the major social institutions in European Christendom were not established by God seems reasonable given their experiences. They found solace in the apocalyptic passages of the Bible, particularly in the book of Revelation's claims that the Roman Empire was bestial, not founded and administered by God. Their lives certainly fitted that scriptural interpretation, but sadly their enemies were not ancient Roman emperors but other Christians.

Lack of political and economic power was one of the most prominent features of Christians in the *eastern Mediterranean*. The fall of Constantinople in 1453 marked the collapse of a remarkable Christian civilization that could hold out no longer. Sacked in 1204 by Western troops on a crusade, the capital city of the Byzantine Empire languished under various Turkish sieges. In 1453 the great walls were breached for good. The Byzantine Empire lay prostrate under Muslim rule. Adjustments were made in many aspects of life, but in Constantinople the limited access to Hagia Sophia and other churches must have been difficult. No longer could the Christian God be worshipped with the splendor of former times. The liturgical vessels and vestments that were of value on a Muslim market were confiscated. The insults must have been painful. The Christian God had not saved this jewel of cities.

In many ways the plundering left Constantinopolitan Christians in positions quite similar to those of Christians further east all the way to China. Since the seventh century most believers in Christ in much of what we now call the Middle East had been under alien political control. By the sixteenth century within the Ottoman Empire their education and diplomatic skills were not strong enough to demand that they regularly be included in Muslim courts. Any with historical memories could grow nostalgic about the early Muslim conquests in which they were respected as people of the book and sought as needed political operatives. Now they were persecuted, often not allowed even to repair their worship or school buildings. Some Christian traders with sharpened eyes made money, but the taxation was heavy and the Christian communities continued to struggle for existence. Yet they were still there to be taxed.

Christians elsewhere than in Europe had learned well in previous centuries what was expected of them as religious minorities under benign or hostile rule. Believers from *Constantinople to Baghdad* had moved with the times and adopted styles of dress in the Ottoman Empire that did not make them stand out. They learned not to wear ostentatious clothes even if their positions as scribes or courtiers would allow it. Whether or not to own a horse remained a difficult decision. Christians' houses and businesses were constructed in ways that would not attract attention. No matter how much they tried to appear assimilated, their place and jobs within the political, economic and social structure of Islamic society continued to be precarious. But inside those nondescript buildings there were often small signs that they were indeed Christians. Many of them were already fluent Arabic speakers and writers. The earliest Christians had adopted Koine Greek, the language of the street. These Ottoman Christians followed that pattern in their own situations. They did their best to sustain existence by finding ways to make peace with the Arabic or Turkish Muslim culture in which they lived.

During the sixteenth century in *Persia*, on the *Silk Road* and even in *China* there were small Christian communities who in no one's memory had ever been more than local minorities, usually tiny groups. They knew what it took to live out their faith without governmental assistance or establishment. Persecutions came and went, often dependent on the whim of national or local rulers. People became and remained Christians only out of deep faith and family relationships. There were no economic or political prizes for continued involvement in Christian community.

When Matteo Ricci (1552–1610) sought to take Christian faith and life deep into *China*, he was recognized as a foreign person who had interest in things Chinese. He used Western technology, however, to his advantage. He brought clocks, astronomical charts, and maps that made him interesting to the inquisitive Chinese. He not only learned their language but also many of the Confucian classics; he eventually adopted the dress of Confucian scholars and thus put himself forward as a lover of their learning. All these were genuine attitudes fulfilled in actions. Even when the Jesuits were disbanded in the eighteenth century and their work in China faded, they left behind a changed Chinese calendar that was both a cultural and a religious artifact.

Japanese converts first grew to numbers that pleased the missionaries in the second half of the sixteenth century. A degree of political tolerance allowed them to flourish so that near the end of the century they had reached 150,000, then 300,000 before the persecutions became intense in 1614. Although those are considerable numbers, all these Japanese Christians were endangered when a majority of their warriors fought in Japanese feuds in which their side lost. The ruling family in Japan then perceived Christians as a strong threat to the country's stability. Unable to defend themselves with the armament and soldiers they could field, they were hunted down and executed.

Thomas Christians in *India* had no great political power. They blended into the larger culture by sharing various cultural artifacts and customs with their neighbors. Much like Hindus did with their scriptures, the Vedas, Thomas Christians had passages from the Gospels placed in gold and silver jewelry which they wore around their arms. When they were ill, their priests would read parts of the Gospels at their bedsides as the Vedas were read in the homes of sick Hindus. Christian prayers were considered so powerful that even some Hindu leaders asked for and received them.

Many Indian churches adopted the architecture of Hindu temples. Some Christian families had documents indicating that they were the property trustees of Hindu worship sites and were regularly invited to the festivals celebrated there. Christian feasts often had Hindu trappings: umbrellas, Indian musical instruments, torches and noise makers. The Hindu *prasad*, in which birds, candies and other edibles were presented to the temple and then distributed back to the people, was also practiced by the churches. Moreover Hindus and Christians used similar but distinguishable crosses.

The Thomas Christians had occasional skirmishes with their Hindu neighbors, but often they lived with them in a harmony that they did not have with the Muslims. In fact many of the Thomas Christians thought of themselves as a special Indian caste and thus fitted into Hindu cultural life in that way. Although they did not let lower caste Indian Christians worship with them, they did attempt to recognize them as fellow Christians. But they had no intention of challenging the caste system that had served them well for centuries.

Various kinds of *scientific* knowledge and technologies were exchanged between Western groups who traveled so far East and the host cultures they met. Christian converts in sixteenth-century China

took advantage of their relationship with Western expansion in unexpected ways. Clever businessmen among them sailed to Macao, where
they could purchase cannon of superior quality and sell them in their
homeland for a good profit. The printing technology of the Europeans
also intrigued the Chinese, who had long possessed a love of books and
their production.

A CHRISTIAN CORE

In the area of *spirituality* Teresa of Ávila (1515–82) may be viewed as
the most important figure of this period. She was a remarkable mystic
and theologian. In 1970 she became the first woman recognized by
Catholics as a doctor of the church. She grew up in a merchant family
with a Jewish grandfather who had converted. Her career in Christian
leadership was blocked by her gender. After her mother's death when
Teresa was fourteen, she decided to be a nun. Her father vigorously
resisted her wish so she ran away to the Carmelite nunnery in the city.
Only a year later illness struck her down with such force that her father
brought her back home. She went into a coma so deep that at first those
around her thought she was on the verge of death. When she recovered,
her lower body was paralyzed for months. She returned to the convent
after three years but the previous events and the present setting did not
seem to have enriched her spiritual life. The convent itself was more a
social club, with frequent male visitors, a place where her vivacious personality had made her a desired conversationalist.

Teresa's conversion from the fear of purgatory to dependence upon
the love of God occurred in her twenty-ninth year when she saw a cru-
cifix and was deeply moved by God's loving gift. She vowed to make that
the center of her life and to spend much more time in prayer. The result
was a continuing series of inner experiences of God's grace and a strong
resolve to reform her Carmelite order. Her talents and these mystical
visions formed her as a virtuous, persuasive nun. The Spanish Inquisition, however, was concerned about anything that appeared to be Protestant. Women with public power were looked upon with suspicion. Most
sadly the 'shoed' Carmelites whom Teresa viewed as deeply undisci-
plined gave her nothing but grief. But eventually the church allowed her
to found the 'shoeless' Carmelites who returned to the more primitive
surroundings of the first Carmel. Sixteen new houses owed their existence to Teresa's influence.

Not only was Teresa recognized as one who had experienced communion with God; she was also loved as a person who was able to use those visions to assist the lives of people who had never had them. Her male spiritual director insisted that she write down her thoughts for the nuns, something she at first resisted. But those writings, now available in various languages, used poetic imagery to move the soul. In her book *The Interior Castle,* Teresa employed the metaphor of rooms at various distances from the center to talk about the levels of prayer along the way from reciting the liturgy to almost wordless communion with God. In a previous work she had described such union as fleeting, ecstatic and harmful to bodily health. But here she insisted that life in the Trinity demanded the incarnation that marked Jesus Christ. In the midst of living within the Trinity the mature believer returned to the kitchen, to the field, and carried on the lowly tasks with new vision and energy. So serious about meditation, she also had a remarkable sense of humor. Spilled from a wagon into the mud, she heard a voice say, 'This is how I treat my friends.' In response she quipped, 'Perhaps that is why you have so few.'

Her companion in the reformation of the Carmelites was St. John of the Cross (1542–91). He is the devotional writer who gave us the concept of 'the dark night of the soul'. Tragically, it was 'shoed' Carmelites who provided him with the opportunity of coming to know such times. They threw him into a windowless dungeon for nine months, fed him only bread and water, and beat him severely. The inquisitorial sense of battering the body to save the soul was their watchword. They missed out on the guidance in meditation that he could have provided. He pushed the union of the soul with the Trinity to the point that a mature Christian could breathe the air of the Spirit that flowed between the Father and the Son. Such a mature soul loved God with the Spirit in a transformation so deep that the soul was, in a guarded way, a participant in the Trinity. The grace of God now lived in and through the human soul.

Although Protestant and Catholic battles over the grounds and limits of reform dominated most discussions about the center of Christian practice and faith in Europe, those conflicts were seldom even on the periphery of discussions among the Catholics who sailed throughout the world on a mission for Christ. For example, the Inquisition set up in Goa, *India* was much more concerned with whether Robert de Nobili or Matthias Ricci had sold out the gospel to Indian and Chinese cultures and religions. Formed to deal with Muslims and Jews particularly in Spain and then later with heretical Protestants, whether Magisterial or Anabaptist reformers, the Inquisition in Goa was not focused on Central European Protestant questions. One reason was that the missionaries who set out for Africa and Asia, even those who first reached Latin America, were Catholics from countries where Protestants were weak. On important occasions they disagreed intensely with each other, becoming angry enough that they enlisted the Inquisition to settle their differences. Each representative insisted that his was the correct side and the other the heretical one. The sixteenth-century struggle between the Jesuit and Dominican orders, particularly in the Philippines and Japan, was legendary but little interested in the Protestant problematic.

The *European Reformation* of the sixteenth century is probably best treated as an extensive debate about 'the core of Christian faith and practice' within particular parameters. The late fifteenth and the sixteenth centuries saw at least three European movements toward reform that finally separated in growing disgust with each other: the Protestant or Magisterial Reformation, the Catholic or Counter Reformation and the Anabaptist or Radical Reformation. The first fitted into important Central European political and economic situations but was primarily interested in religious reform. The second found its early desire for reform dissipated as many traditional Roman Catholics increasingly came to the conclusion that protesters of any stripe were dangerous. Catholic reform would need to have both eyes on the threat. The third option did not involve large numbers of people but was full of interesting visions. Protestants and Catholics alike usually despised the Radical reformers, fearing that they were actually political revolutionaries.

In most treatments of this period, Martin Luther (1483–1546) and John Calvin (1509–64) are presented as the magisterial figures of the *Protestant Reformation*. Luther, a man of deep questions about his own practice and faith, worked through the educational opportunities offered to an Augustinian monk. The hallmark of his reform might be stated as justification by grace through faith. Each person's sin was so deep that it could not be forgiven through any merit or work that the person could produce. The only response from that miserable condition was to accept God's gift and the faith that God offered to claim it. The whole Roman Catholic system of works was evil.

Luther's extensive biblical commentaries would probably place him in the position of an Old Testament professor in a modern Western theological faculty. Yet his enormous influence grew from the occasional tracts that could be printed and distributed among many readers. His translation of the Bible into German could put scripture into almost any German reader's hands. His abandonment of monastic vows and marriage to a former nun set a pattern for Protestant clergy. The attacks he mounted on Roman Catholics, the Anabaptist *Schwärmer* (fanatics) as he called the Radical Reformers, Jews and Turkish Muslims left Protestants with a swordlike edge. At the same time his writings on ethics displayed many deep sensitivities about the human condition.

He worried how order could be maintained when some understood Christian ethics as including a complete ban on taking human life. Cutting the Gordian knot, he introduced an ethic of two kingdoms. His commitment to a society of law under God led him to read Jesus' Sermon on the Mount in two ways. All Christians should respond within their families to God's grace by living out the commands not to kill, not to take other's money, and all the other difficult demands on human attitudes and behavior. But if a Christian were a prince, a magistrate or a soldier, then the killing necessary for that assignment in society did not break the commands of Jesus. Society would be impossible to construct and sustain if its supporters and those who put its laws into practice were not allowed to do what was obligatory. Personal and societal roles must each be given their due, but political rulers had to have order and the force to maintain it. In fact a competent Turk would be a better ruler than an incompetent emperor.

Luther's teaching about the priesthood of all believers marked an interesting change in the lives of ordinary Christians. He had a strong sense of God's working in the world even to the point of directing the place of each baby. If a man were born into a royal family then God intended him to rule. If a boy found himself in the home of a baker then God had called him to be a good baker and in that way fulfill his vocation. This understanding of birth as destiny formed part of the theological foundation on which Luther built his conservative view of society. He was as angry at peasants for refusing to accept the position in which God put them as he was that, during their revolts, they looted the possessions of the rich and killed upper class people. Greater society was meant to function in order and harmony, each segment not only content but also honored to take its place.

John Calvin (1509–64) was raised in a French Roman Catholic family in which devotion reigned. But later he was persecuted, perhaps even imprisoned because his faith had changed so radically. He had to flee France. Those experiences, however did not soften Calvin's view of people who jeopardized the theocracy that he led in Geneva. Heretics who taught false doctrines were the most dangerous. Calvin fervently pleaded with them in person. Visiting their jail cells, he urged them to repent and often brought his own precious books for them to read. Yet however heavy his heart, he oversaw or was complicit in the death of people who claimed they were Christians but did not fit the Genevan theocracy's views of right faith. Calvin's vision of the Christian life had at first been rejected by the Genevans; thus he did not intend for that dream to be sacrificed because of others' wrong teachings. All this is saddening, since a group of bright, well-educated Europeans who had questioned Catholic views and thus been threatened with death or banned from their Catholic homelands gravitated to Geneva as a refuge of freedom. In fairness to Calvin and the other leaders, they banished most of these refugees from the theocracy, but they arrested and killed over fifty.

The early European Reformation had no more learned theologian than Calvin. He had gained much in his humanistic education and wrote commentaries on ancient Latin classics that are models of insight. His own commentaries on scripture overflowed with help for any Christian who could read or be read to. With the kind of understanding that only genius can muster, he used his education to help him read the Bible through the lens of the ancient Latin disciplines of rhetoric and grammar. In unexpected ways he was able to let passages of Holy Writ say things in his commentaries that he could not allow them to mean in his systematic studies, particularly the *Institutes*. This latter work has continued to be viewed as one of the clearest presentations of the Christian gospel ever published, rich in biblical detail and consequent argument. Its edges are softened by the biblical commentaries.

For Calvin the Christian gospel spoke of a majestic God who had decided who would be saved and who would be damned. Humans were too depraved by sin to question God's judgment. That total depravity did not mean that nothing good remained in any human, but that every aspect of any human had been touched by depravity. Without God's rule and his forgiveness there was no hope. Roman Catholics did not grasp the gospel's significance.

Influential *Roman Catholics* constructed their own vision of *reform*. Many of the most powerful conservatives defended much of the political and economic structure of the church against all comers. Things were not all that bad. A group of centrists, however, attempted to stay in touch with various protesting groups. One of the most important was Desiderius Erasmus (c. 1469–1536), a Dutch humanist and devoted Roman Catholic who traveled throughout continental Europe and Great Britain. Remembered often as the creator of the first published critical edition of the Greek New Testament, he used the newly available printing technology to his advantage. Educated leaders of every major group in the Reformation struggles in Europe tended to adopt his edition as the touchstone for biblical study. Catholics and Protestants each used it as a sword against the other. Radical reformers accepted it with great appreciation and found a number of Erasmus's positions helpful. He wanted to read the text in its context and use grammatical analysis as a major tool. So did all the participants, but each group attempted to modify that method to fit its own theological purposes.

In Spain, the birthplace of the Inquisition, some had found Erasmus's works questionable and translations of them dangerous enough to be suppressed. Cardinal Francisco Ximénez de Cisneros (1436–1517), however, had worked for reform and labored diligently with others on a polyglot edition of the Bible. His efforts on the scriptures reached completion before those of Erasmus, but they were duly submitted to the papacy and thus were delayed. The Greek New Testament was finished in 1514 but Erasmus's 1516 edition benefited from a four-year ban on the publication of other editions. Thus the entire Bible of Ximénez was not circulated until about 1522.

Reform within the Catholic Church had representatives other than Erasmus and Ximénez. Cardinal Thomas de Vio Cajetan (1469–1534) insisted well before the changes demanded by the Lateran Council in 1512 that correction was imperative. As early as 1518 he was in conversation with Luther. On one occasion he pithily remarked that the best response to raging reformers was not to deserve their criticisms.

Another centrist, Cardinal Gaspar Contarini (1483–1542), at first had been involved in political diplomacy for Venice, his home city. He had written a tract on church reform by 1510 and in 1529 even rebuked Pope Clement VII for being more interested in power than the truth and virtue found in Holy Writ. He wanted Clement to pay closer attention to the divisions arising within Christendom.

Pope Paul III in 1534 was so interested in change in the church that he named Contarini a cardinal, in spite of his still being a layman, and made him the head of a papal commission for reform. The commission's report included a lengthy group of reprimands centered on the sale of offices and the ordination of unqualified bishops. In 1541 Contarini was appointed the papal legate to a conference of centrist Catholics and moderate Protestants in Ratisbon, Germany that began its work empowered by his graciousness. Cardinal Caraffa assisted in choosing compromise language meant to allow both sides to find an agreeable understanding of justification by faith. But when word got out, opposing forces on both sides reacted angrily. Catholics accused Contarini of being a Protestant, and Protestants denounced any attempt at compromise. The conference collapsed. Cardinal Caraffa became so much more conservative that he threw his support behind the Inquisition. As Pope Paul IV (1555–9), he put on the list of condemned readings the reform documents that earlier he had signed, parts of which he may have written. He warned that he would gather the wood to burn his own father if he found him to be a heretic.

The conservative right had outflanked Catholic centrists. The latter had little or no ground left to occupy. The death of 70,000–100,000 people in the Catholic Inquisition, Protestant trials, and conflicts like the Peasant Wars is one of the saddest testimonies to Christian leadership in this period. Yet from a theological point of view, the collapse of the Catholic center, so open to Protestant reform early in the struggles, only to be abandoned by Protestants and attacked by conservative Catholics, was also a significant loss.

In a strange way, however, the centrist Catholic view, which became a major casualty in European Protestant and Catholic hostility, reappeared on the mission field. Views similar to those of Erasmus and the Spanish circle around Ximénez can be found in the writings of José de Acosta (1540–1600), a Jesuit priest missionary in Peru. Although from different orders, with educations separated by several years, both Ximénez (1436–1517) and de Acosta were Spanish and had studied at Salamanca. De Acosta's work with Peruvian Amerindians reflected few of the major issues that concerned the Council of Trent and in itself demonstrated a remarkable insight into Christian unity and ministry to those of other faiths. He took the Peruvian Amerindian culture seriously and made the theological decision that many of its features needed little change.

The Council of Trent (1545–63), which shaped Roman Catholicism over against Protestantism for at least three hundred years, belongs to this era. Pope Paul III called the council in 1537 but various problems delayed it until 1545. At first only thirty-eight leaders were in attendance. Because each leader was given one vote, the Italian influence was overwhelming. In three separate periods, 1545–7, 1551–2 and 1562–3, the members, ever growing in number, reached important decisions. The Nicene–Constantinopolitan Creed, which many Protestants also would have accepted, was confirmed as the basic statement of faith. The council declared the Latin Vulgate to be the church's Bible and insisted that only the church could interpret scripture. Statements about original sin and the relationship between justification by grace and the merit from good deeds contradicted Protestant positions and were to guide Catholics. All seven sacraments were affirmed and defined. Concerning the Eucharist, transubstantiation (after the consecrating prayer the change of the inner essence of the bread and wine to Christ's body and blood while the outer appearances remained the same) was affirmed. That stood against Protestant views of consubstantiation (Christ's body and blood coexist with the bread and the wine as fire and iron unite in the heated metal) and symbolism (the bread and wine represented the body and blood). Communion of only one kind was declared sufficient; thus the wine could be withheld from the laity. The sacrificial character of the Mass, the regular liturgy that offered Christ each Sunday, was more clearly defined as were the doctrines of purgatory, saints, relics and images as well as the question of indulgences. Various types of reform of a more thorough nature were rejected, but considerable change in the definition of orders, the education of priests, the appointment of bishops and the calling of local and regional synods were demanded.

As significant as this council was and as positive as many of its reforms were, it still missed some remarkable opportunities. Protestant representatives were in attendance during the first two periods. At the second they insisted that bishops' oaths of allegiance to the papacy and the dominance of councils over popes should be discussed. Battered by the decisions on justification and some of the sacraments, furthermore unable to get the questions raised that they thought vital, the Protestants did not return for the third period.

The decade between the second and third sessions elapsed because princes revolted against the emperor Charles V. The conflict made travel and financial support difficult. Pope Paul IV (1555–9) stood against the council for fear of losing both theological battles and power. When Trent began again, there were struggles between the pope and the bishops who opposed him, particularly those from imperial, French and Spanish regions. At the same time, the council reached some interesting decisions that have influenced modern Catholicism. They did not declare that church tradition was a source of Christian revelation that could by itself complete what holy scripture had left unsaid. Seventeenth-century Spanish interpreters insisted that tradition was part of revelation as Trent had said. But in preparation for Vatican II in the twentieth century, historians found that the letters and journals of participants at Trent had a different view. They indicated that tradition as a further aspect of revelation was rejected and the ambiguous concept 'scripture and tradition' was put in its place. That reopened many discussions with Protestants who could see Holy Writ and church teaching working together, but not tradition completing what the Bible had not said. In numerous ways Trent created a foundation for renewed spirituality and discipline among Catholics, both of which were certainly necessary.

As streams of the Magisterial Reformation became raging torrents, the Catholic counter reform built dikes. Patient, peaceful contact with a destructive flood was out of place. The Inquisition became a controlling institution and moved to limit the influence of European centrists like Erasmus and others in order to stop questioning within the Catholic ranks and to hunt down Reformation leaders who had cut their ties with Rome.

The third group trying to spell out the *reform* of a Christian core, the *Anabaptists*, infuriated everyone. Their sense of the gospel was radically different from both Roman Catholic and Magisterial Protestant conceptions. They read Erasmus's New Testament with an intense interest in what the earliest church must have been like and with a deep conviction that contemporary Christians around them had neither understood nor lived according to Jesus' example and teaching. They earned the name 'Anabaptist' because they saw only adult conversion and baptism in the New Testament. In their view, young children could not make the decisions necessary for living out Christian commitments. Many Anabaptists were rebaptized because their family's acceptance of the Roman Catholic sacrament of baptism when they were infants did not seem valid. How could it be proper when they, as babies, did not know what they were doing?

Their early argument was most often with established Catholics; for Anabaptists the Romanists had failed to lead the ordinary believer toward Christ in a way that resulted in mature ethical practice. Their own demands were strict, marked by energetic efforts to follow the deeds of the first Christians. The response to the grace of Christ from a conflicted but free human will, both facets so necessary for salvation, should be a life of good deeds within family, church and community relationships.

The Radical reformers struck both Catholics and Protestants as enthusiasts, as Luther called them, *Schwärmer*. They were perceived as impractical, unreasonable, and thus destructive of both creation's and God's order. Their working definitions of the gospel's core were not only too expansive but also a danger to human life. Protestants like Luther disowned and persecuted them because genuine Protestant reform never intended to turn the world upside down and thus smash orderly existence.

The Anabaptists themselves had vastly different views of what their reforms might be. Some of them earned scathing reputations that tarnished the efforts of the others. Both Catholics and Protestants assumed that if Anabaptists would finally tell the truth about themselves, they would all be revealed as violent revolutionaries. Any claim to pacifism was a ruse.

This third movement in the Reformation had developed from two separate streams. Where we can find information it seems that some of them had read writers from the Magisterial Reformation like John Calvin and Martin Luther. But for these Anabaptists freedom from what they saw as the bondage suffered by Roman Catholics had more features than freedom from sin. It almost always meant some kind of independence from commonly accepted political and economic structures. One stream of Anabaptists, marked by political revolutionaries, emerged under the names of Müntzer and Münster. Thomas Müntzer was the leader of a peasants' revolt in southern Germany. Recommended as a preacher for the town of Zwickau by Martin Luther, Müntzer was a well-educated pastor with a heart for the common people. His plan was to set up a theocracy in the city, one based on the inner light that might dwell in any person. For him and his followers revelations from the Holy Spirit could occur to common folk, particularly in dreams and visions. These ecstatic experiences were the power of life. By 1521 his views so threatened the city officials that they called for his trial. He fled, then returned to the region and called another congregation to his type of theocracy, which demanded shared property and common life. A fiery preacher, he even demanded that a baron in his hearing use his troops to set up apocalyptic rule. Müntzer was forced to flee again, ending up in Mühlhausen by 1524. Outside the city he led his charges on the battlefield against an army of German princes and died there. Remarkably, his concern for the downtrodden led East Germany in the twentieth century to create a critical edition of his works and put him in the place that Luther occupied in West Germany, as a hero from the past to legitimize the present. Müntzer's work as a Christian reformer was usually left in the background – the important thing was his communistic view of society.

In the Westphalian city of Münster during 1534 a group of fanatics drove out the bishop and the political authorities, then set up a Christian theocracy with rules to guide all of life. Led by a baker and a tailor, the workmen's guilds overpowered a small group of Catholics and some conservative Lutherans. They held all belongings in common, called their city the 'New Jerusalem' and taught a strong vision of the last times. They contended that all their views were clearly taught in the Bible. They found Old Testament polygamy advisable and broke many other conventions. Some of their group slipped across the border to Holland in an attempt to set up similar 'biblical' communities there. The passion they aroused among both Catholics and Protestants can be seen in the cages that are still chained to the Münster cathedral. In them the captured leaders of the revolt were starved to death.

Swiss Anabaptists, pacifists with no interest in political revolution, suffered from being identified with the dramas of Müntzer and Münster. We have some of the writings of these leaders but many of them were dead before the age of forty, killed by Catholics and Protestants alike. Often drowned in honor of their espousal of rebaptism, they were hounded from city to city in most of Europe except Holland. Driven out by the decisions and power of others, they spread their views of practice and faith wherever they fled. Conrad Grebel (1498–1526) emerged from the circle of Ulrich Zwingli (1484–1531) in Zurich to become one of the founders of these revolutionary but peace-seeking people. Grebel and his friends separated themselves from Zwingli because he did not follow their more literal understanding of the New Testament descriptions of the church, and particularly their sense that it must be a confessional fellowship free of political entanglements. No one could be born into such a fellowship; all needed to make a profession of their faith and pledge their commitment to a life of holiness. The result should be a visible dedicated group of people recognized by everyone as those who obeyed Christ.

Their services of worship were simple, patterned after the earliest church. Baptism for the adult believer meant a kind of rebirth. The Lord's Supper was celebrated in homes during the evening as Christ and his disciples had done it. It was a memorial of Jesus' death and not a sacrament in which the Lord himself was present in the elements. Anabaptist pastors, paid by the flock, concentrated on the Bible, calling the members to live by its rules. They led worship services organized around prayers and the Lord's Supper and supervised the spiritual growth of the group. The strong emphasis on separation from the world led many of these reformers to a nonviolent reception of the persecution they received from Protestants or Catholics.

The work of Anabaptist theologians was characterized by what moderns might call practical theology. Often their views of Trinity and Christology were orthodox, but they seldom emphasized those doctrines. Menno Simons (1496–1561), one of the few long-lived leaders, refused to use the term 'Trinity' because he could not find it in scripture. Hans Denk (died 1527) discovered that both the visions of Christian mystics and some views from the ancient Platonists – previously adapted by Christians – were of help in establishing the true church. Jakob Hutter (died 1536) set up Christian communes that had success both spiritually and economically.

Some have insisted that the left wing of the Reformation does not merit mention in even larger histories of the period. But these small communities of Christians, straining to live like Jesus in a sinful world, must be mentioned even in the short compass of this volume. They have such similarity to tiny groups of Christians persecuted in other lands, first those around the Mediterranean, hounded by the Roman authorities, and later particularly those in Asia, hunted down by established leaders of other world religions. The oddity of the Anabaptists, however, is that they were martyred primarily by Catholics or Protestants in Europe, people embarrassed by the Anabaptists' simplicity and horrified by the possibility that they would soon move into a revolutionary stage.

Another sad intra-Christian conflict of this period involved Portuguese Catholics and Thomas Christians in *India*. When a Portuguese vessel under Vasco da Gama reached India, its passengers initiated one of the more disappointing debates about the nature of Christian life and faith. After making the difficult journey around the cape of Africa and escaping various Muslim intrigues near Madagascar, they reached Melinda in 1498. Perhaps finding a few Christians there, they sailed on to Calicut. Da Gama's instruction from the Portuguese king John was to make friends with Indian political leaders so that trade would be both possible and profitable. Meeting Christians became an interesting aspect of the trip after a few had been encountered and the mistaken impression acquired that most of the country was Christian. At the same time da Gama and his companions, including some priests more concerned with the spiritual life of the Portuguese than mission among the Indians, had no expectation of meeting Christians so different from themselves. They would hardly have anticipated a group of Christians, perhaps in India since the first century, who had developed their understanding of being Christian almost entirely without European influence.

The self-confidence of the Europeans – they were the ones sailing to India; they were the ones sent with papal blessing – made them poor observers of these Indian Christians. The experiences in Melinda perhaps alerted the Portuguese to some strange customs and practices, ones that eventually could be brought into line. In an ironic twist of history, they were led in Calicut to a place of worship – one of many that they passed. They were not allowed to enter. The Indians who went inside had a thread over their left shoulder and under their right arm, worn much as a European deacon would wear a stole. The Portuguese looked in the building and saw the Virgin Mary and groups of saints represented rather strangely with long teeth and four or five arms. The captain was offered holy water and a type of clay to smear on his head, neck, chest and upper arms, but he said he would do that later. The Portuguese company prayed outside in the church graveyard. Their difficulty in recognizing these unusual Christians might have been understandable had they known they were worshipping outside a Hindu temple within shouting distance of the Brahmins inside. This incident does not give one confidence in their ability to define Christian practice and faith.

There were Christians in India, perhaps over eighty thousand; most of them, however, lived further south in Malabar. Influenced by East Syrian (Nestorian) contacts with churches in Syria and Persia (Iran), these Indians had a different theology, a different sense of community and a different understanding of how far they could be Indian and thus get along with Hindus. They emphasized the human nature of Jesus Christ, but in ways like Babai the Great (died *c.* 628), an East Syrian divine, they balanced that understanding with a deep sense of the Son's divinity and the oneness of his person. Their communities were more like extended families and ruled by a *yogam*, an assembly of wise ones who made the significant decisions for the church. Their dress, their celebration of festivals, their prayer practices and their acts of piety often so resembled those of their Hindu neighbors that it was difficult to tell them apart.

Most of the Portuguese were appalled. Nestorian Christology was one of the severest ancient heresies. Furthermore, bishops, not assemblies, ruled churches. Finally, Christians should be differentiated from Hindu Indians. So offended were these Western Christians, that they held a synod in Diamper during 1599 to settle the issues. Portuguese Christians with their powerful political and economic trade interests dominated the meetings. They had little or no knowledge of Syriac or the local Indian languages. The Thomas Christians knew little or no Portuguese. The interpreters held all communications in their hands and did not serve either side well. The most brazen of the European acts was the systematic destruction of almost all the books of these Indian Christians, writings on various media including copper plates. Their efforts were so successful that no full Indian Christian manuscripts survive dated earlier than the sixteenth century. The only reason some records from that time still exist is that the Malabar Christians eventually learned that they had to keep their current books hidden.

Western Catholics rearranged or wrecked Christian church buildings and treated the Christian communities as heretics who had succumbed to Indian culture and lost their way. Because of this ignorant arrogance it is impossible to write an extensive history of Indian Christians before the sixteenth century. In the same way that sixteenth-century Spanish soldiers burned the books of the Incas and Aztecs as blasphemies, these Portuguese imperialists burned the Indian Christian writings (historical, theological and liturgical) as threats to the true faith. As we have seen, the Portuguese treated the Hindus with similar condescension and probably would have been as cruel as they were to the Amerindians in Latin America had they been strong enough to do so. It is difficult to treat other religions with such ferocity and not follow similar practices against heretics in one's own faith, or vice versa. One reason that the Spanish Inquisition against Christian heretics was so brutal was that the ferocity turned against Muslims and Jews had been God's crusade, a noble and totally absorbing 'holy' task.

In Francis Xavier's mission voyages to *the East*, he demonstrated that at heart his efforts depended upon his deep sense of the need for catechesis – teaching. We have three catechisms from him, two originally written in Portuguese and the third in Latin. He had the first catechism quickly translated into Tamil and Malay, languages of the islands he visited. It included prayers, the Latin creed of his church and a list of commandments. The second was also translated, but this time into Tamil and Japanese with a view to its eventual rendering into Chinese. Its cadence suggests that it was meant to be sung. The third was concerned primarily with how the faith should be taught. Xavier himself worked to educate groups of catechists for each land he visited, indigenous teachers who with some guidance and encouragement could preach the gospel among their own people. His own successes and their results were considerable.

CONCLUSION

With the development of Catholic orders such as the Dominicans and the Jesuits along with the rise of Iberian political and economic power, European Christendom was poised to make its faith a truly global religion. Africa, Asia and Latin America became targets for conquest and evangelization. 'Christianizing the pagans' sometimes brought disaster. Attempts to find a western sailing route to India brought Europeans to Latin America. They offered the 'truth' to its inhabitants, but their 'gifts' led to massive death rates among the Amerindians of Latin America. When the extraction of gold and silver waned, raising sugar cane became the source of money. Black African slaves were needed because the Amerindians did not survive the work. When black African workers also perished, more were enslaved. However, some leaders such as Las Casas fought for the rights of the Amerindians, while still others questioned the inhumanity of the slave trade.

In Asia the arrogant Portuguese Catholics destroyed the literary records of Indian Thomas Christians because the Indians were, in their eyes, clearly heretical. Francis Xavier took advantage of Portuguese shipping and spread the faith to parts of East Africa, India and Japan. He died trying to reach China. He struggled with his own cultural biases but eventually wrote catechisms that made both faith and practice culturally attractive to people in various Asian countries.

The European Protestant Reformation insisted on changing the Catholic Church radically. Its cause was just, many of its insights sound and its results impressive. No reasonable description of Christian faith and practice may avoid its claims. It created Christian communities that now appear throughout the world. But Luther and Calvin neither conceived of nor led world mission. They each extolled political establishment as basic to Christian existence. Anabaptists held fast in the midst of persecution and thus looked more like Christian minorities on other continents.

6 WEAKENED CHRISTENDOM AND EUROPEAN ENLIGHTENMENT, 1600–1800

Some European Protestants and Catholics had serious questions arising from deep convictions about 'the core of Christian practice and faith'. These were tied to a strong sense that it was an advantage to be the established religion in a region. The Thirty Years War (1618–48) roiled around such interests. Reform had been a continuing concern of Western Christians, but especially so during the Middle Ages, when a series of monastic movements worked for that goal. In the sixteenth century Roman Catholics had used their political establishment to set up a thorough Inquisition to deal with heresies, particularly those of Protestants and Anabaptists, and thus to save the faith. At the same time Martin Luther had appealed to German princes not only to crush marauding peasants but also to support the new Protestant movements in their lands. Calvin found a city theocracy to be the best approach for insuring the reform he sought. By the mid sixteenth century many agreed that common people should move to areas where their religious convictions were the convictions of the rulers. Anabaptists had no home except a few places like Holland where religious freedom was honored.

Such peaceful religious coexistence did not hold. By the beginning of the seventeenth century, pressures were building for Protestant and Catholic political powers to put their armies in the field. Spain had failed to conquer England in 1588. The Spanish Armada was badly mauled, primarily by weather. Spain had wanted not only to put England under Spanish political and economic control, but also to bring the English people back into the Catholic fold. After Spain's stunning defeat, England began to flex her own 'Anglican' muscle, but Spain remained a force in continental politics and New World trade. In Europe Catholic power had revived; Poland had been won back from the Protestants and other areas were more inclined to return to their older Christian roots. Most of the Protestants' founding fathers from over half a century earlier had died; they were being led by less imaginative people whose plan was to consolidate the gains.

The Thirty Years War remains one of the bigger blots on Christian history in Europe. It began as a Christian religious conflict fueled by economic and political desires. The Catholic South and the Protestant North were too well matched for either to overcome the other. From the standpoint of village dwellers and struggling farmers a generation was lost as occupying and scavenging armies joined the ravages of famine and plague to make life unbearable.

The conflict erupted in Bohemia during 1618. Protestants accepted the Catholic traditionalist Archduke Ferdinand as king of Bohemia, then later realized that their religious practices and convictions would be jeopardized. They voiced their objections to the agreement but were rebuffed. Eventually, substantial opposing armies met and the Protestants were decisively defeated. Punishments were severe: not only forced conversion, but also expulsion from one's home and confiscation of one's property. Protestants were forced to house and feed Catholic troops; they had no rights, civil or religious. At least thirty thousand Protestant families were expelled. Many ended up in Saxony.

Fighting broke out next in the German Palatinate during 1621. Again Catholic soldiers won, but they did not disband after their victory. Many mercenaries grabbed what they could because too few governments were willing or able to pay them. They took shelter and food where they could find it. As before, the defeated Protestant believers were treated shamefully; their ministers were driven out of the region.

The Danish period, starting in 1625, resulted in yet another Protestant defeat. Christian IV had high hopes, but the English fleet that was supposed to immobilize Spain failed. Furthermore Cardinal Richelieu did not deliver on his pledge of French support for the English and the Danes in order to weaken the Austrian Hapsburgs. King Christian escaped to a Danish island and signed the peace treaty of Lübeck in 1620, which gave him battered Denmark and some northern German provinces. This near collapse of Protestant forces should have given the Catholics a great advantage. They, however, floundered in political squabbles among themselves. 'National' cravings took precedence over religious victory.

Gustavus Adophus of Sweden led the next Protestant resurgence in 1630. His soldiers were hardened through wars against Poland, Denmark and Russia. Catholic armies were reorganizing, so Gustavus was unopposed in Pomerania (northern Germany) for half a year. After his stunning victory, Protestant princes flocked to his cause. But when Gustavus was killed in another battle, the struggles began to look useless. Protestant gains of territory were considerable, yet the outlook suggested that northern German territory would be Protestant and southern German regions Catholic. The Peace of Prague in 1635 was reached because the Germans were tired of fighting. French and Swedish wounds festered, however, because these countries had lost their territorial gains.

The final period of this lengthy war was dominated by an alliance between France and Sweden. There was no longer any pretense that the conflict was a religious one. It was nationalist and political through and through, for France was Catholic and Sweden was Protestant. The battleground was again in German lands, ones weakened and unable to defend themselves. Early on there were efforts to broker a peace, but the emerging frailty of Spain made the resolve of its enemies stronger. The stalemate was finally recognized in the 1648 Peace of Westphalia that more or less ended the carnage.

This peace brought glorious relief. Ground could be plowed, seeds planted and crops awaited. Near the bottom of the social strata were farmers on land that had been ravaged by Catholic and Protestant soldiers in turn. To plant and harvest a crop had been difficult enough when the farmers faced only the threats of exhausted land, bad seed or inclement weather. Those in German territories were most often at risk, but other countries faced similar challenges. This uncertainty had an effect not only on struggling tenant farmers but also on the poor within cities, whose reliance on charity or occasional work became even more fragile. Many of them did not care whether the endless war was fought on political or religious grounds. For whatever reasons, it had made life far too difficult.

Trade on more than the most restricted local level meant that merchants now could invest in the making and selling of products. Stories and economic records help us understand what the revival of hope meant, but the most obvious witness is Baroque art. Churches in southern German areas were rebuilt or remodeled with gaudy colors, pink and white on the outside and brilliant murals on the inside. God had brought peace, and the Christian houses of worship should look like blazing sunrises. The new peace provided the opportunity for Christians to inculturate their faith, indeed their almost unrestrained hope, in brilliant color and pleasing form.

The results of three decades of war, however, could not be covered over with the stunning visions of artisans and artists. The medieval crusades had ruined the reputation of Western Christendom outside its homeland among the Eastern Orthodox and the Muslims. The Thirty Years War damaged the character of Christianity as viewed by the people of Europe who had thought Christian faith was the truth for the whole world. Seventeenth-century weapons of war could not exact the tolls that twentieth-century machine guns, poison gas, airplanes and finally the atomic bomb did, but the damage to life and property was terrible. What started as the defense of religious liberty ended in the emerging but dominant rights of the nation states. Leaders of this Western religious defense of Christendom, who had often found the Church's political, economic and social establishment to be their greatest asset, gradually discovered that they were being pushed to the margins of many significant decisions. Those edges were a painful place, but century by century they grew to be religions' allotted spaces.

The birth of the European Enlightenment gave evidence of how badly the ancient foundations had been shaken. This developing view of the world presented an environment for European Christians quite different from what they had known for well over a millennium. Since the initial preference for Christendom in the fourth century by Constantine and the efforts over subsequent centuries to uproot weeds like Graeco-Roman pagans from Europe, reforms within Christian communities, even in their most radical manifestations, intended to save and cultivate Christian roots. Medieval and Byzantine attacks on heretical Christians insisted that the culprits had become infected by grafting in branches not compatible with the root. They had to be pruned, cut away and burned.

Protection of that perceived root by both Roman Catholics and Protestants during the sixteenth century had taken various forms. Not the least were the massive historical tomes of the Roman Catholic Vatican librarian Caesar Baronius (1538–1607), the *Ecclesiastical Annals* and the *Lutheran Magdeburg Centuries*, published from 1559 to 1574. Both projects attacked the historical truthfulness of their opponents and from their point of view set the Christian story straight. In the seventeenth century the left-wing Anabaptist reformers entered the fray.

They wanted to restore the church of the New Testament so that the early purity could be regained. Thieleman J. van Braght's *Martyr's Mirror* (published in 1660), a Radical Reformation view of Christian history, attempted to demonstrate the truth about the Radicals' understanding of the church's story. Van Bracht carefully selected the heroes who had suffered for the faith and vilified what he saw as continuing Roman Catholic attacks on the Anabaptists.

The Thirty Years War had broken common trust in the authority of the church. In important instances it led to the pulling up and burning of Christian roots so that more fruitful plants could be put in their place. Previous eras had witnessed serious pruning of the Christian tree, but this time the attack went to the root. The war had not disrupted life on every acre of Europe or directly touched every person, but its influence was staggering. The philosopher René Descartes (1596–1650) found his life and thought remarkably agitated by the events. Educated in French Jesuit schools, he made his way to Paris by 1613. He left in 1619 on his travels and returned in 1625. During that time he became aware of the Catholic–Protestant wars and tried to keep out of the way. Paris had offered him a place to extend his philosophical career, but he went to Holland in 1629 to find a more peaceful setting. There he wrote his major works. He had much to teach; one of his classic lines was 'Cogito ergo sum' – 'I think, therefore I am.' In that observation he found the end of his gnawing skepticism, which had arisen in no small part because of the destruction of political alliances, trade partnerships, social relationships and, not the least, religious certainty and faith. Those developments had left him with much deeper questions about what could never be doubted. When he rebuilt his philosophy on that foundation, he had no need to worry about the structures of life that the Thirty Years War had destroyed. Like any good brush clearing done before constructing a house, the failure of those structures had made Decartes's foundationalism even clearer. He had looked for a solid basis of knowledge that could be neither doubted nor destroyed. His discovery was the clear understanding that if he knew he was thinking, he must exist. From that base he could deduce what could be known with certainty. He did not mean to put all Christian revelation and tradition in jeopardy; he saw his work as that of a Christian apologist, an attempt to contextualize practice and faith in this new rational environment. Some early Enlightenment theologians thought that redoing theology on basic premises similar to Descartes's would lead to new opportunities. Right reason was no enemy of Christian life. But Descartes's philosophical foundationalism, centered on the human thinker, needed support from neither religious intuitions nor Christian institutions.

This does not mean that the Enlightenment developments were so jaundiced that none of them brought anything helpful to the world or to Christians. During the period numerous believers found modern life to involve real progress. Immanuel Kant (1724–1804) constructed an impressive system based on the limits and strengths of reason. Any kind of natural theology that theologians previously had used, for example, to offer proofs for the existence of God, did not fit proper rational canons. Only in recognizing the limits of such knowledge could true faith appear. Various traditional props for Christian belief had proved to be either weak or false. If miracles occurred they had no import. Of what use could an incarnate Savior be? Religious or mystical experience, even prayer itself, had little or no value.

The great truth of reason and faith was the moral imperative deeply imbedded in each human being: do your duty. There had to be freedom, the ability to choose the duty, immortality in which the evil of this world could be rectified, and a God who could defend full justice. For traditional Christians Kant's contextualization of the gospel involved unbearable losses. Conservative Lutherans found him quite dangerous. But for many moderns his emphasis on the essential importance of morality that could be defended rationally to and by any human being looked like the best way to keep Christian practice and faith alive in the modern age, whittled down but sharpened.

The apparently objective science of this era nurtured a public square in which all comers could discuss any issues without being encumbered by emotions and previous commitments. Burgeoning senses of human worth and freedom worked themselves out in passionate attacks by these 'dispassionate' thinkers on both slavery and the burning of witches. However misguided their assumptions may appear in the twenty-first century, the values they defended led them to mortally wound some ghastly inhumane practices.

CHRISTIANS AND PEOPLE OF OTHER FAITHS

In many sections of *Africa* the growth of Muslim communities created a number of shifting relationships. For example, in Ethiopia Christians had been a force since the fourth century, often the most significant religious and political leaders of the country. But late in the sixteenth century the Turkish conquest of Egypt and the incessant raids of the Galla people in Ethiopia made Christians ill at ease. The Ethiopian connection with the Coptic Church was still in place, but the Egyptian Copts were themselves a persecuted group. They could not regularly provide theological and administrative assistance. The Galla clans continued to raid Ethiopian villages and monasteries. Although some of the Galla were Christians and some followed their *traditional religious ways*, most were *Muslim* and anti-Christian. Only the decline of the Turks and the inability of the Galla to band together in a centralized government allowed Ethiopian Christians to continue through the seventeenth century.

The creation of the Roman Catholic Sacred Congregation of Propaganda of the Faith in 1622 was a response to the growth of interest in mission. Four hundred Capuchin monks had volunteered four years earlier to work in the Congo, but they were mostly Spanish and were refused entry by the Portuguese. The twenty-four Portuguese priests in Angola were given responsibility for the Congo.

The bishop of São Salvador, Manuel Baptista Soares, had lived in the Congo for years. His 1619 report indicated how much he despised conditions there as well as how difficult it had been to Christianize the people. The cathedral had only a grass roof and a single small bell. When the king came to worship he brought all his wives. Most Christians continued to follow their pagan rites. The Congolese king, Alvaro III, continually wrote the pope trying to get the bishop removed. He had no sense of how much power any bishop might bring to the post.

In *Latin America* during this period Christian leaders had not yet developed a helpful strategy for dealing with *indigenous religions*. The Catholic clergy were often so closely identified with the European powers who had sent them that various rebellions of the indigenous people emphasized their own non-European racial and religious backgrounds. During the 1560s in the Andes mountains, natives in a movement called Taki Onqoy heard the gods calling to them and danced with uncontrolled movement similar to the St. Vitus's dance of fourteenth-century Europe. In that same region from 1780 to 1783, a *mestizo* took the name Tupac Amaru II and claimed that he was descended from the royal Inca family. His actions recalled Tupac Amaru I, who futilely but courageously fought the Spaniards during their sixteenth-century conquest. This mostly indigenous rebellion spawned another uprising in more mountainous parts of Peru and Bolivia led by Tupac Catari. Nearly

100,000 people died, and the Catholic Peruvian elite, mostly of Spanish descent, were terrified. Native religious and cultural features, officially banished but never forgotten, came to the fore again.

Seventeenth-century *Buddhists* in *China* mounted their own critique of Christian views. They distrusted the influence of the Jesuit astronomers in Beijing – Ricci and his successors. Huang Shen in Fukien during 1633–5 warned that Christians not only were teaching about their lord of heaven but also had desecrated various idols of Buddha and had even burned sacred sutras. Buddhists had to defend themselves against these foreigners. The argument was a difficult one to mount because it did not seem to represent the disdain for life in this world that characterized Buddhist spirituality, yet it called close attention to the political dangers that the Christians represented. In 1638 the authorities in Fukien banned Christian missionaries and sent those in the province back to the Portuguese Christian community in Macao.

During the seventeenth and eighteenth centuries Catholic Christians in China were of two minds about whether the gospel could be contextualized within traditional Chinese rituals concerning ancestors. On one hand those who found the Jesuit position of the previous century the most persuasive looked on the rites honoring ancestors as cultural or civil practices rather than entirely religious ones. The filial piety of the great Confucian heritage was no threat to Christian faith. What needed to be done was to strip away the various superstitions that had overgrown the teaching of Confucius and thus to encourage traditional Chinese understanding of family life as fulfilled in Christ.

On the other hand Dominican and Franciscan missionaries found the veneration of ancestors too deeply imbedded in idolatry to be salvaged. The rituals involved pagan spirit worship that could not be tolerated. In 1693 Charles Maigrot, a member of the Société des Missions Étrangères de Paris (MEP), vicar apostolic of Fujian, insisted that Chinese Christians should not attend ancestral rites or make the common sacrifices to Confucius twice yearly. They were told not to display tablets with the word *jingtian* (Maigrot translated it 'worship heaven'). Tablets honoring the ancestors with the words *shenzu* (spirit ancestor), *shenwei* (seat of the spirit) or *lingwei* (seat of the soul) were also not permitted. They could mention the name of the dead and use the character *wei* (spirit), but must also include a Christian statement about death and filial piety.

These rules created difficulties for Christians. Most Chinese found no way to make the distinctions Maigrot and his followers did. Not to perform the ancestral rites, particularly at funerals, not to display the tablets daily meant to some of their relatives and neighbors that these Christians had abandoned being Chinese. In some way this foreign religion had taken away the center of Chinese life. The feelings aroused by Maigrot's demand moved the Kangxi emperor to strong hostility against the missionaries. They were a threat to the Chinese being Chinese. In 1724 Christianity was declared illegal and all missionaries were banned. Not every Chinese neighbor, however, found the Christian practices to be that upsetting. Often they were tolerated by the immediate community and overlooked by the officials. Persecution was sporadic, mounted only when there were disrupting protests against the Christians.

The threat to the presence of Catholic missionaries led to an increased reliance on a few well-trained Chinese clergy. Andreas Ly (1692/3–1774), born into a Chinese Catholic family, left China in 1707 during an outbreak of persecution related to the Rites Controversy. He received an entirely European education in Siam under the MEP and found himself uncomfortable with his native culture. After the 1746 persecution, many missionaries were forced out and he was the only senior ordained priest in Sichuan province for a decade. He refused the traditional Chinese rites but in his journal praised a Christian who attended a non-Christian funeral, helped defray the costs, bowed reverently but not in honor of the tablets, and went to the burial yet avoided the banquet because it fell on a Christian fast day. Ly, when his mother died, put up a tablet with her name, wore the traditional white mourning clothes for one hundred days and refused to shave during that period. His journal after 1751 does not mention problems with funerals. Most Sichuan Christians by then evidently had shifted their practices to the prescribed Christian Catholic way partly because the persecution had waned. They had discovered that they were still Chinese but also Christians standing against the 'superstitions' of their surroundings.

Buddhist and Christian conversations in *Japan* had depended on the toleration of Buddhist monks. But beginning with the rule of the Tokugawa family (1603–1867/8) toleration ended. One important development of the period was the conversion of the Jesuit Fabian Fukan to Buddhism. In 1605 he had written a defense of the Christian God but by 1620 he had penned *Against the Christian god*. In the first work he warned that a spirituality of nothingness would end in inaction or insanity; in the second he turned everything upside down and insisted that Christian teaching about a personal God offered no solution to the deep questions about evil. Well into the nineteenth century his more detailed arguments shaped Japanese Buddhist–Christian debates.

During the seventeenth century Catholic mission in *Indochina* was still primarily associated with Portuguese ships and traders. Portuguese Dominicans had entered the country during the mid sixteenth century; Spanish Franciscans from the Philippines had appeared in the 1580s. In 1615, as an Italian Jesuit missionary watched a Vietnamese comedy, he was overcome by how much the people misunderstood Jesuit work. A local actor, dressed as a Portuguese man, appeared on stage with a child hidden in a bag. He pulled the child from the sack and asked, 'Do you want to enter into the belly of the Portuguese?' The child answered, 'Yes.' Then the actor put the child into the midsection of his baggy clothes. Each time this was repeated the crowd roared with laughter. The Italian missionary recognized all too well that these words were similar to the phrases converts were asked at their baptism. To the local people, becoming Christian meant becoming Portuguese.

Alexandre de Rhodes (1591–1660) and his Jesuit companions made a valiant attempt to change that perception. They sought to inculturate the gospel deeply within Vietnamese life. In his daily practices and in his written catechism de Rhodes gathered up various truths in *Vietnamese proverbs*, even ones from Vietnamese indigenous religions, and also affirmed what he could about their *Buddhist, Confucian* and *Taoist* practices and beliefs. Although he found much in all four areas of religion that struck him as superstitious, he purposefully sought within the ancient Chinese religious classics and in contemporary religious life what he could claim. Those sources were so fully entwined in his presentation of Christian practice and faith that Vietnamese could become Vietnamese Christians, not Portuguese ones.

For example, de Rhodes did not believe in idols but warned Christians not to break them. The cult of ancestors, so deeply imbedded in Vietnamese life, should not be confronted with destruction, but with transformation. The practices of building houses for the departed souls and burning paper clothes made for them seemed to him expensive and useless. But filial piety among Christians, honoring those departed, should be every bit as strong as it was in other Vietnamese households. Prayers for souls in purgatory and good deeds in their names must be offered. One should buy or make real clothes for the poor in remembrance of those souls.

Occasionally, seventeenth-century Portuguese observers said that some of the Thomas Christians in *India* had such a high regard for their

Hindu neighbors that they thought about them as living pious lives. These Christians felt no deep need to convert Hindus. Among the teachings that members of the two religions at times shared were the transmigration of souls, fatalism, rites to drive away demons, and specified days of special honor. It was in part these doctrines which led the Western-dominated Synod of Diamper in 1599 to view the Thomas Christians as schismatics or heretics who must undergo rigorous reforms.

An Italian Jesuit, Robert de Nobili (1577–1656), however, worked in India with a sense of mission different from that of some Thomas Christians and the Synod of Diamper. Hindus needed conversion to Christ, but they should be approached with respect and patience. De Nobili shared certain principles with other Jesuits who preceded him to the East. It was not necessary for Indians to become Europeans in order to enter Christian community. When de Nobili arrived at Madurai in South India during 1606, he met Gonsalvo Fernandez, who had already worked in the region for over a decade. Fernandez had not made any converts primarily because the pearl fishermen among whom he worked thought that his offer was for them to become Portuguese like him, particularly in their lifestyle and eating habits. In many ways they had understood Fernandez properly. The suggestion of such changes deeply offended these Indians, especially their fear that they would have to eat the stinking meat on which the Portuguese thrived. Although these fishermen were far from being high caste people, they were proud of their heritage and considered the Portuguese inferior.

De Nobili took a different tack. He sought to contextualize Christian practice and faith in Indian truths. He mastered Tamil, the language of the region, and learned Sanskrit and Telugu as well. At the end of his life he had published books in all three languages, particularly Tamil. He worked through the Hindu Vedas and studied other Indian volumes concerned with philosophy and religion. In order to seem more a part of Indian culture, he adopted Brahmin dress, appearing in saffron robes, wearing the sacred thread, cutting his hair to their style – leaving only the small tuft – and generally lived as an Indian. For him all these characteristics were parts of Indian culture, not essentially parts of Hindu religion.

Fernandez, both from jealousy and from principle, attacked de Nobili as too Indian and nearly a Hindu convert. He was convinced that de Nobili had syncretized the Christian faith in ways that made what the Brahmins were willing to accept something less than the whole Christian truth. This conflict, known as the Malabar Rites Controversy, centered on the type of worship liturgy that de Nobili's churches adopted. The conflict was significant for Christian relations with Hindus and eventually with other religions. Although the Roman archbishop in Cranganore and the Jesuit provincial in charge of India supported de Nobili, the Inquisition in Goa questioned his efforts. He wrote a series of letters and treatises to explain his positions with the result that in 1623 Pope Gregory XV decided in his favor.

Unlike Fernandez, de Nobili met upper caste Indians who listened intently to his presentation of the Christian gospel most probably because it did not demand that they abandon all their Indian way of life. His respect for their traditions is clear. *Preaching Wisdom to the Wise*, the title given to an English translation of three of his works, captures the sense of his mission. But his approach entailed that, like Gandhi in the twentieth century, he refused to question the justice of the caste system. By 1643 the Jesuits were sending two types of missionaries to India, one group who like de Nobili worked among the Brahmins and another group who labored among the lower castes. Brahmin converts, however, never grew to the numbers hoped for. De Nobili's decision to leave the caste system intact, even to set up churches for different castes, left serious questions about how the gospel should speak to Indian social structures. Like Francis Xavier, de Nobili diligently worked on catechisms in more than one Indian language in order to offer guidance to Indians about the Christian faith. He used his mission position to clarify some points of Christian doctrine through a grid of things Indian.

The seventeenth century also witnessed the colonization of what would become the *United States* of America. Spanish *conquistadores* had set up a fort in northern Florida during the previous century, but they later abandoned it, partially because of pressure from the English. Some English companies planned settlements in Virginia with a view to making profits, but these settlements tended to fail. The most successful incursions were those of the Puritans in Massachusetts, whose purpose in sailing to the New World was to escape the religious persecution that had plagued them throughout Europe and finally in Great Britain.

Battered and ill equipped to be pioneers in the rough New England climate, they fought to survive. Many died. Had the *Amerindians* of the region not befriended them in the unexpected ways of providing food and then teaching them how to plant maize, probably all of them would have perished. The Puritans had no strong inner vision of themselves as missionaries and, as Calvinists, often thought God would evangelize the folks outside their tight circle. They had been steeled to protect their own from persecution by outsiders. Thus only a few of them looked toward conversion of the Amerindians.

John Eliot (1604–90) took up that task by forming a community in Roxbury, five miles from Boston. He worked with Narragansett people who lived in the area, learning their mother tongue and a series of other related Amerindian languages. Starting at Natick, he founded fourteen Amerindian villages that allowed no white residents and practiced a kind of self-government. Amerindian leaders handled most of the evangelization, but Eliot argued their cases before Massachusetts's magistrates concerning property rights that included the land and water necessary for their way of life. He sought mercy for those in prison and freedom for those sold into slavery. As part of his concern he set up schools for all ages, translated scripture and other books into the Amerindian languages and tried to help them learn how to adapt to settled existence. In 1675, however, most of the Amerindian villages were burned in King Philip's war. Some of the Amerindians then fought in the battles, and others went elsewhere. Only a few of the settlements were ever rebuilt.

The Dutch immigrants in New Amsterdam (New York) were not greatly different. They seem to have depended less on Amerindian assistance than the English Puritans did. They were also noted for their negotiations with the 'ignorant savages' in which they traded useless but pretty beads for large sections of land. The Amerindians had no sense of private property that could be owned and sold by anyone. Thus the bartering was marked by misunderstandings on both sides.

Jean de Brébeuf (1593–1649) was called a 'Huron of the Huron'. His work among that people in Canada had some success because he followed the Jesuit plan of inculturation seen in China and elsewhere. He wrote a catechism that was eventually translated into Huron. At the same time his condescending attitude toward these Amerindians appears in his reports to the Jesuit authorities. The Iroquois Confederation looked on Huron converts as sorcerers who assisted the foreigners in their conquests. Iroquois warriors, who believed that the whole enterprise of the mission was evil, finally killed de Brébeuf.

CHRISTIANS AND THEIR CULTURES

At the beginning of the seventeenth century Roman Catholics seemed poised to convert important peoples of *Africa* from their *traditional religions.* Dom Manuel, the Mani Vunda, traveled from the Congo to Italy in order to connect the king and the Congolese church with the pope. In this man were fused the traditional religious authority of his people and the authority of the Christian church. Sick on the journey, he died in 1608 just after his meeting with Paul V. Part of the pope's response was to send Mattheus Cardoso (1584–1625), who learned Congolese, translated a Portuguese catechism into the language, and had it printed in Lisbon to bring back with him on a trip in 1625. That work and Cardoso's history of the Congo – not published until the twentieth century – indicated how the Congolese had contextualized their new religion.

Similar successes were appearing elsewhere. Many of the Mutapa, a people living north of Great Zimbabwe, were baptized. Pedro Paez (1564–1622), a Spanish Jesuit, led a careful mission to the Ethiopian court which saw the emperor Susenyos convert. Paez translated a catechism into the local tongue so that the Ethiopians could better understand Catholic views. Olu Sebastian labored in Warri (south-western Nigeria) and a young Christian king, Dom Jeronimo Chingulia, reigned with his Portuguese queen in Mombasa. The Sacred Congregation of Propaganda of the Faith, founded in 1622, had set up its college by 1627. In time hundreds of missionaries from orders like the Capuchins and the Jesuits were waiting to be sent out.

At the end of the century Christians in several African countries were in jeopardy. All but one of the baptized Mutapa, Mavura, and probably all the members of the court had thought that baptism signified political allegiance to Portugal. The emperor of Ethiopia, Fasiladas, knowing that earlier conversions to Catholicism had been based primarily on such non-religious grounds, threw the Roman missionaries out in the 1630s. Alphonsus Mendes (1579–1639), blind to the life and faith of any non-Roman Christians, demanded that all the Ethiopian religious practices be changed to Roman ones. The Congolese church was prostrate, as was the kingdom, in spite of the efforts of hundreds of Capuchin missionaries. The promising king of Mombasa had apostasized and massacred all the Christians who did not follow him. That group included many African converts, and members of his own family. Muslims took advantage of the difficulties and took Fort Jesus in Mombasa.

In many cases Christian practice and belief had not been well contextualized in spite of brilliant translation efforts. Many of the converts belonged to local courts that had political connections with Portugal but loose ties with the common people. Portugal wanted Portuguese churches with no interference from missionaries from other countries. Catholic inflexibility in Lisbon often kept Christian practice and faith foreign to Africans, not the least by insisting on celibate clergy, few translations into the vernacular and little recognition of indigenous leadership. The greatest evil influence was the slave trade, sanctioned by Portuguese Christians and extremely destructive of native social relationships. African resistance to conversion made good sense.

There were Catholics who found *slavery* both unchristian and an obstacle in the way of conversion. The Capuchins, founded in 1552, lived simply and were at the forefront of preaching and mission. With the growth of the slave trade in the seventeenth century, their outcries against it became louder. Black Catholics also argued the case against slavery. They were significant groups in Brazil and Portugal as well as in Angola and the Congo. Lourenço da Silva, a black leader in Lisbon, was probably born in Brazil; he claimed that he was in the bloodlines of both Angolan and Congolese royalty. The position he held within Catholicism was as the 'procurator-general of the congregation of the Blacks and Mulattos of Our Lady of the Rosary'. He went to Rome in 1684 and decried the cruel treatment of baptized Catholic slaves. In the 1680s such views of blacks and Capuchins persuaded the papacy to condemn slavery both strongly and broadly, but the protests and the papal action had little effect.

Eighteenth-century African leaders also shed light on the practice of slavery. Olaudah Equiano, an Igbo boy (Nigeria) seized by slavers and sold to British slave traders, survived to reach Barbados and then Virginia. A British ship captain purchased him and offered him some dignity and a little education. Equiano sailed widely and learned from that. He had become a Protestant Christian as a boy and had an experience of rebirth later in young manhood. He asked the bishop of London to send him as a missionary to Africa, but the bishop refused. During his stay in London, however, Equiano became a leader of the city's African community, particularly in the fight against slavery. His book *The Interesting Narrative of the Life of Olaudah Equiano, or Gustavus Vassa* (1789) used the form of a travel tale to attack the horrors of slavery.

Equiano's friend Ottoba Cugoano published a scathing attack in 1787, *Thoughts and Sentiments on the Evils of Slavery*. A Fante man from the Gold Coast (Ghana) who wrote in England under the name of John Stuart, he insisted that Protestants were the worst slavers, particularly certain Scots and Dutchmen. The volume was soon translated into French. It pulled no punches.

These two were part of the dozen or so intellectuals of African origin who represented black Protestant Christians in Africa, Europe and North America. Together they articulated in English the case against slavery. Equiano was dead by 1807 when the British parliament made the slave trade unlawful, but he and his friends had helped form the British majority that acted. African Protestants existed, but most lived in North America, not Africa. David George and Moses Wilkinson, black slaves who became Protestant Christians, sided with the British in the American War of Independence. They both settled in Nova Scotia after the conflict and served black congregations, one Baptist and one Methodist, of tolerant dissenters. During the war they fought against the slaveholders who treated black people so viciously. They believed that the British were farther along in the battle against slavery.

Protestant missionaries in Africa before the eighteenth century were sparse. Chaplains had been selected to serve the troops in many of the Dutch, English and Danish forts that had dotted West Africa since the late 1600s. Because few European women lived in those forts, the chaplains found themselves caring for African prostitutes and common-law wives. They baptized the mulatto babies and taught them along with the white children in small schools. Like the Portuguese Catholic chaplains before them, they were in Africa because of the slave trade and were forced to face its atrocities either believing that it made Christian sense or recognizing that they had little voice in its decisions. Occasionally, black chaplains served in the forts, usually men who had a European education and were married to white women. Philip Quaque had such a ministry for fifty years and married a black woman after his first wife died.

The first Anglican missionary to Africa, Thomas Thompson, sent out in 1752, had worked with black slaves in North America, but his later book – *The African Trade for Negro Slaves Shown to Be Consistent with the Principles of Humanity and with the Laws of Revealed Religion* – made his views clear.

One of the more remarkable stories of African Protestants involved Granville Sharp's intention to resettle London blacks in Africa. The 1787 attempt failed miserably because many of the people did not have the requisite skills for creating a colony. The more hardened took advantage of the situation, even themselves becoming slavers. But when the Sierra Leone Company sought Nova Scotia blacks who possessed the needed talents, a society emerged in 1792 that looked promising. Many of the Nova Scotia blacks were Christians whose Protestant experience in Canada led them to lives of virtue. An English lady, Mrs Falconbridge, who was a severe critic of most Christians, was astounded at their godliness.

In *Latin America* Juana Inés de la Cruz (died 1695) was probably the most significant Christian *woman* known in this period. Born into an upper class family, she began to read at the age of three. When she was seven she declared that she would study in the University of Mexico (founded in 1553). At seventeen she was given the opportunity of standing before forty university professors. She repeatedly asked them questions they could not answer; in their foolishness they barred her from university study for her own good. The poetry she wrote as a teenager caught the mood of the Mexican public.

Sor (Sister) Juana chose a nunnery rather than marriage because she thought it would provide more freedom. At first it did. She read voraciously, even in difficult disciplines like mathematics, wrote and played music and created a new kind of musical notation. Her poetry matured and was published in Europe. In some of it she attacked male views of women. She asked about the practice of using a prostitute and then looking down on her, which partner was the worst: 'She who sins for pay or he who pays for sin?'

Her brilliance emerged in nearly everything she did. She undertook various experiments in her kitchen, noting that Aristotle would have discovered more had he cooked. She responded so persuasively to one biblical scholar that she made him look inept. Her male superiors warned her that she was not living as a woman naturally should; her place was in prayer and contemplation. Resistance was unthinkable, so she let go of her library and scientific and musical instruments, and turned to what she was told to do. Not long after that decision she caught the plague while caring for others and died. Her life illustrates both the disdain for women and the fear of science that too many church authorities had.

Antônio Vieira (1608–97) received his education from the Jesuits. In 1640 when John IV became the new Portuguese king, Vieira was invited to be the court preacher and a diplomatic adviser. While in Europe he demanded that the Inquisition stop persecuting Jews and new Christian converts. As a result the Dominicans responsible for the Inquisition bitterly hated him. In 1652 when the king was failing, the Jesuits sent Vieira to Brazil as the leader of Christian mission there. Soon he was defending the *Amerindians* against Portuguese settlers. He traveled into the Amazon, not only evangelizing, but also learning Amerindian languages and cultures. In 1661 King John died. Without his protection, the colonists almost lynched Vieira, but sent him back to Portugal for trial by the Inquisition. He was sentenced to silence because he thought that the prophecies of a sixteenth-century shoemaker named Bandarra about the resurrection of John IV to fight the final battle with the Turks were true. His struggles to preserve Amerindian cultures and rights remind one of Las Casas and the approach of Ricci in China.

Jesuit mission in the capital of *China* did not end with the death of Matteo Ricci in 1610. Johann Adam Schall von Bell (1592–1666) and Ferdinand Verbiest (1623–88) both proved their mettle by defending Christians in the midst of persecution and demonstrating to the Chinese authorities that their *astronomical calculations*, so important to Chinese culture, were superior to those made at the Beijing court. In 1623 Schall assisted Hsü-Kuang-ch'i (1562–1633) in a calendar recalculation, but their reforms were bitterly contested by Muslim and Confucian astronomers.

Hsü, earlier unsettled by passing the lowest level of official examinations in 1581 but failing the next, met a Jesuit some fifteen years later. Encouraged by that meeting and his years of teaching in the provinces, he tried the city exams in Beijing in 1600 but failed again. He met Matteo Ricci in Nanking, was baptized by another Jesuit, and in 1604 passed the highest examinations. From then on he held various high offices in Beijing, particularly in astronomy. He helped Ricci translate Western scientific books into Chinese and predicted a 1628 solar eclipse that stood against the expectations of Muslim and Confucian scholars. Hsü was the most highly regarded Chinese Christian of the era. He not only contextualized Christian views within the science, particularly the astronomy, of his day; he also led both his father and his son to conversion and twice went back to Macao to assist the churches there.

Schall continued the scientific work of Hsü and founded a Christian church in the Beijing palace complex. He offered various scientific treatises to honor the emperor and also published a series of books on religion. In 1644 when Beijing finally fell to the Manchus, Schall was the only leader in the capital to protect the Christians. Once more proving his scholarship to be necessary, he was allowed in 1650 by the Manchus to build a Christian compound in the city. In 1664 when a stroke paralyzed his speech and movement, *Muslim* astronomers again attacked him and his religion before the young *Buddhist* emperor. Schall was stripped of his honors, brought to trial and condemned to death. But in less than two weeks an earthquake and the subsequent fire led the court to reverse its decision.

After Schall died, Verbiest requested and received the restoration of Schall's reputation. He then became the highest official responsible for mathematics and visited various Chinese provincial officials to recommend missionaries. He worked tirelessly to have Christianity declared a legal religion, and pleaded with the Jesuits to send more helpers, but full success on both fronts evaded him.

During this period China's borders were not far from eastern Russia's southern boundaries. Fur traders from the border areas made their way to Beijing, sometimes because of their business and sometimes because the Manchu Empire, which had arisen in Manchuria and now ruled China, took them captive. In 1683 Grigorii Mylnikov was traveling to Albazin, a fort in easternmost Siberia, with a party of some seventy men which included a priest. Manchu soldiers met them in a forest, offered them a feast, but then took them south to Beijing as 'guests' of the emperor Kangxi. As captives they became one spark for the Russian–Chinese Albazinian War.

The priest in the group served these hostages. Given an old Buddhist place of worship, the community of Russian Christians converted it into an Orthodox church named for St. Nicholas. In 1676 an embassy to China headed by Nikolai Spafarii had noted that the Russians in Beijing had attended worship in Jesuit churches. He would have been happy with the St. Nicholas chapel, but his own view was that the Orthodox should match the vision of the Jesuits and look for ways to convert the Chinese, particularly their emperor.

In 1700 Peter the Great ordered the metropolitan of Kiev to send a devout and learned leader to Tobolsk so that there would be a Russian representative in the East to mediate disputes between Russia and China and to provide translators for both governments' representatives. He was also to serve the Russian Christians and to evangelize the Chinese. Not much came from that venture. But by 1728 the Kiakhta treaty between Russia and China included Chinese agreement that the Russians could have a hostel in Beijing and would be allowed to worship in their own way. Four 'lamas' (priests) could live there and six students who knew Russian and Latin could pursue studies in the important languages of the Chinese Empire. Apparently no provision was made for any evangelization of the Chinese. The learning of languages and cultures was meant to support trade and political needs.

The eighteenth century in China brought intense persecution of Chinese Christians and their European colleagues. Catholic priests saw the signs and planned for their replacements to be smuggled in. They taught their fellow believers not only what they considered to be the necessary aspects of Christian life and faith, but also a spirituality that supported the communities in their suffering together. They helped them see that their allegiance to Christ could be demonstrated even by martyrdom. Some recanted under such pressure, but others held on and gave Chinese Christians a legacy that served them well in the trials of the next two centuries. One of the sad failures of European mission work in the country, however, was the inability of Protestant missionaries who arrived in the 1800s to recognize the deep commitment of Chinese Catholics. Their European background caused them to see even Catholic martyrs as unfaithful.

Alexandre de Rhodes (1591–1660) is another of the important Jesuit missionaries, a Frenchman whose field was *Vietnam*. He moved into the country in 1624 and was able to serve only four short terms, the final one ending in 1645 when he was finally banned from the people he so loved. He and his fellow Jesuits had by 1640 won over 100,000 converts, mostly in the north of the country. An inveterate missionary, he died in Persia after having mastered enough of the language to talk with the shah.

He is noted for two strong commitments that eventually got him into trouble with his Jesuit superiors. First, having mastered twelve languages well enough to speak all of them with some fluency, he was insistent upon presenting the Christian gospel in the language and the culture of those whom he served. Before he came to the Vietnamese, their language had been written in Chinese characters even though the Vietnamese had no great love for the giant neighbor who so often wished to rule over them. He latinized the script and published a French–Vietnamese dictionary and a Vietnamese grammar. Had he been granted more time, he doubtless would have produced a Vietnamese translation of the Bible. Second, he argued for ordaining Vietnamese leaders as priests. For him that was an important part of properly inculturating the gospel. The Portuguese were so upset with his refusal to abide by the *padroado*, an agreement between their nation and the papacy to restrict clerical offices to Europeans (particularly Portuguese), that they would not allow Alexandre to book passage from Vietnam on their ships. Thus he was forced to return to Europe overland. Both in Rome and in Paris he made his case for indigenous ministers.

The Jesuits in Vietnam wore the gowns of the literati and the slippers (without heels) of middle class folk. De Rhodes let his hair grow long as

Vietnamese men did, a custom forbidden to missionaries before his birth because of regulations set up in Europe at the Council of Trent. He and many of his companions ate the local food. He went further by trying to give Christian meanings to various cultural customs. For example he transformed the three-day celebration of Tet – devoted first to ancestors, then relatives, and then the dead – into a festival of the Trinity. At the same time he insisted that Christians should not take over European practices that would set them apart from their neighbors. The country's rulers forbade Christians from wearing images, crosses or rosaries around their necks. Some believers wanted to make this a point of potential martyrdom, but de Rhodes, who found these objects helped his own devotional life, argued that even they should be abandoned. No possibility of affront about these material articles should be provided.

In *Japan*, the Christian community had grown to 300,000 by 1614 but the reticence and racism of European missionaries had produced almost no native Japanese leaders, only seven diocesan priests and a few Jesuits. Christians still appeared to be followers of a foreign cult with allegiances that were suspect. Toyotomi Hideyoshi, the most important Japanese leader in the late sixteenth century, had allowed Christian soldiers and Jesuit chaplains to serve in his armies during his failed invasion of Korea. He had even invited Franciscans to enter Japan. These Franciscans thought that the Jesuits were too timid, so they pushed a bit harder. When a Spanish galleon ran aground on the Japanese coast, a ship filled with padres and a rich cargo, some of its officers tried to influence the local Japanese authority by showing him how worldwide Spanish power was and how vital the Franciscans were to Spanish conquest. Hideyoshi heard that as a threat and became furious. He had the crew imprisoned, took the cargo and demanded that all the Franciscans in Japan should be executed. A friendly local officer quietly reduced the number until only twenty-six Christian martyrs were crucified at Nagasaki in 1597 – tied to crosses and killed with lances. This show of power against any enemies continued as Hideyoshi became aware of the need to protect the way for his son, Hideyori, to follow him; he ruthlessly dispatched all who seemed to be in the way, whether family, advisers or Christians. But in 1598 he died.

Hideyoshi's friend, Tokugawa Ieyasu, worked to make himself shogun, not to protect Hideyoshi's beloved son as he had promised. In 1599 he reopened the connection to Spain by allowing a Jesuit, Jeronimo de Jesus, to re-establish trade with the Philippines. After a decisive battle in 1600 with Hideyori, he ruled, and held the highest title in 1603. By 1609 he had opened up relationships with the Dutch so that neither they, the Spanish nor the Portuguese could force him to depend on only one of the international traders. In 1615 a final battle at Hideyori's castle saw Christians in both armies but more on Hideyori's side. The government was centralized in the hands of the Tokugawa family, and they were convinced that Christians were a threat.

By 1614 Christians in Japan were under strong political pressure. Various local leaders were worried about the believers' foreign connections and spasmodically persecuted them. More significantly, in 1639 the worship of Christ was banned in the country; no one was allowed legally to participate in a Christian community. That ban was not lifted until 1873.

The Christian Suppression Office of the Japanese government, established in 1640, carefully searched for Christians. Monetary awards offered earlier were continued; missionaries and priests listed as the most valuable prizes. In strongly Christian areas, all the inhabitants were organized into units of five families. If a Christian were found in that unit, all five families were punished. At random times the authorities would require all people to walk on a sacred Christian image. Also each family had to register in a Buddhist temple and receive a certificate that they had done so. By 1659 this final step had become a national law for all Japan, not just areas where Christians were strong.

The British explorer James Cook's three voyages to the *South Pacific* between 1768 and 1779 held that area of the world before British eyes. Peoples whom he and his crew considered to be primitives lived on each island that his ship touched, including massive Australia. Initial reactions often seemed cordial, but on occasion there were armed skirmishes brought on by the indigenous people's anger at the ways in which they were treated by the British seamen. Sailors are notorious for letting all inhibitions go when they reach land. Cook's crew was no exception. Some of them died from sickness on the long journeys, but others ended their lives killed as thieves and rapists.

During this period some academics in *Europe* became unsure whether faith in the Christian God was a proper or a helpful assumption for *science*. Galileo Galilei (1564–1642) believed in God and felt free to investigate whatever he could observe. He had no intention of disrupting Catholic faith; his arguments were primarily with Aristotelian science. Like many scientists whose work proves to be fruitful, his conclusions were at times speculative, moving beyond what he had demonstrated. Some arguments mounted by his opponents were cautious and sensible. But the final Catholic reaction to him lacked proportion to the point of unreasonableness. He was not executed, but he was forced to deny his work defending Nicolaus Copernicus (1473–1543), who had insisted that the Earth was not the center of the universe. The affair put a blot on the church that often is recalled.

Isaac Newton (1642–1727), the most significant mathematician and physicist of his day, not only remained a Christian but claimed that at the points where his theories did not explain all, God himself had made the adjustments. Because he did not believe in the Trinity and had views of the millennium that seemed odd, he was not considered a man of orthodox faith. Yet he did not see the logical conclusion of his scientific efforts to be the claim that 'God' was not a necessary hypothesis for science.

François-Marie Arouet (1694–1778), the French writer known as Voltaire, praised Newton but thought that Deism was the only proper religion. God made the world but left it to its own desires; God was no longer active in the universe. With rapier-like ridicule in *Candide,* he dismantled the claim of Gottfried Leibnitz (1646–1716) that the present world was the best possible one. For Voltaire, only someone disconnected from contemporary life or history could ever believe such an idea after the Lisbon earthquake. He despised the Catholic Church as full of lies, mysticism and emotionalism. Their persecution of the Huguenots was inexcusable. He chose Pascal as a particularly bad representative; Pascal's Augustinian views of humanity stood directly opposed to Voltaire's hope in the future of rationalism. Life would be much better if Christian practice and faith, as he saw them, were eliminated.

A CHRISTIAN CORE

In the seventeenth century European Christians would pay dearly for Descartes's philosophy so carefully erected in response to the disruption of the Thirty Years War and the apparent collapse of the intellectual foundation of Christian faith. But they could not avoid paying the bill because they had accrued the debt. Catholic and Protestant hatred of each other smashed the structure of community in Western Europe. As Christians adapted to these new developments, many rejected years of communal teaching about a core of Christian faith and its disciplines that answered how they could carefully respond to any culture in which they found themselves. Their practice and faith had been shamed. They thought that they had to renew their reputation not by returning to the vaunted sources, but rather by entering the neutral public square where each person could objectively argue on the basis of universal reason for the truth of any position. Too seldom did deep prayer, active ethical life, scripture and the witness of the ancient saints seem to be powers for sustaining existence and persuading others. The European crucible that formed Anselm, Aquinas, the Catholic reformers, the Magisterial Reformation and the left-wing Anabaptists had been badly cracked if not finally broken.

Blaise Pascal (1623–62) stood against that destruction in his own way. He fitted the new Enlightenment pattern by being a brilliant mathematician and scientist. He had finished problems of geometry before his father had finished teaching them to him. He had invented the barometer. He appeared to be attacking the very root of Christian faith when he battled Roman Catholic Jesuit casuistry. For him what the Jesuits intended as providing substance to Christian theology proved itself to be an impediment to Christian truth. His *Pensées*, collected thoughts on religion with no set sequence, showed the same brilliance that marked his mathematical and scientific work. For him the truth that 'the heart has its reasons that reason does not know' was based in experiential knowledge of the most reasonable sort. The fullness of God was not open to the human mind, but our thoughts could give evidence for certain aspects of God. The genius of Augustine in many ways reappeared in Pascal's work. Here Enlightenment science worked together with an ability to investigate ancient Christian faith with its trust beyond what could be proved.

Other European Christians, particularly the theologians, continued to argue throughout the seventeenth century about the character of orthodox faith. In many ways the battles were extensions of the wars fought in that century, but now involving professors and preachers rather than troops. Massive tomes charted the topography and pointed out each place in which aggressive arguments – the 'soldiers' of Protestant orthodoxy – should be stationed. Protestant systematic theology has seldom been pursued with such a belief in its worth or commitment to spelling out its details. The German Lutheran theologian Johann Gerhard (1582–1637) took twelve years (1610–22) and nine volumes to create his *Loci communes theologici*. He had written a masterpiece of Lutheran orthodoxy that became the standard for generations. It was difficult to plow through, but another book of his about sacred meditations was quite popular and also appeared in a series of editions in English translation.

Not all the systematicians, however, were as gifted as Gerhard. The dryness of detailed doctrine led to the emergence of what is often called 'Pietism'. Philipp Jakob Spener (1635–1705), a devout Lutheran, emphasized the heartfelt, meditative aspect of Christian practice and faith, over against the professorial and clerical insistence on exact statements of faith. His *Pia Desideria* (1675) laid out the principles that he found important; the devotional group that met in his house twice a week encouraged lay people to become more fully involved. Their intent was to reform Lutheranism. Many local ministers in Frankfurt and beyond found this movement reviving, but others, schooled in orthodoxy, were threatened by Spener's views. He moved to Dresden, then Berlin, and finally was the primary influence in the founding of the University of Halle.

But at the University of Wittenberg the faculty heard an account of the movement by Professor Deutschmann that charged Spener with 283 counts of false doctrine. To avoid further difficulty, Spener retired from the battle and spent most of his final years in pastoral ministry. When August Hermann Francke (1663–1727) joined the Halle faculty, however, Pietism had another champion. He attacked orthodoxy in the university faculties by suggesting that meetings for prayer and Bible study were better than most lectures. He was so interested in the poor that he started an orphanage, a school and a small hospital. His academic interests led to the founding of a publishing firm. In 1713 when Frederick William I of Prussia visited Francke's institutions and used some of them as models for his own educational reform, much of the criticism of that kind of Pietism ceased. The University of Halle became a center of Christian world mission.

Count Nikolaus Ludwig von Zinzendorf (1700–60) studied in Francke's school. After his marriage he made his home in Berthelsdorf, a center for Moravians, who represented the suppressed Hussite Brethren. Together with German Pietists they built the town of Herrnhut. Zinzendorf traveled the world founding and visiting Moravian settlements that believed in the importance of Christian community for the practice of the faith. He insisted that cross-cultural mission was basic to the church.

In its later manifestations Pietism recognized prayer and Bible study as fundamental, but put more and more effort into social involvement.

Christians could not withdraw to small conventicles and live among themselves. They needed to be at the forefront of movements that worked for justice and reconciliation.

In the eighteenth century a great reform spread through *Great Britain* and parts of the British colonies in the Americas. Centered in the work of John Wesley (1703–91), his brother Charles (1707–88) and the evangelist George Whitfield (1714–70), it not only exposed features of doctrinal difference within Anglican communities but also included a compelling awareness of the degrading conditions of the cities in which so many people lived. John and Charles were graduates of Oxford University; Whitfield was a servitor at Pembroke College who met them and attended their study groups. This circle sought to approach the discipline of Christian practice and faith methodically, to discern a core of things and to make that clear not only to the privileged but also to the underprivileged. John wrote most of the Bible studies and the tracts of theology, Charles turned his talents to hymnody and George pursued stump evangelism.

John could do nearly any task. His booming voice allowed him to speak to crowds even of 100,000 without worrying about being heard. His heart, 'strangely warmed' at an Aldersgate street meeting after his failure as a preacher in the American colony of Georgia, made him a man of compassion for those without Christ, particularly the poor. His scholarly mind served his arguments well. The Methodist revival probably brought the most penetrating Christian presence ever into the British cities that had been founded in the Middle Ages. These cities and others like them elsewhere in Europe had not necessarily been lost; they might never have been fully won.

Elsewhere in *Europe,* Tikhon (1724–83) of Zadonsk (now Gdansk, Poland) was a Russian saint who came from a very poor family. A church scholarship allowed him to study at Novgorod. Ordained a priest, he took monastic vows and was asked to teach in the seminary, a task that did not suit him. But his appointment first as an assistant bishop and then as a full bishop in 1763 was even more difficult for this man who so loved solitude. He discovered, however, that he could help members of his church to deepen their faith and take responsibility for the starving peasants around them. He believed that all men and women were equal in God's sight.

By 1769 Tikhon's health had broken and he retired to the monastery at Zadonsk. At first he lived alone as a hermit and at last enjoyed the solitude he had wanted. He had dreams of the baby Jesus, who warned him about his temper and called him to a life of charity. As his soul calmed, he opened his door to any who sought his help, particularly in spiritual matters. The rumor spread and thousands made their way by foot and wagon. His funeral attracted 300,000.

Within Eastern European Orthodoxy, the practices of the Hesychasts, the Quiet Ones, had included attention not only to posture and breathing but also to the repetition of the Jesus Prayer. This use of the body in the *practice of prayer* seemed silly to some, but it fitted with the understanding of Jesus Christ having a body during the incarnation. Lying down and concentrating on slow but unlabored breathing could put anyone in a better mental and physical state for meditation. The repetition of the Jesus Prayer – 'Lord Jesus Christ, Son of God, have mercy on me, a sinner' – focused on a central truth of Christian faith. What became known as Hesychast practices and sensitivities had probably begun in the fourth century with Gregory of Nyssa. Gregory Palamas (*c.* 1296–1359) had defended them well; by the eighteenth century they were a staple of monastic practice.

The *Philocalia*, collected by Macarius Notaras and Nicodemus and printed in 1782 at Venice, included writings on Hesychast themes. Translated into Slavonic in 1793 by Paissy Velichkovsky and into other languages later, the *Philocalia* became the backbone of Eastern Orthodox spirituality. The mystical and ascetic writings it contains are a treasure chest of Christian spirituality, available for many Christians, not Orthodox monks alone.

In this period European missionaries often took their idiocies with them. The contrast between the work of Pedro Paez (1564–1622) and that of Alphonsus Mendes (1579–1639) in *Ethiopia* is one between dusk and night. Paez, a Spanish Jesuit, did not allow enslavement by Turkish pirates for nearly seven years to keep him from his mission in Ethiopia. Entering disguised as an Armenian merchant, he learned Amharic and Ge'ez. His report on the errors of the Ethiopian Orthodox Church indicated that he deeply disagreed with many aspects of their practice and doctrine. But he concentrated on winning the court and had some success because of his gentle persuasion. The emperor Susenyos converted to Catholicism and banned the slave trade. Although Paez insisted on the inculturation of what he understood as the Christian gospel into the language of Ethiopians, he was not able to encourage religious reform without thinking in terms of conversion from Ethiopian Orthodox to Roman Catholic principles.

Mendes, who knew no Christians but those in agreement with Rome, followed Paez. A Portuguese Jesuit, he insisted that all Ethiopian Christians be *baptized* and all clergy be *ordained* as Catholics because the Ethiopian sacraments were invalid. He replaced the Ethiopian calendar of church feasts with the Roman one. The old practices of circumcision and worship on Saturday were banned. The emperor Susenyos tried to follow those rules, but the people rebelled. Susenyos withdrew the laws, abdicated, and gave power to his son, Fasiladas. In response ham-fisted Mendez petitioned the Portuguese to dethrone Fasilidas. The result was the banning of Roman missionaries in Ethiopia for two hundred years. When Mendez wrote a history of his mission, he was able to see some of his mistakes. But he remains one of the ignorant defenders of the Europeanization of every church, in this instance the Portugalization of Ethiopians who had been Christians for over a thousand years.

Christians in Ethiopia at the beginning of the eighteenth century might have seemed prosperous to a Westerner visiting the court, but Muslim advance through the infiltration of the Galla people caused weakness and even the loss of the coast. To make matters worse, Roman Catholic and Protestant missionary influence persisted in questioning the core faith of Monophysite Ethiopian Christianity. When pressed, leaders of the Ewostathian monasteries, known as the Kebat, insisted that the anointing of Jesus involved the divinization of his humanity and thus the union of the divine and human into one nature. Their opponents, the leaders of the Takla Haymanot houses known as the Tewahdo, said that the anointing only made Jesus the Messiah or the second Adam and had nothing to do with the formula of two natures in one person. After a struggle about such things in the last half of the seventeenth century, in 1720 the Kebat massacred a number of the Tewahdo leaders when the two groups were meeting at the Kebat capital in Gondar. The 'right' view of Christ brought death to those holding 'wrong' views. The Muslim pressure and the inner theological conflict hastened the constriction of Ethiopia. The Shoa region was lost. The only bright light at the end of the century was the strong abuna Yosab (served 1770–1803), but his efforts were overwhelmed by the continued strength of the Galla people, among whom Christians were few and Muslims many. At the dawn of the nineteenth century the Christian stronghold of Ethiopia was at its weakest in hundreds of years.

In the *Congo* at the beginning of the eighteenth century a strong Christian movement emerged in response to the Portuguese defeat of the

Congolese army in 1665 and the continued desolation that followed. The capital, São Salvador, was nearly empty and Christians found little solace. In 1704 a Congolese woman, Kimpa Vita, with the Christian name Beatrice, said that she was possessed by St. Anthony. Watching her behavior, the priest declared both her and her interpreter heretics, but she persisted. She burned crosses and fetishes that she thought were superstitious, gave away her possessions and began preaching. Common people followed her back from Mount Kimbangu to the capital. Beatrice insisted that Jesus had been born at São Salvador and baptized in the Zaïre river. St. Francis had been part of a Congolese clan. God was interested in intention, not outward symbols or rituals. Beatrice's perception of Congolese Christian practice and belief as a veneer was acute. Her social understanding that the capital should be repopulated was also correct.

When she had a baby with her companion John, she was tried under Congolese law with the assistance of the Catholic missionaries who so despised her work. At the age of only twenty-two, she and her lover were burned. But the Antonian movement continued for at least a century, with its odd practices and its ability to give Christian faith an internal Congolese authenticity.

When the strongest ban against Japanese Christians was put in place during 1659, closing *Japan* in particular to Portuguese traders but actually to all but the Chinese and the Dutch, only about 150,000 Christians remained. Most of their upper class leaders and supporters had either been killed or left the church. Those remaining were primarily merchants and peasants. There is some evidence, however, that the European missionaries had tried to organize and teach the Christians in ways that would serve them during persecution. The Japanese Christians themselves developed helpful approaches to life as threatened criminals. The seventeenth- and eighteenth-century communities hand-copied small manuals – for example, one on penance – and surreptitiously had small Christian symbols carved on statues of Buddha to allow them to worship Christ while being publicly observed as devout Buddhists. They also followed their own secret lives of prayer and virtue, but their numbers continued to dwindle.

Alexandre de Rhodes (1591–1660), the Jesuit missionary to *Vietnam,* wrote a remarkable *Catechism* for Vietnamese people. His outline covered eight days ending in preparation for baptism. The spirituality that informs it is warm, filled with common examples that move the

reader. He carefully distinguished between worship of God and veneration of the saints because the Vietnamese had only one word for the two
acts. He also coined a new Vietnamese phrase *Duc Chua Troi Dat* – 'the
Noble Lord of Heaven and Earth' – rather than using the transliterated
Latin *Deus* or the Chinese *Thien Chu*, 'Master of Heaven'. For de
Rhodes the use of Vietnamese proverbs, traditional Confucian books,
and Buddhist writings allowed him to appeal to what his audience knew.
Occasional employment of aspects of his Western education did not
overpower that work.

Fifty years after the 1599 Synod of Diamper, many of the ancient
Indian Christians fought to keep their own identity and tradition. A
century and a half earlier they had welcomed the Portuguese, both as a
military protection against the armed Muslim traders who on occasion
attacked their settlements and as intriguing Christians with whom they
shared important aspects of the faith, but whom they also found to be
rather strange. At first they received the Roman Catholic bishops with
honor and tried to find ways in which their unity together could take
first priority.

Decades later, however, they finally discovered that they could not
retain their tradition if they did not attack Archbishop Garcia and the
Jesuits in order to make their independence plain. A metropolitan of
the Syro-Antiochian patriarchate, Mar Aithalaha, came in 1652 from
the Middle East to take leadership of the Indian churches, but he was
locked up at the Catholic seminary at Mylapore in eastern India until
the Roman Inquisition from Goa could properly investigate him.
Aithalaha claimed to be a Roman convert with papal authority. Archbishop Garcia refused his authority because it was not also from the
Portuguese king.

The Thomas Christians, who for over a millennium had accepted
the leadership of Syriac-speaking bishops from Syria or Persia (Iran),
were furious. They did not deny their allegiance to the pope; the archbishop, however, had thwarted the pope's intentions. They became
incorrigible when the Portuguese fleet supposedly bringing Aithalaha
to them at Cochin did not enter the harbor, but sailed on to Goa. The
result was that Archdeacon Thomas was ordained a bishop by twelve
priests on the basis of a forged letter apparently signed by Aithalaha.
Thus imperious actions on one side and deceitful decisions on the other
led to the strong division between Catholic and Syrian Orthodox
Christians in India.

CONCLUSION

The Thirty Years War in Europe, which started in the midst of religious disagreement, ended in national causes and the marginalization of religion. Those results form part of the context for Christians in the twenty-first century. Developments in science and philosophy during the Enlightenment further weakened Christendom. Being reasonable often seemed to involve the spurning of Christian intuitions and institutions. But various scientists and artists as well as ordinary people kept Christian claims alive. Some Protestant theologians created large theological systems to make faith and practice compelling; others found the heart, the spirit, to be the arena of appeal. Pietists became famous for their social works. They organized for Christian mission and pursued its goals around the globe.

Roman Catholic world mission had a series of leaders who understood the importance of moving Christian faith and practice into indigenous cultures. In India Robert de Nobili studied Indian classics and lived much like a Hindu Brahmin. His vision was stronger than his results. Alexandre de Rhodes mastered Chinese classics and Vietnamese proverbs, created a printed Vietnamese language, and made Christian faith and practice Vietnamese. Matthias Ricci, because he was a Confucian scholar, was able to introduce European scientific instruments to China and became an influence in the Beijing court. But traditional conservative Catholics, some well placed in the hierarchy, insisted that too much of the faith had been sacrificed. They rejected the efforts of their best missionaries and set back Catholic world mission for centuries.

7 WESTERN MISSIONARY EXPANSION, 1800–1920

The last quarter of the eighteenth century witnessed two cataclysms that had an impact on Christians in North America and Europe. The growing British colonies along the Atlantic coast of North America did not mind the cultural and religious ties to Great Britain but some of their leaders chafed at the decisions made in Britain that were imposed upon them. British loyalists could hardly imagine independent existence but were eventually forced to accept it or move. The United States was born in conflict that many feared would lead to war. The outcome was not really determined until France offered funds after 1776 and the British were beaten back in a second war during 1812.

The congress that put together the constitution insisted that there should be no established religion in the country. The discussions in Philadelphia show, however, that most decisions about the character of this new country were reached in a milieu that had little interest in living a religion. Many citizens were Christians who centered their existence in God, but some important intellectuals were Deists. There was a divinity who made the world and then left it on its own. Thus humans should take responsibility for their own lives. Religious language was included in various documents; letters indicate the influence of Christian practice and faith. Yet the foundation for a civil religion with trappings of Christian faith rather than one based primarily in Christian communities was there from the beginning.

The French revolution at the end of the century convulsed the country and much of Europe. The enemies of the revolutionaries were many, but monarchy, a privileged elite and the Roman church absorbed much of the anger. Marie Antoinette's purported comment, 'Let them eat cake', summed up the issues. Common people could not find bread and sometimes were forced to steal it when it appeared. Moneyed landowners lived in luxury, their peasants in squalor. Monasteries owned large blocks of land as did the Roman church under its bishops. In some French counties nearly ninety percent of the tax base belonged to the untaxed church. Its consumption of wealth and its perceived lack of concern for the poor, even the merchant class, made it a major target.

The goals of the revolution were humane: liberty, equality, fraternity. They became a clarion call for others in various circumstances around the globe. Yet the reality of the deluge in France expressed revenge more than high-minded ideals. Order eroded or was enforced with arms. Property rights for the nobility were declared 'holy' but were not always protected. Recovery was long in coming. Perhaps it is fair to say that the institutions of the rich, including the Catholic Church, deserved to be brought down, but the cost in human life was severe. Catholicism in France has not yet recovered.

Battles for independence spread elsewhere. During the first half of the nineteenth century nearly every country in Latin America had at least one war in which liberals tried to oust conservative elites who depended upon their landholdings and the support of the Roman church. The descendants of the invading Spanish and Portuguese looked to Europe for their culture and religion but came down on both sides of the conflict.

The political instability of Europe became manifest in the Napoleonic Wars. Napoleon was a brilliant general who believed in himself and the cause of France. He put troops into the field all over Europe, from Spain to Russia, and into the Mediterranean all the way to Egypt. Only his bad judgment in invading Russia close to the onset of winter and his final defeat at Waterloo ended his rule. The disruption that he considered to be the forming of a peaceful empire upset the lives of many, including Christians. Nationalistic identities that worked toward military coalitions dominated the times. Individual congregations in the way of the marauding armies suffered immensely. Any sense of international Christian unity fell afoul not only of Protestant and Catholic division, but also of national squabbles. The stage was set for European colonialism played out as competition between nations.

European and North American economic expansion became a major influence after the mid nineteenth century. In Africa the scramble for colonies that occupied European countries in the last decades of the century has led to ruinous consequences in the twenty-first century. For many European and North American businessmen in the nineteenth century, African people might no longer be the best investment for making the highest profit; the slave trade was waning. But the promise of precious metals, gems and other raw materials led to rampant speculation in those markets and the demand that governments help finance and defend such interests. The boundaries of the present African countries drawn by Europeans confine together groups of peoples who have been sworn enemies. These boundaries made little or no sense to Africans. They were questionable from the beginning and help explain why the modern nation states in Africa have been so difficult to govern.

Foreign policies toward Asia tell a similar story. British takeover of India, European opium treaties in China and other stories in the region had a direct impact on Christians because both at home and abroad they depended upon colonial expansion. Winds were whipped up that bore whirlwinds.

CHRISTIANS AND PEOPLE OF OTHER FAITHS

In *Africa* Christians found two major religious forces to contend with: *traditional* tribal religions and Islam. The first came in nearly as many shapes as there were tribes. But there were common features. The tremendous respect for the world, its spirits, animals and plants meant that in many ways Africans cared more for the land than did the North American and European entrepreneurs or missionaries. Though the Maasai, for instance, might raise cattle and at times overgraze the grasslands, their long knowledge of the regions in which they lived allowed them to survive flood and drought. Nearly every clan had worshipful respect for their ancestors, often as a response to their fear of the bad individuals who in life had already made existence miserable – now that they had died, they still needed to be placated. Other ancestors had been good, supportive influences, and some tribes developed rituals and fetishes to honor them.

One remarkable aspect of many but not all peoples living in Africa was a deep sense of a creator god, above the spirits and ancestors, who at least made the world before he left it alone. Some clans thought humans had dishonored him, poking him in the eye while they were working or making him angry in other ways. Such stories often included a name for this one overpowering deity. For instance the Kikuyu, when asked if they worshipped a supreme god, answered that they could tell narratives about his actions, knew his name, and prayed to him with deep commitment and ceremony, particularly for the rain that sustained their crops.

The Africans could defend their beliefs. David Livingstone (1813–73) had a conversation with a native shaman who was proficient in making rain. Livingstone lived within his European worldview and believed that the medicine he had studied in London and practiced in Africa represented a superior, civilized understanding of reality. But the rainmaker pithily pointed out that his own assumptions and practices brought rain just as surely as Livingstone could trust his medicines for their results. Neither religious leader could vanquish the other.

Some foreign missionaries to Africa found the tribal life around them so different and so clearly inferior that they discovered nothing of much use for picturing, conceptualizing or living out the gospel. This was particularly true of some later nineteenth-century European missionaries who came from the upper class established churches and were confident that making people first-rate Europeans was intrinsic to spreading the faith. They were content to build a mission station that looked as much as possible like the home they had left, to wear their own clothes and to 'civilize' the savages. They were convinced that they had come from a society where logic and rationality ruled, where human existence was clearly at its best. Compassion for the Africans was nearly always present, even if in a condescending form, but these missionaries thought that the natives must be raised to a higher level of genuine human life in order to make a decision for Christ. When that sense of the world dominated their consciousness, missionaries could hardly conceive of authentic stories of the one true God actually being a part of African traditions. When they saw similarities, they too often resisted the use of the African names for that one God or the narratives about him because they sincerely believed that had those features been powerful and valid a different kind of life would have emerged.

For reasons that are not always clear, other missionaries were impressed with the overtones of African traditional religions and were happy to use African tales and names as the starting point for preaching the Christian message. Some of them came from underclass life in Europe. They had possessed little and had worked hard just to exist. Often they had the good sense to learn the languages along with the cultures in which they now lived so that they could translate Christian faith and life into the African worlds.

Some missionaries well positioned in the upper strata of European society somehow got the point that African life was anything but inferior. Johannes Van der Kemp (1747–1811), born in Rotterdam, arrived at Cape Town in 1799. The son of a theological professor, he had become a dashing military officer with a passion for the conquest of women. When he married he left the army and its temptations, studied philosophy and medicine at Edinburgh and made significant contributions in both fields. His life as a doctor in Holland (1782–95) should have been fulfilling, but the drowning of his wife and son in 1791 led to a deep Christian conversion. Moravian Brethren told him of the London Missionary Society. He gained the society's trust and was ordained for mission ministry in 1797.

At Cape Town he was overwhelmed with disgust for the slave economy. Work among the Xhosa in Kaffraria for two years seemed ineffective, so he moved to the Graaff-Reinet area where the Khoikhoi (Hottentot) people were in deep need. He built a mission station at Bethelsdorp and at first was resented by nearly everyone: the Dutch settlers, the Xhosa and the Khoikhoi. But Van der Kemp identified with the Africans and took on their fight against slavery and for recognition of their social and economic disadvantage. He did not view other humans as inferior.

This Dutchman had charismatic qualities, not the least his active prayer life and his recognized ability to make rain. He learned the Khoikhoi language and composed a catechism in it. He adopted their ways, ate their food, wore their clothes (no shoes or hat) and lived in their huts. Finally he married a Malagasy slave girl he had purchased along with her family and thus raised the wrath of almost all the European settlers. Yet his work was deeply set among the people he loved. At his death, large numbers of both blacks and whites from the Cape attended the funeral, and his Christian community was led by indigenous Khoikhois whom he had given the freedom to develop.

In Van der Kemp's view neither Khoikhoi nor Xhosa had first to become European in order to convert to Christ. The gospel could be contextualized in their practices and faith. Indeed one of the great African prophets, Ntiskana, a Xhosa warrior and councilor, heard Van der Kemp preach and eventually attended the services that Joseph Williams held among the Xhosa. Ntiskana had a deep spiritual experience that led him to immerse himself in a river and never again paint himself with the ochre that was proper to his position. He gave up one of his two wives because polygamy now seemed unsuitable. Rejecting the warlike teaching of the Xhosa prophet Nxele, who also showed traces of Christian influence, Ntiskana taught his disciples that war was evil. His group named themselves the 'Poll-headed', cattle without horns, real pacifists. Ntiskana's greatest talent was his ability to compose hymns, particularly about God and creation, some of which are still sung in African Christian worship (and should be sung elsewhere). He is an example of an African who was never formally baptized by an ordained minister, who neither accepted European education nor adopted European culture, but who understood the power of a saving God in his own Xhosa way. He and his followers represented a fragile Christian flower that grew in African soil, demonstrated its own beauty and deserved careful cultivation.

The story of African Christians cannot be told without reference to African *Muslims*. In Nigeria a Yoruba diviner had chosen the child Adjai for worship of the high god Olorun alone, not the entire Yoruba pantheon. Enslaved by Muslim raiders when he was about thirteen, he only became a Christian in Sierra Leone three years after his liberation. The adult conversations of Samuel (Adjai) Crowther (1807–91) with Muslims were never vengeful. He emphasized what Muslims and Christians shared and avoided talk of Trinity because Muslims were offended by the thought that Allah could have a son. He asked within a Nigerian Muslim court in 1872 if Jibrila (Gabriel) told the truth when he he announced the birth of Jesus the Messiah. The Yoruba Gospel of Luke and the Arabic Qur'an were similar on that point so the Muslims agreed. Then Crowther read John 14 and Matthew 28. The first noted that Gabriel called Jesus 'the way, the truth and the life,' the second commanded Christians to teach all nations about him. After other questions were given biblical answers, the emir asked for prayer. Crowther offered 'The Prayer for the Queen's Majesty.' He explained that outside England the name of the local ruler was put in the place of the queen.

In some places the advance of minority Muslims in the interior of Africa was suppressed by the emergence of Christians. The two minorities among the majority of people following their traditional religious customs could look remarkably similar. Both were book monotheists worshipping one God and denying the power of idols. But their similarity could also result in strong antagonism as it had in other areas of the world.

African Muslims displayed various African characteristics, but their maturing in Islam led them to adopt Arabic as their language and the culture of the Qur'an as their own. The insistence on Arabic as the tongue of God led various tribes to forsake their traditional cultural heritage and to let their stories about and words for the one God atrophy. Members of the Dinka tribe, for example, have little or no memory of those features of their tradition from before they converted to Islam. The many Dinka Christians feel that loss.

The nineteenth century saw much decay in Islamic regions and the rise to power of 'Christian' Europe. The Ottoman Empire wheezed toward death. France dominated Egypt and North Africa; the British Empire included India. In each of those countries political weakness fostered religious reform. Allah would smile more on a people who had returned to him.

In Africa south of the Sahara a revival of Islam was in process, particularly among the Fulani, who as wandering herdsmen had moved out of the Senegal valley across much of West Africa. They had become Muslim early on and had kept a rather pure form of Islam, less dependent on African traditions than the people of a more mixed Islamic background among whom they lived. One Fulani leader, Shehu Usuman dan Fodio, after visions occurring in 1789–94, withdrew in 1804 from the Hausa people and called for a jihad against Muslims who would not enforce the *sharia*, the laws of daily life that he and other purists held to be necessary. There were at least two other jihads led by archconservative Fulani tribesman that gave Muslims strength to reform their lackadaisical brothers in the faith and to evangelize pagans. Islam became a powerful force involved both financially and militarily in conquest. In East Africa, Arab traders took their religion with them as they sought goods, including ivory and slaves. There was reason to think that Africa might well become primarily Muslim.

One Christian rock in the continent was *Ethiopia*, but it cracked and in places crumbled. The disintegration of central authority, including religious leadership, was serious. Tribes ruled themselves. For the first four decades of the century Ethiopia had no abuna, no single Christian leader. Worshippers of the old tribal religions and the Muslim Galla people had taken many Christian areas and forced the Christians into isolated conclaves. But the appointment of a new Ethiopian bishop in Cairo during 1841, a young man of vigor and vision, began to change the situation. Not until Tewodros was crowned king after a series of military victories over separate tribes, however, were throne and abuna united. 1855–68 saw the revival of the Ethiopian Christians. Tewodros was a firm Christian, faithful to his wife although she bore him no children. He helped the poor, rebuilt churches, pressed the Muslim Galla to convert, but in the end committed suicide as his army devastated the country by pillaging for income. A British force bent on releasing European hostages found almost no resistance. The Ethiopian people had no loyalty for this failed prophet and ruler.

By 1896 Ethiopia had recovered enough unity among king, abuna and people to repel an Italian army. King Yohannes IV had died in 1889 fighting Sudanese Muslim Mahdists, but the army had been toughened and armed with European weapons. He had set up a policy of converting the Galla by either suppression or persuasion. His successor, Menelik, continued that policy. A description of its effects, however, shows how resilient both Muslim and tribal religious practices were. Ethiopian Christians stayed with their tradition, its liturgy, music and church buildings. The Galla, who accepted baptism under threat of losing land and property, built churches and even paid for Christian priests. They fasted, confessed their sins and celebrated the Christian festivals, but their marriage ceremonies were according to the old tribal customs. That could not be challenged because most of the Christians in the region did the same. Christian persecution of Muslims brought neither authentic nor full conversion.

In *Latin America* during the nineteenth century social unrest did not often lead to revolutions. Most of the conquered peoples, who had never recovered from their defeat and conversion, continued their wretched lives under the rule of local or national elites. Those upper classes most often were Spanish or Portuguese and had within their group only a few of the middle or lower castes of the region. The only people who could muster the energy for conflict were those motivated by religion. In the Caste War of Yucatán, Mayan people rebelled against the highest caste. The Maya lived in a different cultural and religious situation. Their conversion to Christian faith left them in touch with their own sense of clan. A talking cross prophesied that they should drive out the whites and the mixed racial inhabitants of their land; the rebels called themselves *Cruzob*, 'people of the cross', but their central core was Mayan. In one tragic way they looked like their 'Christian' conquerors, whose main interest revolved around Spain and gold, not Christ.

The Bahian conspiracy in Brazil also pitted the lowly against the powerful. But this time it was black, Arabic-speaking Malês who stood strong against any attempts at Christian conversion. Their revolt failed on that count, however, because black Christians rejected the rebellion primarily on the grounds that its leaders were *Muslims*.

In *China* Yang Wen-hui (Jen-shan, 1837–1911), who directed the office for technology in Nanking, developed a great interest in Western science. He learned English and visited London but his greatest contribution was his printing and distribution of the *Buddhist* canon. He privately published a new edition and gave copies to temple monasteries; he has been called the 'father of modern Chinese Buddhism'. Yang suggested to his friend the Christian missionary Timothy Richard (1845–1919) that he read the sixth-century Chinese Buddhist text *Awakening of Belief in Mahayana* and the Lotus sutra. Yang saw those texts as reason to think of Buddhism as the religion for all peoples of the world. Richard saw them as the foundation in Pure Land Buddhism for the building of Chinese Christianity. The two friends parted each saddened by the other's view. Another reformer, T'an Ssu-t'ung (1866–98), had studied with Yang and Richard. He found a unity in Confucianism, Buddhism and Christianity in the area of *dharma*, 'the view of the world', and accepted Martin Luther's emphasis on the freedom of conscience. He was executed by the government for his participation in what they saw as revolutionary activity.

The interlocked religious and cultural festivals that were held around temples and in public spaces raised difficult questions for Christians. Both Catholic and Protestant missionaries studied these phenomena and usually concluded that Christians not only should avoid participating but also should not pay the support expected from all village or city inhabitants. Christians rejected these festivals as religious rites; *traditional Chinese* responded that only because of their acceptance of a foreign, both devilish and seditious, religion did they refuse. To honor Confucius, to hold the important local operas with all their music and finery, was necessary. All citizens should help.

This tension simmered throughout the second half of the nineteenth century and boiled over at various times. As early as 1862 the Chinese government tried to understand French criticism of these practices as 'pagan' in terms of the criticism made by modern Confucians that they were 'useless'. But among the common people, they were seen as needed Chinese rites, not susceptible to separation into 'secular' and 'sacred' categories. In Shanxi province, persecution was intense though sporadic, breaking out into widespread killings during the Boxer rebellion at the turn of the twentieth century. There and in other provinces Christian converts faced such bitterness openly because they and particularly their lay leaders had never seen themselves as anything but Chinese. They evangelized their kin and their neighbors; they did business with other non-Christians. The idea of a compound in which they lived only with Christians did not take hold.

Christians in *India* were surprised to see their evangelistic efforts coopted by a *Hindu Renaissance* in which many Christian views were infused into Hindu thought. Ram Mohan Roy (1772–1833), an orthodox Brahmin Hindu, studied Islam and Hinduism thoroughly by learning Arabic and Sanskrit under Muslim and Hindu scholars. In Calcutta in 1815 he began his reforms. He found a unitarian Christian congregation in the 1820s and was taken by their sense of God's unity, a concept similar to the Islamic monotheism he had also found fascinating. His *The Precepts of Jesus* made Jesus a powerful teacher of monotheism and morality whose divine acts, including his death and resurrection as a savior, were not the point. Without those, Jesus (like Muhammad) would serve as a teacher of Hindus whose faith needed to be turned away from polytheism. Jesus could help Hindus purge their lives of superstitions.

Keshab Chandra Sen (1838–84) followed Roy's emphasis on reason and ethics but also insisted that faith and revelation were crucial to Hindus. He sought to weld British science with Indian sensitivity to religion. Christ was the most significant teacher of religion, but the amalgamation of most of the world's religions should be the goal. Christian views of Trinity were important but the unity of humanity and divinity in Christ made the most sense of the complete pantheism found in the oldest Hindu texts. Sen fought the caste system, refused to call any 'untouchable' and insisted on schooling for women.

Ramakrishna (1836–86) and his pupil Narendranath Datta (1863–1902), known as Vivekananda, both emphasized the oneness of all religions in the search for divine–human union. Ramakrishna claimed to have a deep mystical experience of Christ that involved a vision of and participation in spiritual union with the divine. For Vivekananda, Jesus was a mystic who showed all people that they too were God.

The power with which these Hindus absorbed understandings of Jesus and Christian revelation was countered by various Christian leaders, particularly those like Joshua Marshman (1768–1837) who found the uni-tarianism of Roy too limited. But the ways in which these leaders could claim Jesus as yet another *avatar*, another incarnation of what was best in religion, and employ his deeds and teaching as the light for the reform of Hinduism, remain a stunning if questionable set of proposals.

In *Korea* foreign missionaries and the struggling Christian communities regularly lived under persecution. Many of these Catholic disciples had an understanding of practice and faith that resisted the ancient cult of ancestors and thus had angered both cultural traditionalists and Confucians. Some Korean authorities worried that these small coteries must be breeding grounds of rebellion and for that reason may have accepted the decision in China (and possibly the similar judgment in Japan) that Christianity was an illegal religion. The result was a steady killing of martyrs. The Napoleonic Wars had made it impossible to put a bishop in Beijing, so an appeal to Chinese Christians for help was futile. Andrew Kim, the first ordained Korean priest (1845), had traveled in and out of his country for education, but was martyred in 1846. Some Catholic missionaries entered the country in the 1850s, but another persecution broke out in 1866. The 1880s, however, brought more openness both politically and culturally so that by 1900 Catholic conversions were increasing.

CHRISTIANS AND THEIR CULTURES

Only in the nineteenth century did trade in the South Atlantic between Africa, Europe and Latin America cease to be primarily in *slaves*; it did not end officially until 1886 in Cuba and 1888 in Brazil. Pressure on that commerce from European countries like Great Britain had slowed the traffic, but even in the 1830s and 1840s Africans were shipped west by the hundreds of thousands. The estimates from 1500 to 1870 range from nine to fifteen million who arrived alive; those who died during the struggle of capture, the trek to the ports, imprisonment there and the journey at sea are almost impossible to judge – perhaps two million or more. The indigenous Amerindians of Latin America did not live long in the fields; the Africans survived only a bit longer but they were easier to find and ship. The Portuguese dominated the traffic in the sixteenth century, the Dutch in the seventeenth, the British and French in the eighteenth, and traders from the United States, Cuba and Brazil kept it going in the nineteenth.

This commerce showed no understanding of the rights human beings should have, yet Christians have had as much difficulty in recognizing others as human beings as have those of other religions. Europeans' sense of their own excellence linked with enormous greed blinded many to anything but the gain. The capacity to view humans only as beasts made for work is not singularly a Christian failing. African chiefs sold their captives from wars to slave traders. Islamic Arab traders in East Africa killed elephants for the ivory, then used Africans to carry it to eastern ports and finally sold both to other traders. The country that we now call Malawi had areas in the nineteenth century that were no longer inhabited. Almost all the members of some tribes had been captured and sold.

In the eighteenth century the Quakers had mounted some of the earliest modern Christian arguments against the slave trade and continued to do so in the nineteenth. How could Christ's disciples hold slaves? If all God's creatures were intended to be family, how could one group enslave another? In the nineteenth century a number of European Christian groups discovered that they had a mission responsibility to the less fortunate people in Africa. They joined together in voluntary associations that allowed the poor and middle classes to aid in this work of God. Too often the wealthy Europeans' mindset of superiority remained, but now some Europeans took the gospel seriously and gave it to those in need. The whole enterprise also gained strength from sanguine economic sense that trade in human flesh did not fit well with the growth of capitalism and its world markets.

David Livingstone (1813–73) has the largest reputation of any missionary connected with *Africa*; he was involved in the European mission to Christianize and civilize the continent. His mission began in South Africa, where he met and married the daughter of Robert Moffat. In terms of winning converts, his efforts were a disaster. The rigors of travel to the north cost him his wife. His primary contribution was making Great Britain aware of Africa's natural grandeur and breaking that continent out of its place as 'darkest Africa'. He died in Zambia and was buried in Westminster Abbey. One of his strongest battles, however, was against the ruin that the slave trade produced. His stand threatened other whites in Africa, who tried to avoid him. He vigorously insisted that Africans should be free in their own lands. Too often forgotten is his acknowledgment that had his friends in the Kololo tribe not accompanied him on his walking trips first west to Angola and later east to

Mozambique, he would not have been able to complete the journeys that made him famous.

Many European missionaries in Africa and elsewhere suffered from a deep conviction of their culture's superiority. They often brought medicine to aid African people who already had remedies for certain diseases that had worked quite well. Whether Catholic or Protestant, when the missionaries set up village compounds that replicated as far as possible their homes in Europe and offered Africans the opportunity of becoming European in order to become Christian, even their successes were marred. For the missionaries Christian education was the hope of the world, an education that civilized the savages, and taught them languages that opened them to the best values in life. These Christians congratulated themselves for helping such different people to catch the vision. At times Africans did so well even in European universities that the prejudices were either shaken to the ground or could only be sustained by discounting the individual success as an anomaly. How could a black man be first in his class?

The greatest threat to European pre-eminence, however, emerged in the many *translation projects*. Both Protestants and Catholics wanted to get Christian literature into the hands of Africans, printed in their vernacular languages. Protestants thought mostly in terms of the Bible; Catholics often focused on catechisms and liturgies. Whether these missionaries were aware of it or not, they soon had to acknowledge that the final experts in any translation project were the native speakers. What a missionary viewed as both proper and clear statements were often either deep offenses or hilarious jokes. Every line had to be tested by the Africans themselves. Hundreds of translations occurred, often among people who had never had a written language. The results must be counted among the greatest gifts that these missionaries offered the people they served. Languages and cultures were saved from extinction. In the twentieth century, nationalist and communist activists, who despised the 'Christian' colonialism of the nineteenth century, themselves depended on missionary writing and printing of their languages for the traditions they wanted to salvage or reintroduce.

The Victorian missionaries, though so often maddening in their condescension, were well aware of the importance of Christian practice and virtue. Christians emerged from their compound life who thought themselves not inferior but equal Christians. During the scramble of European countries for African colonies, Africans were horrified as, for example, German and British Christians battled each other for control. But missionaries who fought the slave trade and who dealt compassionately – though sometimes condescendingly – with the natives laid out a gospel that could be learned and practiced.

As importantly, much of the spread of Christian practice and faith deep in the African interior was accomplished not by foreign missionaries, but by *indigenous Africans* who could be far removed from any contact with European missionaries. Christians emerged in various places because the gospel was not limited to European cultural trappings. Their life was African, not European.

In *Latin America* a number of the wars for independence relied upon a call to *nativism,* a sense that the best of the region was in the indigenous blood. That allowed the few Creoles, who still valued their place as being nearly 'white', to call on the natives, the *mestizos* of mixed racial background, and even the children of black slaves. Such forces had more than limited success although the Creoles never intended to participate in any way except as rulers. Christians did fight in these conflicts, but they seldom had the insight to reject the basis of the coalition and its rather unusual interpretation of the Latin American caste system. Too few Christians thought that in the first place Christ stood against the separations of brothers and sisters within his church into such castes. Even the impressive Father Miguel Hidalgo, himself a Creole who had studied the languages and cultures of his region of Mexico, told his followers that the problem was the 'Americans' against the Europeans, the Virgin of Guadalupe against the Spaniards. It took Father José María Morelos, a *mestizo,* to see that the fight was against slavery, the caste system and the crippling taxes. He rejected all the social classes carefully constructed along racial lines. Both priests, however, were executed during the second decade of the nineteenth century and their movements eventually faded.

The strangest North American mission in Latin America was that of William Walker in mid-century. This Tennessee archconservative Christian, at the request of liberal politicians in Nicaragua, assembled a tiny army and invaded the country in order to make it a colony of the United States. He claimed to represent progress and instituted freedom of worship so that his conservative Protestant views could flourish; he also insisted on making English the primary language, offered grants of land to U.S. citizens who would immigrate, and made slavery legal. In 1860 an army from several Central American countries defeated Walker's forces and executed him.

Russian presence in Beijing, *China*, which began in the later seventeenth century and was expanded under treaty rights in the eighteenth, became particularly fruitful in the nineteenth. Father Iakinf (Hyacinth) Birchurin (1777–1853) was the son of a village priest in Kazan. He received a church education, and served as an abbot and then rector of a seminary before he was named an archimandrite. He caused difficulties in Irkutsk, was transferred to Tobolsk in order to teach, but was forbidden to preach. There he proved himself and was appointed the head of Russia's mission in China, where he served for fourteen years.

In Beijing he angered the Russian authorities, but his accomplishments were important. He immersed himself in Chinese language and culture. When he left in 1821 he loaded fifteen camels with his library. Imprisoned for a time, his linguistic work led to his freedom and recognition by the Russian and French academies. He had developed his skills by dressing in Chinese clothes, frequenting the markets and asking anyone to tell him the name of the thing he pointed to. Then he would ask for someone to write the sign and repeat the pronunciation. Over four years he and his Chinese teacher created a small Chinese–Russian dictionary. With that type of investigative technique he composed many writings not only on Chinese language and culture, but also on the people of Tibet, Mongolia and other parts of Central Asia. He was the foremost European Sinologist in the first half of the nineteenth century.

A later leader of the Russian mission, Archimandrite Carpov, *translated* the Gospel readings of the liturgy into Chinese. The usefulness of these Russian translators and their dictionaries was finally rewarded in the Tianjin treaty of 1858 in which mission representatives were allowed to evangelize in areas outside Beijing. Thus in the 1860s Chinese participated in the Orthodox worship services at Dunding'an village. Archimandrite Palladii also had liturgical pieces translated into Chinese and had some families baptized. In the late 1880s and 1890s Orthodox liturgies were performed in Hankou, Tianjin, Kalgan and Urga. But the Boxer rebellion of 1900 decimated the Chinese Orthodox through outright murder or fearful abandonment. The mission had created Russian Sinology and served Russian political and economic interests in Beijing well, but its Chinese Christian communities did not grow strong.

Christianity had been banned in *Japan* since 1639. Thus there was joy in Christian communities the world over when Japan was reopened to the West in 1859. Roman Catholic missionaries set sail and arrived in some numbers during the 1860s. Their European mindset, however, had a strong and rather negative influence on their sense of mission. The papacy feared the developments in Europe and set itself against nearly all aspects of Modernism. So certain was the pope that European culture was a vicious opponent that papal advice about Japan could hardly have been open to Japanese culture. The strategy was to re-enter the country and pick up the pieces from the great successes of the sixteenth century. Also the Rites Controversy that involved names for God, the proper celebration of sacraments, and Asian, particularly Buddhist, understandings of funerals and ancestors was still perceived as settled in favor of European decisions. The Jesuit missions of Francis Xavier, Matteo Ricci, and Alessandro Valignano, which chose to work from within Asian cultures toward an Asian Christianity, were despised and branded heretical.

There were several difficulties with the application of that official strategy in the Japanese context. First, the 1614 law that made becoming a Christian illegal was not repealed by the 1859 agreements. From 1869 to 1873 four thousand Christians on Kyūshū were exiled to the northern regions. None was slain but all suffered and some died in the harsh climate. The results were not all negative, however. In the 1880s those laws against Christian conversion were seldom enforced. Second, a growing group of upper class Japanese found aspects of Western cultures both interesting and acceptable. In those circles there seemed to be little point to making Christianity look more Japanese. It was more attractive when it was Western. Third, Catholic missionaries not only discovered Protestant Christian groups but also remnants of the seventeenth-century Japanese Christians who during persecution had kept and developed their grasp of practice and faith. Neither of these surviving groups of Christians automatically accepted nineteenth-century Roman teachings as the entire truth.

Catholic missionaries had widely differing views about how to proceed. Some of the French found Japanese far too difficult to speak; others thought that they must develop fluency at all costs. In Nagasaki one group insisted that the Latin–Portuguese tradition of the seventeenth century must be followed because it was the culture of Japanese Christians who had suffered through two hundred years of persecution. But others in Yokohama wanted to use an alphabet of Chinese characters, employed successfully in China, to write Japanese because the Yokohama peasants had had no contact with the seventeenth-century Catholic mission.

As attempts were made to enfold the Japanese Christians in contemporary Catholicism, some believers who had come through the fire of persecution saw no reason to be assimilated into this new Catholicism. They wanted to be left alone to live out the faith that had served them so well. These *kakure Kirishitan* – 'hidden Christians' – feared the return of oppression.

Other problems emerged. The hidden Christians had developed their own offices, one man responsible for leading worship and another for baptizing. If their baptisms were invalid because proper priests did not administer them, all would lose face. Marriage was viewed not as a sacrament but as a contract that could be invalidated. No Eucharistic celebrations were a part of their worship. The people celebrated various indigenous festivals; they often recited prayers in butchered Latin that they could not understand. They had their own Bible, the *Tenchi*, that included concepts, terms and stories from Buddhism and Japanese folklore. Furthermore they had learned to make crosses of paper that could be concealed in various places, particularly in the sleeves of a kimono. In numerous ways they had become an indigenous Christianity that few of the Catholic missionaries knew how to reform without mortally wounding. Perhaps most importantly, the missionaries had no education in Shinto or Buddhist teachings and practices. They knew nothing of Japanese folk culture. Thus they could neither recognize the interweavings nor ask proper questions about the inculturation of Christian practice and faith that had already occurred. Their authoritarian background in European Catholicism and their sense of their superior culture did not serve them well. Catholic missionaries found no way to develop the pastoral care that would have strengthened the Christian characteristics of these believers and critically encouraged their attempts at contextualization.

Protestant missionaries accepted much of nineteenth-century Japanese culture as well as that of their own homelands. The more conservative among them were on guard, but, unlike the Roman Catholics, Protestants had some mass conversions. At times they also had intensive discussions with leaders of Japanese religions.

Protestants made some missionary attempts in *Korea* even as early as the 1860s, but the first real penetration came with the entry of Horace Allen (1858–1932) in 1884. A medical doctor, he cured a prince in the Korean royal house. That led to his appointment as court physician, then to diplomatic service first as the leader of a Korean legation to the United

States and then as ambassador from the United States to Korea. The Korean court set up a Western hospital so that Allen's approaches to illness would be available. His elevation into the highest levels of Korean politics was a cultural coup for Christians who for so long had been treated as pariahs. The contacts made by the Korean delegation that Allen led to his home country resulted in a series of modernization projects undertaken by United States business firms in Korea: railroads, bridges, electrical plants, water systems. Allen also supported Korean independence from China and Japan. He was viewed as a Korean patriot.

Mission work among the Maori in *New Zealand* had experienced some success near the beginning of the nineteenth century, but missionaries were uncertain of its depth. The Maori had their own aboriginal culture that had served them well since at least the tenth century. The sea and their land produced the food they needed; their society was organized in ways that usually supported peace. Even their wars to avenge damage done to kin, and thus to avoid shame, were fought with wooden clubs so that death was not regularly the result: most battles left warriors wounded and bruised. The Maori heard what various missionaries said but they did not find much if any of it significant. Only a few converted to the new faith; most stayed around just to get the iron artifacts that helped them with their daily tasks.

The increasing availability of guns changed the situation in a dramatic way. When the Maori factions found that they could compete on the field of combat only if they had firearms, many died in each skirmish. Eventually a large group of the Maori came to the missionaries asking for more teaching about loving one another. They had calculated that if they continued to live with their warring customs of revenge now enacted with guns, they might annihilate each other. They needed radical change to survive. When they arrived at the mission station to proclaim their decision, the missionaries were overwhelmed. They had never anticipated such a mass conversion and still wondered why it was not like their own evangelical conversions through facing up to guilt for personal sin.

As might be expected, other Maori fought to keep their ways and used firearms to protect their land from invading whites. A series of wars marked the last half of the century. Yet peace eventually prevailed. During that peace the former mission work of translating scripture into the Maori tongue, creating hymns and finding ways in which the Maori could keep much of their culture became invaluable assets.

Russian Orthodox missionaries started the most successful Christian mission to any North American Amerindians on Kodiak Island, *Alaska* in 1794. Drawing from the deep Orthodox missiology that went back to Cyril and Methodius among the Slavs during the ninth century, these missionaries were balanced and effective. Their overland travel toward Alaska allowed them to see how monks in different places had learned indigenous languages, affirmed all they could of those cultures and supported vital churches of native people.

Hieromonk Joasaph and nine others, four of whom were priests, represented the first overseas mission of the Russian Orthodox Church. They went to work at the Kodiak trading outpost of Gregory Shelikov, who had bragged to the St. Petersburg metropolitan that many natives had been baptized and needed spiritual direction. He promised all the supplies the party would need. What the missionaries found upon arrival, however, were no church buildings, no supplies and an outpost culture that had little interest in Orthodoxy and less respect for the Sugpiaq people of the island. Trappers considered nothing to be the property of the Amerindians, cheated them in trade, and took their women as concubines whom they had no intention of marrying.

After their experience with the traders the Amerindians found the kindness of the monks unexpected and received it openly. These Christians, at first working through good interpreters, wanted to learn the Amerindian's language and culture. Their worldview had many aspects that were compatible with Christian practice and teaching. Their family structures and their ethical lives would have put the traders to shame had the traders believed enough to be shamed. The monks went round the island and moved into the interior with their message. Within two years, seven thousand Sugpiaq had been baptized. Their villages were left intact and their culture was supported in many important ways. The Sugpiaq became Sugpiaq Christians, not 'Russian Christians' who would be even less esteemed than Russian Christian serfs. The Amerindian godson of a monk, a young man known to Bishop Joasaph, became an important chief. He understood that he had the power and the position to resist the trading company and its leaders.

As Orthodox missionaries moved throughout the region into areas occupied by different Amerindians, they were not always well received. Hiermonk Iuvenalii, who tried to preach from his kayak, was killed by arrows launched at the command of a shaman. But other tribes, particularly the Aleuts, found so much of their own religion enhanced or fulfilled in Christian practice and faith that they converted village by village. The inspiring life of the Orthodox hermit Father Hermann, who healed the sick with the sanctified waters of a spring near his dwelling, fit the best ideals of the shamans. In similar ways Father Hermann so impressed the Russian governor of Kodiak that the relations between Europeans and Amerindians were improved.

William Carey (1761–1834), a Baptist missionary, was sent from England to *India*. His family was Anglican and accustomed to books in the home, but their poverty meant that the bright lad served as a cobbler's apprentice rather than going to school. In young manhood Carey became a Baptist and was impressed by some Baptist and Dissenting pastors who were insightfully and passionately interested in mission. He rejected the more prevalent Calvinist Baptist view that if God wanted the nations to be saved, God would do it. In 1792 he published *An Enquiry into the Obligations of Christians, to Use Means for the Conversion of the Heathens*. He successfully urged other Baptists to organize a mission society for the purpose of training, supporting and sending evangelists. The society eventually carried the name Baptist Missionary Society.

By 1793 Carey and his family arrived in Calcutta, but only survived because he got work as the manager of an indigo plantation further inland in Bengal. His unsuccessful struggle to obtain the proper permits led him in 1799 to locate at Serampore, thirteen miles upriver from Calcutta, in a Danish colony. His major contribution lay in the study of language. He not only taught Bengali and Sanskrit at Fort William College in Calcutta, he also, with a group of helpers that included Indians, created biblical translations into dozens of Indian languages. Serampore College was one of his educational ventures.

In many cases Carey urged missionaries to accept much of the Indian culture. *Sati*, the burning of a man's wife on his funeral bier, sickened him, and he vigorously opposed it. But the eventual split in 1827 between the experienced missionaries at Serampore and the young evangelicals sent by the Baptist Missionary Society grew out of the newer colleagues' sense that much more cultural change, viewed as proper piety, should be demanded of the Indians.

Adoniram Judson (1788–1850) led the first mission effort of American Baptists. Educated at Brown University and Andover Newton Seminary, he failed in his application to the London Missionary Society. The group that eventually supported his family and the Newells for service overseas was the American Board of Commissioners for Foreign Missions that he and fellow college students had founded in 1810. During the voyage the Judsons, who were Congregationalists, studied Baptist positions on baptism and then followed them in their mission. The East India Company refused to let the couples enter India, so they made their way to Rangoon, *Burma* (Myanmar) in 1813. By 1824, Judson had finished an English–Burmese dictionary and some translations of scripture. But his wife, Ann, who early on had trouble with the language, had become a better speaker because she ran the household. She also founded a school and was responsible for the translations of the biblical books Daniel and Jonah.

Not long after they moved to Ava, the seat of the Burmese government, Adoniram was accused of being a British spy. Badly treated for twenty-one months during the Anglo-Burmese war, his survival depended on Ann, who took the children with her from prison to prison and provided him food. Worn out by her labors, she died at age thirty-eight, so much a part of the mission that her dying words were in Burmese. After losing her, Adoniram moved to Moulmein in 1828, where he started a church and a school and finished the Burmese Bible in 1834. He also published a Burmese liturgy, a life of Christ and completed the English–Burmese section of a dictionary.

While in Rangoon, Judson built a *zayat*, the type of building in which Burmese men sat and talked. By accepting both their architecture and their notion of a gathering place, he had created a space where he could teach Christian practice and faith more as an insider. Later he traveled to the larger cities in order to talk with non-Christians and made a series of visits to the Karen people.

Robert Morrison (1782–1834) reached Canton, *China* in 1807, the first recorded Protestant missionary in the country. Selected as a missionary by the London Missionary Society after not only a theological education in an academy linked to the society but also studying medicine, astronomy and Chinese in London, he became a translator for the East India Company, a position with legal status. Chinese officials, however, stood against his having any relationships with Chinese. A remarkable linguist, by 1813 he and his companions had translated the New Testament and by 1819 the entire Bible. He also compiled a three-volume Chinese–English dictionary (1815–23) and a Chinese grammar. Furthermore he translated English hymns and an English prayer book into Chinese.

Some Protestant missionaries derided the Catholics in spite of Catholic acceptance of persecution even to death. To these Protestants, the Catholic strategy of invading the country as Confucian scholars, depending upon unspiritual scientific means, may have taken them to Beijing but had not enabled them to convert the common people. Catholic missionaries insisted that the Protestants did not come with the spirituality necessary to stay and die. The Protestants worked like merchants in centers along the coasts, throwing Bibles from ships to shore. Since the nineteenth century brought waves of persecution for all Christians, it is shameful that more missionaries could not find ways to honor each other's efforts. Some Protestants like Karl Gützlaff (1803–51) acknowledged the Catholics' ability to accept martyrdom. He called other Protestants, however, to do better because they were not restrained by following the pope but were freed by their devotion to the true prince of the church, Jesus Christ.

Recognizing that they could not penetrate the inner provinces of China, Protestant missionaries constructed a 'wall of light' including some of China's coastal cities and other centers nearby: Singapore, Penang, Malacca, Bangkok, etc. Macao usually provided a safe harbor but was subject to the pressure of the eighty-five percent Chinese population who ruled themselves and treated foreigners with suspicion. The attempt within this wall of light was to bring European culture, with its apparently superior science, to the Chinese as a type of natural theology from which the gospel could be preached. Too few of the Protestants attempted to learn the Chinese classics and employ them as a bridge for bringing in the gospel. They learned the language, produced dictionaries and grammars, and thus positioned themselves for good communication. But they too seldom thought of their Western culture as one among many; to them it was the best of all. As part of his mission effort, Elijah Bridgman (1801–61), an expert in Chinese and a Bible translator, also wrote a two-volume history of his homeland, the United States, in order that the Chinese might receive a proper view of this Western nation which they might emulate. Catholic missionaries might have lost their seventeenth-century position in Beijing as experts in the transfer of Western science to the Chinese and been compelled by threatening circumstances to deal more often with more common folk. But the Protestant efforts to engage the Chinese intellectuals, particularly in Canton through the Society for the Diffusion of Useful Knowledge, never recognized fully the rich wisdom and religious heritage of the Chinese.

The largest single blots on Christian expansion in China during the nineteenth century were the Opium War of 1839–42 and the treaties between the Western powers and China that followed during 1842–60. British naval power proved supreme. Ships blockaded the ports and sailed up the rivers to gain the victory. For Western political and economic experts, the purpose of the war seemed reasonable. The balance of payments created by the goods that the British bought could be turned to their favor if they could sell opium to the Chinese. What was an English gentleman without tea at a proper price? Protestant missionaries, who often had little understanding of such things and trusted their governments to save them, waited for the conflict to subside. The French put their toe in the water and during the process created various treaties that protected Catholic missionaries.

Almost all missionaries knew that opium addiction was an evil. But the Protestants neither accepted the long Catholic tradition that emphasized suffering for Christ nor were especially adept at questioning economic and political power. Nearly every missionary of whatever stripe found God's finger in the new legal standing that the treaties had secured. Even Catholics, after years of unsettled and usually illegal existence, were pleased to see they could work well in this new context. But it was a context of power, not of weakness, not one that featured commitment unto death as the key to life. Now it was political agreements and armed force that created the climate for evangelism. In ways that few Westerners in that century could appreciate, foreign Christian missionaries and indigenous Chinese believers were often perceived as agents of foreign destructive might. As more than one Chinese national claimed, the West brought two gifts that the Chinese had not asked for and did not want: opium and Christianity. What a tragic pairing.

The missionaries who worked in China had some insight into the issues of the day. Those who spent the bulk of their time in translation projects had to pay attention to Chinese language and culture; they had to listen to native speakers who could tell them if their attempts induced anger or laughter. Such conversations often turned to wider questions about life. No mission that tried diligently to communicate in the various tongues of China did total harm. Some individual missionaries like Karl Gützlaff had a humane vision. An independent missionary, supported by no society, and finally a Chinese interpreter in the British foreign service, he called for every Christian effort in China to be based on justice and toleration. Believers in Christ should be noted for their generosity, honesty and work for reconciliation. And as quickly as possible, indigenous Chinese should be responsible for the task of evangelism. He was so dedicated to that principle that young leaders with too little training soon failed in the field. He wrote back to Europe and insisted that China was not closed and thus he had strong influence in firing Christians' imagination about the possibilities. But neither his vision nor its execution was strong enough to win the day.

The largest, perhaps the only, indigenous movement of Chinese people toward belief in Jesus occurred in the mid 1800s. The effect of the Opium Wars in South China was dreadful. In the 1840s silver followed the opium, trade became difficult to sustain, and many found no work. A devastating famine made all conditions worse. When the Manchu authorities tried to restore order, common people simmered with disdain for rulers who had signed away their livelihoods to the foreigners. Change was in the air.

Hong Xiuquan, born in 1814 in a small village into a lower class Hakka family, tried to better his life by passing the civil service exams in Canton. When he failed he collapsed from mental and physical exhaustion. During his recovery he had a vivid vision of being carried to heaven, meeting the aged Creator and watching him rebuke Confucius for not keeping people from demon worship. Another figure in the dream, the Elder Brother, called Hong to kill demons. What Hong had seen made little sense to him until he read some Christian tracts he had acquired in Canton. Then he realized the Creator was God, the Elder Brother was Jesus, and the demons were the idols so commonly worshipped. Hong and some of his cousins became forceful iconoclasts who destroyed idols, renounced a number of Buddhist practices and won thousands of followers.

Contact with an archconservative Baptist missionary in Canton for the purpose of learning more about Christian practice and faith turned sour. Hong did attend Bible classes that depended upon memorization. But problems in language (he spoke Hakka; the missionary Issachar Roberts [1802–71] primarily spoke Cantonese) and petty jealousies kept him from further instruction. Even his request for baptism was rebuffed. When the Taiping Movement grew strong, controlling much of central China through successful battles against the Manchu armies and thus attracting dissidents from many corners, Roberts went to Nanking and stayed for almost two years. But once again Roberts's strong beliefs and Hong's passionate vision proved to be at odds.

For most of the Taiping Movement's leaders Jesus was not fully divine like God. They often thought of themselves as divine figures. Hong said he was the second son of God, a brother of Jesus. At times he said he was Melchizedek. Others in the forefront of the group claimed that God came down to earth, took over their bodies and spoke through them. The Old Testament dominated their teaching; more Old Testament texts than New Testament ones may have been available to them in translations they could understand. In many ways they tried to take the teachings they had learned from Holy Writ and favorably compare them with Confucian practices and doctrines that the people already knew.

The Taiping Movement had features of Christian teaching that were characteristic of heretical movements. As Arians of the ancient period did, Hong and his followers insisted on Jesus being a secondary figure in order to demand the worship of one God in the midst of Chinese polytheism. Taiping visions and incarnations sound like those of Montanist prophets. Their view of Mary as the wife of God allowed the divine family to be properly balanced. It was not too different from the practice of some Irish Catholic mothers telling their children to pray to God's mother because she could persuade him.

The Taiping Movement's practices, however, reflected in so many ways the best that Christians have ever offered. Some of their morality might be seen as too strict: no intoxicants, whether opium, tobacco or wine. They stood against gambling, slavery, polygamy, foot binding and prostitution. Setting up a theocracy based on the Old Testament and following ancient Chinese administrative codes, they brought in social revolution. They tried to displace the landlords' and thus the warlords' power by rebuking private ownership. Women held positions of authority in both military and civil arenas because they were equal. Jesus' preference for the helpless was also honored with special care for the downtrodden.

Indigenous Christian movements often have such varied features. Sadly in this case no missionary was able to stay in contact with these folk long enough to assist them in what they did well and to guide them in the doctrines where they were weak, even wrong headed. It might not have been possible. But the Taiping reforms, if followed throughout China, would have put in place on a Christian/Confucian platform many of the changes that Mao later erected on a Communist base.

Conflict between nationalist Chinese and Christians, both foreign missionaries and indigenous believers, intensified during the last decade of the nineteenth century, starting in central China and ending with the Boxer rebellion centered in Beijing. The anti-Christian, anti-foreign forces were strong in parts of the provinces of Shandong, Zili, Shanxi as well as southern Manchuria. The battles were finally won by the troops of eight foreign nations, partly because the rebels' vicious attacks on people and property infuriated the non-Chinese, and partly because those nations still thought that their treaties from the Opium Wars were worth defending. Both foreign missionaries and diplomats had paid little attention to the rising anger. Between 1860 and 1874 over four hundred incidents are recorded in which missionaries and converts were killed and anything that seemed Western and modern was destroyed. Most of the Westerners could not believe that their 'superior' way would be rejected.

In the *United States* during the nineteenth century many Christians found both the culture and the political system of the country to represent the best of Christian practice and faith. Such views did not, however, entail that all the citizens of the democracy were Christian through and through. A series of revivals before mid-century called people to change their practices and renew their faith. In the eastern, western (now called 'midwestern') and southern sections of the country outbreaks of enthusiasm marked by singing through the chest, barking up trees and falling down in a faint showed the power of these movements. They attacked prostitution, alcohol – any practice they considered to be a major vice.

The traditions and viewpoints that led to the Civil War formed the most difficult problems in the culture. Slavery issues, seen as both Christian and economically necessary by the South and both unchristian and economically weakening by the North, focused the conflict. But regional and even topographical situations aggravated almost everything. All along the Appalachian chain from West Virginia into Tennessee and Alabama, small farm families shared nothing vital with Southern planters and thus either stayed out of the Confederacy or had their men shanghaied into service. The industrial strength of the Union eventually settled the conflict. Reconstruction in the South wracked an area already exhausted. Most Protestant denominations broke apart. The different regional cultures tended to shape Christian practice and faith.

One of the most influential cultural changes in Europe and North America during this period centered on the evolutionary theory of Charles Darwin, specifically his *Origin of Species* (1859). The work relied upon the observations that Darwin had made about animal life on the Galapagos Islands. Some of the first Christian reviewers found good sense in the volume. It represented no threat to their belief or practice. Previous critical reading of the Bible, championed by a handful of European scholars, had opened the way. But other Christians saw the entire structure of their faith endangered. Science and religion seemed to be on a collision course. Darwin's own view of Christian practice and faith was mixed. The virulent attacks on his theory and its implications could not have pleased him. But for whatever reasons, perhaps only his belief in the spreading of British culture as a help to humankind, in 1872 he wrote in support of the Tierra del Fuego Mission and requested that he be elected an honorary member of the South American Mission Society. In this instance and in others like his support of Christian missions for the hungry and homeless in British cities, he saw no reason to attack believers as the enemies of his science.

A CHRISTIAN CORE

This great century of *European* Christian world mission led to a number of questions about the central features of practice and faith. Many of those leaving their homelands took their denominational and national understandings with them. The mission societies that supported them warned about the importance of not making the new Christians in foreign lands first into Europeans and then into Christians. Such advice appeared in more than one society constitution. But because missionaries most often were true believers, they had a sense that their vision, even in intricate detail, was the correct one. The consequent struggles were not merely between Catholics and Protestants but also between Catholic orders like the Dominicans and the Jesuits, the latter fully restored by the papacy in 1814 after being suppressed in 1773. Disagreements between Protestant denominations also marked the landscape. As large as the globe is, many missionaries from the different groups popped up alongside each other with conflicting views of what it meant to be Christian. What made baptism and the Eucharist valid? Who could preach and teach? How did an authentic church emerge and carry out its life together?

The competing national interests of European and North American countries added fuel to these fires outside Europe, but they were burning with destructive force in Europe itself. Among Catholics, the first ecumenical council since Trent, designated as Vatican I, met in Rome in 1869–70 to discuss numerous issues of theology and ecclesiastical discipline. The revolutionary character of politics in Italy made a strongly conservative position most attractive. It looked as if the freedom fighters who wanted to unify Italy into a single nation found the Roman church to be a hindrance. War between France and Prussia broke out in 1870 just one day after the important decision on papal infallibility; the conflict took French troops out of Rome and in effect ended the council's major decisions.

The affirmation of *papal infallibility* came from the center of this conservative gathering. A majority of the French delegation in particular wanted the pope to be able to speak without opposition on any topic he chose, from positions of both primacy among the bishops and an inability to make errors. A small minority of the council, including John Henry Newman (1801–90) and Johann Joseph Ignaz von Döllinger (1799–1890), thought that the infallibility of the church, not the papacy, was the major doctrine; a pope in concert with councils and bishops could state incontrovertible teachings. The accepted document, however, declared that when the primary bishop, the pope, spoke from his throne, *ex cathedra*, on matters of faith and practice, he could not be opposed. In the midst of the ever-shifting European conflicts in culture and war during the nineteenth century, many thought that something solid needed to dominate the church. This understanding of broad but limited papal power seemed to fit the conditions. It led to declarations concerning a series of dogmas that the council proclaimed in response to Modernism. But it made the already difficult claim of Catholicism to be the true church one that many more Christians would oppose.

Catholic missionaries re-entered *Ethiopia* during the nineteenth century and found enough success that they had dreams of moving the entire country toward Catholicism. The country was economically weak and Ethiopian Orthodox bishops and priests offered little assistance. Despite previous débâcles when Roman missionaries entered the land, the people seemed willing to listen. The Italian Justin de Jacobis (1800–60) was a man of deep spiritual gifts and discipline. He loved the people and their culture so much that he worked for reform (conversion) from within the Ethiopian Orthodox Ge'ez liturgy. He persuaded several influential individuals to become Catholics, particularly political leaders, and was wise enough to ordain many priests, including married men. His arrest by the Orthodox abuna Salama in 1855 ended his ministry. His most significant convert was the Coptic priest and later martyr Ghebra-Mika'el (1791–1855), who died after months of torture by the Coptic authorities. During his eleven years as a Catholic, Ghebra-Mika'el wrote a catechism and translated into Amharic a volume about ethics.

About a half-dozen missionaries from the Protestant Christian Missionary Society entered Ethiopia in the nineteenth century. Plain biblical people, they hoped to reform the Ethiopian church by ridding it of its errant practices: prayer to Mary and various saints, 'worship' of icons, kissing the cross, excessive fasts and strong support of monasteries. But although these missionaries created a translation of the Bible, eventually with parallel columns of Ge'ez and Amharic, and thus demonstrated their recognition that vernacular translations were necessary in various regions like Tigre, they ultimately failed. Johann Martin Flad (1831–1915) was one who accepted a mission to the Falashas, an Ethiopian Jewish minority. Being forced to baptize them into the Ethiopian Orthodox Church greatly displeased him. Indeed some of the Protestant missionaries had an arrogance that exceeded even the seventeenth-century haughtiness of the Catholic Alphonsus Mendez. At least Mendez knew that liturgy and ritual should not be disdained. Samuel Gobat (1799–1879) could not stomach Marian devotion and thus alienated many Ethiopian Christians despite his open personality, good intentions and later success in Malta, where he edited a translation of the Bible into Arabic.

The *African* Samuel Adjai (Ajayi) Crowther (*c.* 1807–91) was born into an Egba family, part of the Yoruba people in present-day Nigeria. Sold into slavery by Fulani and Yoruba Muslim traders, he was resold many times, finally to Portuguese slavers. A British vessel rescued him, and the captain gave him his freedom in Sierra Leone. Converted to Christ, he showed himself to be a brilliant student and became a teacher. Particularly gifted in language studies, he assisted two English missionaries in learning African languages, eventually traveled to England for an education with the Church Missionary Society in London, and finally was ordained to ministry. Only a few Africans had attained that Anglican recognition.

Returning to Yorubaland, he had the privilege of leading his mother and sister to faith in Christ. His part in translating a Yoruba Bible of remarkable quality that influenced other African translations was most significant. With the assistance of the Church Missionary Society, led by Henry Venn (1796–1873), Crowther set up a mission station in 1857 on the Niger river. No English workers were involved, only Africans, some from Sierra Leone. Venn saw in Crowther the chance to have an African 'three-self' church: self-governing, self-supporting, self-propagating. By

1864 Venn had achieved Crowther's appointment as 'Bishop of the countries of Western Africa beyond the Queen's dominions'.

The success was short-lived. During the 1880s British missionaries doubted both the moral fiber and the efficiency of the mission. Racial attitudes reared their ugly heads; a conservative evangelical theology found the African theology deficient. The policies of the mission society had shifted after Venn's death. Money was sent with destructive conditions. Young European missionaries assumed control, and the African leaders were let go or sent elsewhere. When Crowther died in 1891, his successor was a European bishop. The death of this mission had much more to do with European attitudes of superiority than any lack of effectiveness in the work of Crowther and his staff. A stunning opportunity was forfeited.

William Taylor (1821–1902) embodied a challenge to Methodists and their mission work. Born in Virginia, he worked in San Francisco (1849–56) in a street mission to native Indians and Chinese immigrants as well as the diseased and poverty-stricken, but his building burned down. Traveling to raise money for his work, he went to Australia, New Zealand and finally South Africa. In 1866 his preaching to blacks in South Africa stirred many. In South India (1870–5) he founded self-supporting, self-governing and self-propagating churches under the name 'Methodist Episcopal' that paid no attention to established denominational agreements about where they could be planted. Methodists tried to declare these churches part of their mission work but the churches refused such designation. In their eyes they were authentic without Methodist oversight. After being elected the Methodist Episcopal missionary bishop for Africa in 1884, Taylor started other churches in Liberia, Sierra Leone, Angola, Mozambique and Belgian Congo (Democratic Republic of the Congo). Radical Methodist, Holiness and pentecostal missions around the world saw Taylor as a hero because he resisted church hierarchies and succeeded in planting congregations.

The mission activity of the Russian Orthodox throughout the massive *Russian Empire* seldom receives the attention it deserves. Perhaps because Russian church leaders viewed their church as the third Rome and were constantly involved in translating various Greek and Slavonic Christian documents into Russian, they had a mind for the need of translating scripture into local tongues. That was an enormous task, given the numerous peoples who lived within mother Russia from her western borders in Europe to her eastern border in Alaska with Canada. In the early twentieth century when thorough German scholars wanted to write a complete history of biblical translation, they wrote a rather perfunctory letter to the Moscow patriarch inquiring if the Russian church had made any transla-tions of scripture. The patriarch responded that he would send copies. The German team was rather shocked when what arrived was a railroad boxcar of books, packed with one volume per translation. The apparent conformity of Orthodoxy has often concealed a rich inculturation that has valued the local culture as it insisted on conciliar faith.

Russian Orthodox spirituality was enhanced by the project of Bishop Theophan the Recluse. He found the *Philocalia* of Macarius Notaras and Nicodemus so important that he spent years translating the Greek into Russian and enlarging the body of mystical and ascetic writings until it reached five volumes, published in 1876–90. His efforts, now available in a series of languages, have enriched the devotional life of many beyond Russian Orthodox circles.

CONCLUSION

The nineteenth century saw the greatest Christian missionary expansion in history. Christians in Europe and North America organized to send committed missionaries everywhere. Tales of obstinate superiority and gracious service came back from far away places. Catholic orders trained men and women to live the Christian gospel. In China they taught young people well and suffered martyrdom along with them. Yet neither they nor conservative Protestant missionaries found a way to assist the Taiping Christians, the only large indigenous Chinese movement toward Christ that appeared in that country.

Much of Christian mission growth occurred among Protestants. They went out into the world to save the heathens. Some from upper classes went teaching European achievements to the 'poor devils' who needed that advancement in order to qualify for Christian faith. Their schools did much good; indeed their myriad scripture translations into native tongues kept some of their cultural superiority in check. Only the native speakers could tell them if their attempts were helpful or ridiculous.

Missionaries who were not honored within their home cultures found the ways of those they went to serve to be extraordinary. They tried to live out Christian virtue and thus faced conflicts, for example with Indian *sati*, the burning of the widow with the dead husband. But often they dressed as the indigenous people did, ate their food and lived within many of their customs. As a result Christian faith and practice took on many native forms and in different places emerged within indigenous movements.

The best Christian works found aspects of the great world religions or the native traditional ones that could be affirmed without threatening the authenticity of Christian faith and life. Sometimes the conflicts were bitter. But those who stayed long term sometimes did act as midwives in the births of Chinese, African or Indian communities who loved both Christ and their cultures. They encouraged new and older Christians in those cultures (and in others) to live out and believe in a Christian existence that was not Western. Along with their family members in Latin America, they were growing toward becoming the majority of Christians on the globe.

8 POST-CHRISTENDOM WEST, NON-WESTERN CHRISTIANS, 1900–2000

Two world wars and the threat of global annihilation during a third conflict, the Cold War, dominated the twentieth century. In 1914 the European monarchies, interlocked by marriage and treaties, honored their commitments and began what each alliance thought would be a short conflict decided by their own dominating military force. The First World War burned over Europe for four years with an unimagined carnage. Technology had advanced so far beyond the Napoleonic Wars and even the Prussian conflicts of the previous century that no one had any inkling of what would occur. The battles soon settled down into trench warfare that the new machine guns, tanks and poison gas could not break. Only the entrance of the United States offered enough men and weapons to tip the scales. Yet even the winners suffered in ways that had not been predicted. One English writer Vera Brittain (1893–1970), who had studied at Oxford in the new women's college, went to the front as a nurse. The butchery broke her health. Not long after the end of the war, not a single man was alive from her circle nor any from that of her dead brother. A spirit of dread fell on Europe which did not extend to the United States. Christian hope and resurrection seemed broken reeds.

One of the most unexpected results of this bloodbath was the rise of Marxism in Russia. Marx and Engels thought their views would eventually prevail in the British Isles. German assistance put Lenin in Russia, and European volunteer armies did not bring victory for the Bolsheviks' opponents. Orthodox Christianity was not prepared for the rancor that many poured out on its centuries-long support of the czars.

Japan saw its chance and hacked off chunks of Russian territory that had been in dispute for years. Its invasion of Korea put the Christians there in mortal danger and welded their fate to that of Korean nationalism. Christians created printing that used Korean script rather than Japanese. Becoming a Christian often involved being a Korean patriot.

The war of 1914–18 was a world war not simply because anything involving Europe and the United States was a world affair. Christian missionary expansion had sailed on the ships that the great economic powers had sent round the world. New African Christians struggled to understand how Christians from various European nations could fight it out on African soil for supremacy in Europe. The power of European nationalism to undermine ecumenical Christian commitment had been unknown to them. They learned a sad lesson. Christians could have overriding concerns that brought them into deadly combat. When the pressure of economic and social change intruded and nationalistic dreams were involved, European Christians had no difficulty killing each other.

After only twenty years of respite the Second World War broke out. This time the conflict was even more global and the atrocities more frequent. The human dimensions of the Holocaust were astounding, even more so if non-Jewish victims are included. The Nazi attempt to create a pure race involved the annihilation of any who were weak or deformed. Poison gas did not dominate the fighting, but air power brought saturation bombing of civilian targets. Clausewitz's total war approached. The end came in Europe with Allied forces overwhelming Germany and in Asia with the United States dropping two atomic bombs on Japan, the second one, ironically, descending on the very city, Nagasaki, that in the sixteenth century had been home to most of Japan's 300,000 Christians.

The Cold War saw the Soviet Union and the United States squared off to determine the ruler of the globe. Conflicts like those in Korea and Vietnam pitted the two political systems and cultures in regions where influence was the issue. In both the United States and Russia, Christians often supported their own. Capitalism as a 'Christian' cause was defended against 'godless' Communism. Russian patriots backed mother Russia through a system that depended on tyranny and persecution, led for years by a dropout from an Orthodox seminary, Josef Stalin. The cause of Christ suffered in both countries.

CHRISTIANS AND PEOPLE OF OTHER FAITHS

At the beginning of the twentieth century, European missions to *African* peoples were still not the highest priority. The Protestant mission conference held at Edinburgh in 1910 hoped to focus the evangelical interest of Europe on presenting Christ to all nations by 2000. Enthusiasm was high, but the conference had rather small interest in Africa. African-American delegates and foreign missionaries who served in the continent were invited. For years, however, missionary societies and individual Christian leaders had insisted that the most talented candidates should be sent to areas of high culture like China or India. There the struggle to demonstrate the pre-eminence of European culture over long-established cultures would be a demanding task. Students recognized as having lesser gifts were sent to Africa, but neither in the numbers nor with the support of those sent elsewhere.

Two ironic consequences of this conference have been, first, that Christians have not taken over the globe and displaced other world religions, and second, that in the twentieth century Africa has seen the greatest growth in Christian communities of any continent on earth. The number of Christians in Africa now is greater than the number of people who live in the United States. Missionary activity after 1885 grew extensively to the point that in 1910 perhaps ten thousand people – four thousand Protestants and six thousand Catholics – were working in the continent. About three thousand of these missionaries, however, worked in South Africa, enjoying its mild climate. They had taken advantage of the political and economic interests their countries had in Africa, not the least its gold, and had flowed in with the tide. But a force of nearly seven thousand Christians, including some Jamaican blacks and African-Americans particularly in Cameroon, Belgian Congo (Democratic Republic of the Congo), Sierra Leone and Liberia, served in other areas – though only a few in French West Africa (Niger, Mali, Mauritania). The foreign blacks too often were nearly as inculturated in the ways of their Jamaican and American homelands as were the whites. Both groups had difficulty understanding the native Africans. The Roman Catholic priests and nuns might not have been as attuned to the need for truly African Christians as a few Protestants were, but their lifetime vows put them in places where they stayed for decades and became familiar with the local culture. They were well organized and regularly trained local catechists to practice and teach the faith, although they were reluctant to ordain indigenous priests. In the Belgian Congo, for example, 6,400 catechists were largely responsible for the considerable growth of Christian communities.

After the Second World War more North American missionaries went to Africa, some of them still wanting to 'civilize the savages' but many others passionately committed to the emergence of genuine African Christian faith and practice. They often came from conservative Protestant groups in which missionary societies were seen as inefficient if not heretical. At the end of the century these independent approaches to mission represented the bulk of Christian mission from North America to the world.

Some of the most important communities among twentieth-century African Christians were the *African independent churches*, perhaps better called African-initiated or African indigenous churches. Although they might be noted for attractive parades through the streets of their local towns, dressed in white and dancing toward their area of worship, they also appeared in strength before they were widely noticed. Some missionaries from the United States who had been expelled from Ethiopia when a Communist government triumphed asked foreign missionaries in Tanzania whether a particular area of that country would be a good place to locate. The tribes among whom they had worked in western Ethiopia had clans in that region of Tanzania. The resident missionaries, reflecting life in their compounds, said that this would be a good region for evangelization, since they had had only moderate success. There was great need. But when the American missionaries went to the market in the largest town, they found that one African had been converted and had raised his sons to preach the gospel and now there were over two thousand Christians in the immediate area. The point of this example is to indicate how often indigenous African congregations grew up without foreign assistance and in the process became attractive to native peoples. The evangelization of the interior of Africa often occurred through such movements.

The charismatic character of many of these African-initiated churches points to both the experiences that led a number of their leaders to their powers of persuasion and also to the blending of African prophetic traditions and Christian experience in these congregations. These churches have been creative in assimilating features of African religious traditions into their practices in ways that have frightened European and North American missionaries. Their sense of contextualization has been penetrating, but never without difficulty. Drumming and dancing, so much a part of most African festivals, can dominate the Christian worship. The designation of Jesus Christ as *the* Ancestor has allowed the ultimate Christian claims for Jesus of Nazareth to appear in African dress. The respect for powerful nature, so strong in some equatorial areas with lush vegetation, has found a home in the acknowledgment of God the Creator, who may have already had both name and narrative in tribal lore and language. Even the Christ can be described as the forest canopy that brings coolness and protection, but also as the python who cannot be driven away with sticks.

As would be expected, some missionary leaders viewed these indigenous churches as wracked with syncretistic tendencies that did not distinguish properly between culture and faith and thus became subject to pagan formulations and practices. Occasionally, African evangelical Protestants have themselves asked penetrating questions. Are there not drum rhythms that should never be used in worship? But the power of these popular movements that could grow rapidly – like the Kimbanguists, for example – led to questions about the syncretism of the missionaries, their commitment to North American and European colonialism, and even queries about how African some Christian communities were. The African-initiated churches, whatever their stripe, found ways to operate within the demands for local, tribal and national identities. They are not a foreign religion with ties to colonial cultures. They are not pure and do present various practices and doctrines that need pastoral attention. But they cannot be ignored.

Christians in *Latin America* have had considerable contact with people who practice other religions. In Brazil the Afro-Brazilian religions like *Macumba*, *Candomblé*, *Xango* and *Umbanda*, represent the integration of religions brought to the country as the practices and beliefs of African slaves and religions already present as the indigenous practices and beliefs of Brazilian Amerindians. People who were formed by these religions often kept away from Christian influence or moved into Christianity and retained their previous ways. Probably the most important factor in these religions is their recognition of spirits, both benign and destructive, that dominate all of life. Many West African tribes that acknowledged a single high god, named and storied, also accepted a world of numerous spirits that demanded attention. Among Brazilian Amerindians there was a spirit reality that expressed itself in various forms. Mediums and prophets spoke the words of these spirits, sometimes clearly and at other times ambiguously in forms worthy of the Delphic oracle.

Portuguese Catholicism had its own idea of saints who influenced the lives of common people. At times a modern Brazilian Catholic procession seemed to carry not only that European tradition but also the fearful power of African and Amerindian spirits. Evangelical Protestants, who have become perhaps twenty-five percent of the Christians in Latin America, question such parades. Church of God missionaries arrived in Brazil as early as 1910. Now a strong influence in Brazil, such evangelicals have perceived both the Afro-Brazilian religions and their assimilation into Catholicism as dangerous and heretical. Many of these Christians have had pentecostal backgrounds; they have depended on the Holy Spirit and accepted charismatic gifts – spiritual powers – as vital to their sense of both themselves and their 'enemies'. In their view, spiritual warfare is central to the Christian life. Many who led this kind of Christian existence represented the lower classes of Brazil and have only recently begun to see the kind of influence they might have in public life. They have never been without social conscience, but have sometimes been unaware of all they might be able to do in the national arena.

Occasionally in Peru the stubborn persistence of old Inca customs has had frightening results. In the religious practices of that ancient tradition, human sacrifices were made to insure both the weather and the fertility of the soil for the coming season of raising crops. In the mountains – where the dirt is thin, the time of warmth necessary for plants to grow is limited and thus the whole process is always one of duress – human sacrifice ensured the crop. A young girl or a mature man was ritually killed at one of the sacred high places; the throat was slit, at times the head totally removed, and all the blood drained out. Even in the twentieth century Christian farmers disappeared and then were found mutilated in that way. The resulting grief was intense. But during a Christian funeral, not led by a priest, the response to the killing was a recognition of that person as more than a martyr. The Lord's Prayer could be offered with the person's name in the place of God: ' _____ our father, hallowed be your name. Your kingdom come, your will be done on earth as it is in heaven...' At the local level the sacrificed person had become another god.

Various twentieth-century Roman Catholic leaders have tried to work within the context of spiritual activity and to think through their relationship to political and social problems. *European* Catholic reaction to social reform has been too slow and at times extremely reactionary, not the least because Communism was viewed as a pagan atheistic religion. In many cases, however, that blinded some Catholic leaders to the plight of the poor and oppressed. For instance, in France worker-priests sought to live out their ordination in factories alongside the workers. They listened to descriptions of those people's lives, saw some good in Marxist critique of the conditions, but primarily embodied the gospel. Yet they were quickly perceived as a threat to conservative Roman Catholic truth and ecclesiastical power. They were disbanded.

In *China*, Chang T'ai-yen (Ping-lin, 1868–1936) was imprisoned by the Manchu government in 1904 for three years. He defended the non-theism of *Buddhism* and found its practices and teachings satisfying during his sentence. He wrote *On Atheism*, not in connection with the rise of Communism, but in an attempt to show that Christianity was an inferior form of Hindu theism. He found creation, incarnation and change odd for a God that was said to be changeless and self-sufficient. His views, however, were too rational for most Buddhists and his position on Christian theology too pointed for dialogue.

Karl Ludwig Reichelt (1877–1952), a Lutheran missionary from Norway, studied Buddhist texts and talked with Buddhist monks. He was encouraged when Kuan-tu, a monk in the monastery at Pi-lu, indicated how much he admired the Gospels. Kuan-tu became a Christian and was instrumental in the change of heart of the abbot and many fellow monks, but those were the last conversions influenced by Reichelt's efforts. He set up a center for conversations between Buddhists and Christians in Nanking and eventually moved it to Shatin near Hong Kong, where it is now known as the Tao Fong Shan Christian Center. His inculturation efforts followed much of Matteo Ricci's practice. He used the symbol of the cross growing from the lotus blossom which East Syrian (Nestorian) Christians had adopted; he also thought, like Timothy Richard, that East Syrian Christian truths were still available in various Buddhist practices and teachings, particularly in their Mahayana form. But his efforts were anathema to many conservative missionaries.

At the turn of the twentieth century, the missionaries and indigenous Chinese Christians asserted themselves. The missionaries were still protected in some ways by the force European governments threatened to use on the basis of older treaties. Protestants were no longer sitting on the edges of China, but had moved inside setting up hospitals and schools. They were working to change the religious allegiance of both the Chinese elite and the peasants. The rise of the warlords and their rapacious troops put everyone in danger, but that was only a foretaste of the violence that came with the Japanese invasion. The bombing of cities and events like the infamous rape of Nanking disrupted Chinese life, no matter what ultimate beliefs a person might have professed. The European countries allied with the United States backed Chaing-Kai-shek, one of the warlords, and thus made no headway with the popular movement led by Mao Zedong. Chairman Mao received ground support from peasants who had no hope otherwise and also welcomed the urban anti-Christian youth who had risen against Western ideals in the 1920s.

When European Christians awoke to the events of 1949, they were shocked that the weak China they had supported against Japan was now a feisty giant whose government was Communist and anti-Western. Modernization would have to come through its ally, Communist Russia. Taiwan became the center of political opposition. Christians, particularly in North America, felt betrayed and often took anti-Communist stands that made Chinese Christians look like a fifth column to their neighbors. Christians in the United States often grieved about the closing of China to missionaries and thus about not only the persecution but surely the death of Chinese Christianity.

Three Chinese Christian intellectuals, however, had already left a legacy that attempted to incorporate *Chinese religious traditions* and other things Chinese, sometimes including *Communism*, into Christian practice and thought. T.C. Chao (Chao Tzu-ch'en, born 1888), educated in China, Great Britain and the United States, wrote his *Life of Jesus* (1935, reprinted four times) in order to 'remove the Western veneer and look at the subject matter through purely Chinese eyes'. Each chapter carried in its title a phrase from the Chinese classics. A number of Chao's descriptions depended on Chinese customs.

Jesus intended to 'create a new spiritual mentality' based on God as love. The result was a 'kingdom of heaven movement'. Jesus had no interest in eschatology (the end of the world) and refused the political sense of 'Christ'. His miracles were primarily those of healing and exorcism; the others require rational explanation. Jesus' life for others demonstrated the Confucian concept of staying true to principles and through them serving others. He was the model for the Chinese eldest son.

Jesus' death should be best understood by Orientals: the sacrifice of life in order to preserve virtue appears in the Confucian *Analects*. In that way Christ embodied God's love. His resurrection was not an event of the body but one of his spirit, now freed from time and space. Through him his disciples anywhere can receive new life with power.

L.C. Wu (Wu Lei-ch'uan, 1870–1944), converted in 1915 by Protestant Episcopal missionaries, found Christianity to be in many ways the fulfillment of the Chinese classics. His *Christianity and Chinese Culture* (1936) was written to show 'how Christianity can serve the interests of China'. Although he knew that he would be branded a heretic by many, Wu insisted that the salvation of the soul, the doctrine of Trinity, church organization and ritual taught by Westerners were not the significant characteristics of Christian life. Looking at the words of Jesus in the New Testament, any reader would not find these things and at the same time would find considerable agreement with the Confucian tradition. The Holy Spirit in a believer's life is like the Confucian *jen*, 'perfect virtue, benevolence'. That includes forgiveness and the ability to love, not hate, just as the *Analects* indicate. It leads to the fulfillment of Chinese views.

L.C. Wu insisted in his book that although Communism had been one of the strongest opponents of Christian life and faith, the two belief systems should find many points of similarity that would allow them to work together. 'The integration of theory and practice', and the question of people and society, such strong themes in Communism, were part of Jesus' concerns. Jesus unified knowledge and action by calling for communities of social reform. He was concerned with the poor and the unequal distribution of wealth.

In a different paper Wu also insisted that both Buddhism and Christianity would need to be 'integrated to some extent with traditional Confucian thought'. Only then would they reach their Chinese fulfillment.

Y.T. Wu (Wu Yao-tsung, 1895–1979) was born in a non-Christian family and converted on the basis of Jesus' Sermon on the Mount. He studied in the United States, where he learned more about radical social reform. Eager to talk with the leaders of the People's Republic, he became president of and wrote the manifesto for the Three-Self Movement. His *No Man Hath Seen God* appeared in six editions between 1942 and 1950. The existence of God was not antithetical to scientific reasoning. Indeed God could be represented in different concepts and various names. By claiming that 'Heaven', 'God', 'the Way' and other terms that represent the highest reality are all helpful, he stepped beyond the Western insistence that there was no legitimate Chinese word for 'God'. In his view anthropomorphic conceptions of God had led to incessant prayers about our own well-being. A new prayer life should be marked not by our requests for help but by the search for God's true will.

Y.T. Wu also used the Chinese classics to explain Christianity. Christian love was *jen*, a term that better explained God's compassion than the Greek word *agape*. *Jen* represented a wider conception. Furthermore Wu found dialectical materialism not only a major force in China and the world but also a movement that brought both problems and opportunities. Religions had been the opiates of the people when they were overgrown with superstitions and false, unnatural concepts. True worship of God involved both the vertical and the horizontal. Materialism concentrated almost totally on the horizontal. Religion and materialism, however, need not be in total opposition, but could 'supplement each other'. Christians tended to forget social reality and Marxists tended to take the relative for the absolute. When enough time had passed, even Communists would find the teachings of Jesus to be the best way. Conservatives could argue that each of these intellectuals gave away too much of the Christian core. They did, however, offer interesting points for dialogue with Chinese religions, including Communism.

During the formation of the People's Republic of China after 1949 a government committee was established to force believers in all religions into the Three-Self Movement: self-governing, self-supporting, self-propagating. The first meeting included five Protestant leaders and two Buddhists. Groups of independent Christians, who had refused the attempts to form one Chinese Christian Church, signed on to the government plan only after their leaders were imprisoned. Some Buddhists, particularly those in Tibet, rejected attempts to make their beliefs more Chinese. The Chinese invasion of Tibet forced the Dalai Lama into exile. Troops were used to break Tibetan culture and its Buddhist religion, although the destruction of Buddhist temples eventually stopped. Although oppressed, underground Christians surely have had some common cause with suppressed Buddhists, both in Tibet and in China, but there has not been much evidence of internal Chinese cooperation between the two religious communities.

The Cultural Revolution (1966–1976) disrupted all of China. Anything that smelled of imperialism, older feudal systems or bourgeois influence was attacked. The ideal of confidently watching all religions fade away was replaced by vicious pounding of any aspect of these 'superstitions'. Protestants mainly went underground because the most frequently attacked leaders were those who had been active in the Three-Self Movement that previously had governmental sanction. Some Catholics had set up the Patriotic Association of Chinese Catholics

(PACC) in 1957 under the oversight of the Religious Affairs Bureau. A large group of Catholics resisted that solution and went underground, not the least because the PACC agreed to relinquish its connection with the Vatican as a tie with a foreign power.

Finally, powerful Chinese officials banded together and ended the Cultural Revolution. Even Mao's wife was prosecuted in an attempt to show that the movement had failed. With Mao's death in 1976, Deng Xiaoping and his cohorts sought relations with the outside world and relaxed some restrictions in China. In 1979 the Religious Affairs Bureau, disbanded during the Cultural Revolution, reappeared and encouraged the Protestant Three-Self Movement, the Catholic PACC as well as Taoists, Buddhists and Muslims to reorganize. In the 1980s between four and five thousand Protestant churches were reopened with governmental approval; nearly five million Protestants cautiously emerged from their house churches. Many Catholics strengthened their public worship, but a large segment stayed underground, not satisfied that the government-acknowledged Catholics were authentic or that the oppression was over.

The martyrdom of Chinese Christians, the persecution by Communists who as believers in revolution were unbelievers in all other religions, had forged Christians who did not seek death but also did not buckle before it. Many who went underground practiced their Christian faith in a confidence that drew energy from realistic fear met through trust in God. Others had learned to live within the laws of the regime, moving above ground but quietly making their witness. Chinese Christians had survived without foreign missionaries. Because there were nearly thirty million of them, Protestants and Catholics, some regional universities now have faculty members who have wanted to study these people and their religion as a part of Chinese culture.

Twentieth-century *India* not only felt the effects of the Second World War but also moved violently toward its independence from Great Britain. Mohandas Karamchand Gandhi (1869–1948) proved to be a world class leader who lived nonviolently, finally martyred by an assassin. He had deeply considered the compelling beauty of Jesus' Sermon on the Mount but could find no Christian communities that performed its principles. Influenced by the *Hindu* Renaissance of the nineteenth century, he found the cause of breaking the British grip so important that he purposefully avoided the plight of lower caste people. He did not call Hindus to divest themselves of their deeply rooted views of society. When Bhimroa Ramji Ambedkar (1891–1956) broke with Gandhi over these issues, Christian congregations might have been one of Ambedkar's options. He had studied for eight years with Christian leaders and twice had nearly converted. But finally he led those among the lowest castes who heeded his advice to *Buddhism*. He did not find Christians working powerfully enough against the caste system to justify the conflict within families and the consequent damaging of their Indian identity that Christian conversion would bring.

At the same time one of the most interesting developments among Indian Christians was the emergence of Dalit theology, a view of God and life from the untouchables. A group of indigenous leaders began to emphasize the preference of Jesus for the poor and desolate. With power they have insisted that any follower of Christ can neither overlook the injustice of the caste system nor support it in any way. This problem left over from the fight for independence continues to take center stage within this vital form of liberation theology.

One contrasting work with the poor was that of the remarkable Mother Teresa (1910–97). As a teenager growing up in an Albanian family in Macedonia, Agnes Gonxha Bojaxhiu showed strong religious interests. At eighteen she joined the Sisters of Loretto at Rothfarnham, Ireland and was sent to Darjeeling, India. Within a year she was teaching at St. Mary's School, responsible for the education of students who had few financial problems. But she saw the plight of the poor. In 1948 she received permission to leave her order and concentrate on teaching destitute children. In Calcutta she founded the Missionaries of Charity for women in 1950 and for men in 1963. International Co-Workers of Mother Teresa followed in 1969. Mother Teresa did not so much call for political action to change the conditions of the indigent but rather cared for those whose circumstance had pushed them close to death. She wanted no one she could reach to die without care. Her attention was focused on those beyond political assistance. In 1979 she won the Nobel Peace Prize for her efforts.

In north-eastern sections of India where tribal religions have been more likely to be the controlling practices and beliefs, Christian missionary effort has continued to have an impact. The Christian gospel has an appeal for these Indians that has been difficult to understand and is far different from the rejection of the gospel which so often occurs among Hindu and Muslim communities in the Indian subcontinent. Missionary-supported orphanages, educational institutions and medical clinics have touched people at least to the point that indigenous leaders in the region have honored missionaries as people of high virtue, worthy of praise even if their religion still seems questionable. The place of nature in the traditional religions of the area seems not to have been effective enough to meet continuous human needs. In that arena, Christians have made their claims.

Brilliant Christian monastic theologians like Thomas Merton (1915–68) and Bede Griffiths (1906–93) continued the tradition of Christian–*Buddhist* dialogue. Merton, known among Christians perhaps most for his insights into spirituality, found precisely those interests to be enhanced in conversations with Buddhist monks, some of which he pursued in Asia. Griffiths spent most of his adult life in India living after the manner of a Hindu monk. But discussions between followers of Buddha and Christ have not proved to be as productive as hoped, especially at a more popular level.

The beginning of the twenty-first century finds numerous religious conflicts in process. *Islamists* in the Sudan continue to attack Christians in the southern part of the country, perhaps as much for the food they grow as the religion they practice. Often men are killed while women and children are enslaved. Conflict between Muslims and Christians in Nigeria has erupted again with death and arson the response of each to the other. Taliban Islamists in Afghanistan have demonstrated that they are capable not only of blowing up centuries-old statues of Buddha, but also of imprisoning foreign Christian missionaries and sending them home. Afghan evangelists and converts to Christ live under the threat of death. The Taliban's rule has been ended in war.

Indonesian Muslims burned Christian churches and homes in bloody outbreaks during the 1990s. Muslims have also suffered retaliation in kind by Christians. Tension with less destruction of property and lives occurs in Muslim Malaysia. *Hindus* and Muslims fought tooth and nail during the creation of Pakistan in the mid twentieth century. Now Hindus view themselves as dominant and have attacked both Christian and Muslim communities in India. Many of these conflicts depend upon the notion that all Christians are foreigners, possibly Western agents of cultural and political destruction. As in ancient Persia, when being a Christian meant one supported the Roman (Byzantine) Empire, allegiance to Christ has been perceived as commitment to outside interests.

In the twentieth century, missionaries particularly from the United States were concerned about the religious practices and beliefs that they found among *Koreans*. It was not unusual for conservative Protestants to demand that any Korean convert abruptly stop religious ceremonies in the home and particularly at temple funerals, rites that were marked by *Confucian* or *Buddhist* features. That understanding of the inculturation process created Korean Christian communities who learned boundaries to set themselves off from their 'pagan' neighbors. Such struggles continue at the beginning the twenty-first century, but groups of Korean Christian leaders have developed an understanding that Confucian tradition should not be treated primarily as a religion but as a cultural system that presents much less danger to Christian existence. This view of Confucian practices and teachings has allowed Christians to absorb some of its wisdom about families and relationships and also to carefully tailor practices to honor ancestors and shape Christian funerals. The result has been impressive. It shows how Koreans as Asians can allow the gospel to grow in their soil.

Korean discussions with Buddhists, on the other hand, have often attempted to deal with Buddhist practices and teachings as those of a different religion. In some cases that has meant a call for radical change of life among Buddhists who become Christians. At times those conversions were even more difficult because evangelists found that Korean Buddhists lived a religion that itself had been taken over by other ancient traditional religious customs. Some Christian circles, however, have been attracted to the wisdom of Buddhist texts and accept the idea that the Christian God has spoken truth through individuals who themselves were not Christians. In that way they re-enact various biblical texts in which the truth comes from people outside the Jewish or Christian communities.

Changes in the religious landscape of *European and North American* countries have had an increasing influence on the character of Christian communities in those areas. In the twentieth century the overwhelming force has been secularization, a religion to end religions. The advance of secularization has propelled many establishment churches into long periods of decline. At the same time many believer-based churches have come to the fore with their own responses to secularization. But no Christian group has gone through the past century without both defeats and victories. Nearly all 'first world' Christians have had to ferret out which ways they would live in such strongly secularizing cultures. Their widely differing perceptions of the needs for contextualization are interesting to observe. For some Christians, religion is an individual question seldom to be asked about. Toleration is the key. To absorb cultural values that work toward freedom and progress is sound. For others, Christian commitment demands a counter-cultural life, suspicious of riches and privileges.

The influx of *Muslims* and *Hindus* into *Great Britain* out of the former empire or the present Commonwealth nations has made it more difficult to think about that great nineteenth-century bastion of Christian mission as primarily Christian. The mosques in cities such as Birmingham, Edinburgh and London make clear to any eye that this country is no longer devoted entirely to one religion. The percentages of Muslims and Hindus are not large, but their influence continues to grow. Common courtesy makes it less and less accurate to equate being British with being Christian.

The *United States* also has seen glacial shifts in the religious affiliations of its citizens. The civil rights movement of the 1960s and its ineffectiveness in later decades have demonstrated to many blacks that their future does not lie with racist white Christians. A glance at National Basketball Association teams or National Football League rosters shows that Muslim names have either been given to or in adulthood chosen by some black athletes. The conversion of African-Americans to Islam and the immigration of Asian Muslims means that *Muslims*, rather than *Jews*, at some point in the twenty-first century will become the second largest religious community in the United States. Followers of Muhammad still represent a much smaller group of people than those who claim to be Christian. But again Muslim growth continues to demand that living in the United States does not necessarily involve being a Christian.

CHRISTIANS AND THEIR CULTURES

There are sparkling examples of Christian contextualization among *African* cultures. Perhaps the most successful, and in the views of some the most questionable, have occurred in the African independent churches. Often the understanding of Christian practice and faith there has emerged either from converts who were not deeply catechized into an existing Christian community and its tradition or from people, with negative experiences of church leaders, who found their catechism too Western to be authentically African.

The most devastating struggle of Christians with their cultures appeared near the end of the twentieth century when Hutus and Tutsis, primarily in Rwanda, erupted in a civil war in which perhaps two million people died. Many of the victims were Christians, both Catholic and Protestant. The trials have shown that priests and ministers wielded machetes causing the same terror as soldiers who fired their guns. Young African Christian leaders all over the continent and around the globe are questioning what kind of Christian community had been created among these two peoples that they returned to tribal identities as primary and tried to annihilate each other as tribal enemies. Part of the problem began with the unreasonable national boundaries set up by Europeans such that a number of countries around Rwanda became involved in this conflict. But the deepest question remains how Christians could miss so completely the gospel of loving your enemies that this genocide of 'brothers and sisters in Christ' could occur. Before and during the First World War, some European Christians had taught a bad lesson well, particularly in Africa, where they killed each other to defend their colonies. In the Rwandan battles, however, old tribal hatreds were doubtless the strongest cause. Missionaries had tried to make it plain that the most authentic Christian communities must embody forgiveness and love. Without such habits of the heart and practices to guide all life, the Christian gospel offers little to blunt such hatred.

In *Latin America* the battle over the limits and liveliness of the inculturation of Christian practice and faith remains strong. More than half the Roman Catholics in the world live in Latin America. Much of their worship and service is worked out in terms of the culture in each country. Music, architecture and festivals reflect the contemporary views of each group of people. The colors, the textures, the sounds of Catholicism are Latin American. In some ways it is still odd that world Catholicism does not more fully reflect the accomplishments of Catholic contextualization in this region.

In various evangelical and mainline Protestant traditions, the twentieth century had seen splits deeply influenced by cultures. Missionaries from the United States have brought their hymnbooks and spiritual practices with them from their home country. Sometimes even those who passionately loved the people have been willing to translate only hymns written in the United States and Europe into Portuguese or Spanish. The rhythm and poetry of the local cultures have seemed too emotional to be adopted. The myth of the dangerous Latin temperament has precluded the adoption of Latin music and rhythm. For example the Brazilian samba, like various drumbeats in Africa, has so captured the soul of the people that puritanical missionaries could imagine nothing but sexual promiscuity as the result. That observation seems to have had some merit even for those who wanted to be, say, more Brazilian or more Chilean in their embodiment of spirit and service. One indigenous pentecostal pastor suggested that when Christian music was sung and danced to the samba, at least the women should put their backsides up against the wall. But Brazilian hearts must sing and dance to Brazilian rhythms.

Conservative Protestants in Latin America have not only let the culture in; they have also moved out into the culture. The worship bands of some charismatic Christian churches are remarkably skilled in playing the music of Brazil, Argentina or elsewhere. They clearly encourage the idea than no one need adopt a foreign European religion or the European culture on which it depends. During the major Carnival parades in Rio de Janeiro in the last decades of the twentieth century, floats built by such Christians won major prizes. The attempt is to reclaim these rousing festivals that are noted primarily for the celebration of human vitality and sexuality before the onset of Catholic Lenten restraint.

With about thirty million Christians in *China*, it is reasonable to presume that these indigenous Christians have worked out ways to live as authentic Chinese. Among Catholics the government-approved church has been able to convince government leaders that Christians are not a threat to the ruling regime. When Bishop Aloysius Jin Luxian spoke at the Chinese Catholic Patriotic Association's (CCPA) anniversary, he quoted the Confucian *Analects* as Chinese wisdom and rooted his thoughts in Catholic sources like Thomas Aquinas and Vatican II. He also insisted that a Chinese church must be Chinese just as the early Christian churches were Greek and Roman. For him the CCPA is self-governing, not government controlled and it is also characterized by its deep love of the motherland. It has studied the government documents and can work with its policies

Underground Catholics in China probably experienced the persecutions more deeply than did the CCPA because they have continued to resist what they see as an atheistic ideology that refuses to allow Catholics to claim the pope as their leader. Important people in the government see the papacy as the seat of a foreign power. Allegiance to him amounts to some form of sedition. Thus underground Catholics do not think that persecution has passed; it has only relented until a more opportune moment.

Protestants have emphasized the character of their congregations as authentically Chinese and have worked out various relationships with both the culture and the government. The Communist leadership has swept away some of the more questionable aspects of culture and religion that Protestants fought, but it is not yet clear whether the days of terror have passed.

South *Korean* Christians have been the powerhouse of Asian Christianity. In the twentieth century they experienced two invasions by Japan, one early in the century and another just before the Second World War. Then they lived through a different kind of ravaging during the Korean War that left them a partitioned country under two opposing types of governments: indigenous Communism with support particularly from China, and indigenous democracy with support particularly from the United States.

The appeal of the gospel preached and lived by Korean Christians appeared most clearly during the times of Japanese occupation. Many Christian communities with their schools and publishing houses came to the conclusion that struggling to keep Korea from being absorbed into Japanese life was a paramount value. So many of these Christians had found ways to be Korean Christians that their sense of nationalism did not stand against their understanding of Christian faith commitment. Political leaders like Syngman Rhee, first president of South Korea, and others had been educated in Christian schools. Installed with support of the United States, Rhee viewed Korea's future through his Christian commitments. Many Christians accepted such a view. They usually published their books in Korean characters that had been clearly differentiated from the Chinese and Japanese alphabets.

During and after the Korean War, Christians in North Korea suffered persecution that probably exceeded that experienced during the Japanese occupation. Even though the citizens of the two countries have now been divided for nearly half a century, the small openings for travel in either direction on certain days have justified the observation that many Koreans see themselves as only one people. It is difficult to project how much the different ideologies of the twentieth century can be overcome if the spirit of unification lives to become the reality. If North Koreans have difficulty seeing the Christian gospel as genuinely Korean, it is because they question the authentic Korean character of South Korean culture. South Korean Christians insist that they have struggled for Korean values, not just imported Western ones.

The number of Korean Christian missionaries active throughout the globe has risen dramatically. The growth in the Korean economy after

the Korean War, although the country is now in recession, was phenomenal. Money has been available for travel overseas; the struggles of these
Christians during two wars have given them spiritual strength for missionary efforts. Many of these missionaries know that Christians are a
minority in Asia and that they are still not a majority in South Korea.
Thus they often have a better understanding of their tasks than European
missionaries from the sixteenth century and beyond who too often went
out thinking they were exceptional in every way when compared with
the people among whom they would live. The cultural and social history
that Koreans have experienced has sharpened their own sense of what
the Christian gospel is and how it might be embodied individually and
corporately. Some who have become more and more Western have developed their own brand of condescension, but the suffering of Korean
Christians was long and is still imbedded in stories the old tell the young.

In both *Europe and North America* (here excluding Mexico) the phe-
nomenon of people being Christian through cultural formation has continued and been transformed. Various citizens of the United States and
Canada have thought that something about their life would be less satisfying if the Christian character of these nations were ever totally
denied. That did not mean that those holding such opinions should be
directly involved in any Christian community. Even the rebellious French
of Quebec would not see their struggle with the rest of Canada for political rights as primarily an anti-Catholic or anti-Protestant conviction. In
the United States telephone polls have consistently indicated that a high
proportion of the population believe in God, sometimes in the region of
ninety percent, and that over forty percent of people attend church regularly. The only time the latter figure was actually tested in the twentieth
century – in Ashtabula County, Ohio – the actual number of believers
who attended church represented only twenty percent of the county's
population. Canadians seem not to have made such claims on either
count. Indeed most North American cities have a very low number of
Christians who gather for worship on any Sunday; Seattle figures suggest
about one percent.

At the same time a sense of the need for some kind of Christendom
has remained. The epithet 'culture Christians' used for those who supported the Nazi ideology in Germany has left a stigma on that term. The
culture Christians supported Hitler's program even to the point of prop-
agating strong anti-Semitism in life and literature. But though few
modern Germans are interested in becoming Christians, the recognized

need for Christendom to continue in German culture still exists. At birth Germans are designated either Protestant or Catholic – now more Catholics than Protestants. Seldom have the *Gastarbeiter* – 'guest workers' from Muslim countries like Turkey who have settled in the cities and birthed 'German' children – been officially recognized according to their religion. The inclusion in that category of guest workers of many Orthodox believers from Eastern Europe make the binary categories of either Protestant or Catholic appear even more odd. However, the official status of churches and their service institutions, supported by the tax system, raises much less opposition than might be expected. Some committed opponents of Christianity pay the tax because they think that hospitals, homes for children and the elderly, etc. would have to be replaced if the tax were withdrawn. Pay it and get the service. It's a bargain.

In *Great Britain* the importance of Christianity's place in culture was well illustrated by the lightning fire at York Minster. In a nation where church involvement has dropped steadily since the First World War, it was unthinkable that this ancient site of Christian presence should not be repaired. Attention to the sagging towers demanded a remarkable feat of engineering that sunk new concrete foundations under the building and connected them to the existing structure. In the process pre-Christian Roman ruins and Christian burials were found underneath and older Anglo-Saxon sections of the towers were discovered. Wealthy upper class families provided the tall timbers from their private forests and craftsmen worked on the repair and refurbishing of this Christian structure. They all knew that it was important for England but not necessarily the home of a congregation one would want to join.

The decline of Christendom in Europe must be put alongside the recovery of more vital Christian communities in most parts of the region, not the least in the countries of Eastern Europe where Christians suffered persecutions under Communist rule. Canada and the United States did not experience the near collapse of Christian churches that Europe did after the First World War. Neither the Korea 'police action' nor the unpopular war in Vietnam left the United States in any condition like that of early twentieth-century Europe. But the erosion of Christian commitment in the cities of North America and the secularization of much of life in Canada and the United States still mean that Christian communities are not viewed by the majority as offering important solutions to common problems. In the United States evangelicals still sound the battle cry for a return to 'American values', always with some effectiveness – often because of their ability to move quickly into modern technologies like television and now the internet. But their insistence on returning to the religion of the founders, as if authentic Christianity would appear from that myth, is a sad dream.

Christian *women* in the twentieth century have made significant strides, particularly in Europe and North America. Congregations that recognize what they call 'spiritual gifts' have nearly always encouraged women to do whatever God calls them to do. The Holy Spirit selects leaders some of whom are women. Conservative Protestants often insist that women must be in the home caring for husband and children, but many of them honor female missionaries, married or single, who serve almost anywhere in the world. Pope John Paul II has written strongly defending the priesthood as open only to celibate males, but he has insisted that women have many important ministries in the church.

One of the most interesting discussions in the sadly named 'first world' cultural arena has been the burgeoning study of the relationship between *science and theology*. Some scientists continue to find such discussions absurd. Science and religion are incompatible aspects of human life, the first objective and debatable, the second subjective and untestable. In response to that position, fundamentalist Protestants have funded the Creation Institute that has fought evolution in North America and across the globe. The assumptions of its members usually include the idea that the account of creation in the biblical book of Genesis is historical description and that evolution is only a theory, not well founded on fact. In a different approach the Templeton Foundation has supported efforts to find areas of compatibility between science and religion, specifically between modern Western science and informed Christian theology. This latter attempt and others like it have opened up dialogue on a scale seldom seen before, which has invited scientists and theologians to emphasize the data and methods that they share. Three significant scientist-theologians have given the prestigious Gifford lectures during the second half of the century: Ian Barbour (born 1923), Arthur Peacocke (born 1924) and John Polkinghorne (born 1930). They are helpful guides.

This many-pronged development has provided enhancements in theology. Evolutionary theory need not be judged a demonic force. It helps Christians discover the ways in which scripture and early theologians like Basil and Augustine use different models for talking about creation.

Genesis 1–2, Ezekiel 38 and the creation Psalms offer at least five pictures of how God acted. A modern physics that speaks of indeterminacy and views black holes as phenomena that conceal knowledge about themselves because of their intense compactness is often open to entertaining confessions about a God whose nature is at bottom incomprehensible. If dark matter constitutes as much as ninety-five percent of our universe and little is known about it, the older Enlightenment theories that claimed to know what was possible in nature and thus what could be definitely excluded now seem threadbare. Some participants in these conversations have recognized the possibility of using complementarity in physics as a way to talk about the two natures and one person of Jesus Christ. The study of Christology has not been presented with such fascinating images in a thousand years.

A CHRISTIAN CORE

In *Africa,* William Wadé Harris (c. 1860–1929) led one of the most significant indigenous Christian movements to appear on the continent, one that depended upon *spirituality and evangelism.* Born in Liberia to a pagan father and a Christian mother, he claimed his mother's Methodist heritage. He received his formal education, baptism and appointment as a lay preacher within that tradition. But when he married an Episcopalian, he began working with the Episcopal mission as a teacher and an evangelist among his Glebo people. As the official translator for his tribe he was supposed to further the plans of the Liberian bishop Samuel Ferguson, who had first supported the Glebo but later backed the political leaders of the black immigrants. Harris became so disheartened with Ferguson that he supported a pro-British plot to overthrow the government. Thus, during the tragic 1910 Liberian–Glebo war, he was imprisoned.

Before that conflict his views had slowly changed. He found the apocalyptic teachings of Jehovah's Witnesses valuable and began to share the deep misgivings about the arrogance of Christian missionaries that Edward Blyden (1832–1912), a Virgin Island black who worked in Liberia, had forcefully expressed. He may also have countenanced some of Blyden's interest in the truth of Islam. But during his imprisonment Harris had a vision of the angel Gabriel calling him to the Great Commission of Christ as 'the prophet of the last times'.

The appearance of Harris in any village caused quite a stir. His band included women singing comprehensible songs. He dressed himself in a turban and white robe and walked barefoot carrying a cross-headed staff, a rattle, a Bible and a ceremonial baptismal bowl. He allowed people to feed and house his group, but he took no money for anything. He preached against fetishes and other native religious customs he judged to be evil, but unlike most missionaries he backed up his words by casting out demons and healing the sick. The Lord's Prayer, the Ten Commandments, and Sunday as a day of rest were important aspects of his teaching. At the same time he was open to many things African. Unlike the missionaries he did not question the social structure of the villages. Harris introduced a different God, a different Spirit and different taboos in place of the old religious customs that he discredited with power. But the leaders of his churches previously had been leaders of their social groups. The picking apart of African traditions, so prevalent among the missionaries, was not the thrust of his ministry.

Thousands responded to his person and message in the Ivory Coast, Ghana and Liberia. Harris often sent these folk to Catholic and Protestant missionaries for further teaching, but he had given them a sense that they could be African and Christian. Twenty years after his death as many as two million Christians in those three countries were part of his heritage, some in various Catholic and Protestant churches, others in the Church of the Twelve Apostles in Ghana and the Harrist Church in the Ivory Coast. The latter group, led for fifty-seven years by John Ahui (c. 1888–1992), an illiterate chieftain whom Harris had appointed as his successor, became a multi-ethnic grassroots movement.

The movement supporting *base Roman Catholic communities* in *Latin America*, in which faith and practice were centered on deep spirituality and social/political action, showed serious promise in mid-century. They originated, as did much Latin American liberation theology, with priests who worked in the poorest quarters of the cities and knew first-hand the level of injustice that prevailed. These priests began to write *theologies of liberation* and found particularly in the biblical stories of Jesus a preference for the poor and oppressed. Sunk in the tragic situations of the people they served, theologians like Leonardo Boff in Brazil, Gustavo Gutiérrez in Peru and Juan Luis Segundo in Uruguay – to mention only three – found their European-oriented educations of less worth than they had hoped. Political, economic and social structures that kept the poor down should not only be studied but also abolished. Christians of proper practice and faith should not stand by and do nothing in the midst of such suffering.

Latin American aristocrats saw in that movement shadows of Communism and a type of economic reform that would threaten, perhaps destroy, their livelihood. Groups of bishops, who were drawn from the landed and powerful, attacked such practices and ideas as Communist inspired. The right-wing death squads were not sent directly by the established Church, but they were not always disowned by the Church either. Bishop Oscar Romero (1917–80), who loved his people and embodied the power of Catholic spirituality and sacraments to inspire economic and social relief, was assassinated in his cathedral in El Salvador while he was celebrating mass. Others who encouraged Catholic youth to take their faith seriously and live as Jesus did were pressured, some even killed, when their vision and energy seemed to threaten traditional upper class values and the structures that supported them

John Paul II, firmly opposed to Communism through his Polish experience, has had as much to do with the fall of Marxist governments in Europe as any other leader. Following his practice of trips to support reconciliation, he went to Cuba to affirm Fidel Castro's decision to allow more religious expression, specifically Catholic services. But this remarkable pope, so helpful an example in his own repentance for Christian killing of Jews and Catholic violence toward the Orthodox, eventually demanded that priests pastor their flocks and not be significantly involved in politics. At least one priest who served in the Congress of the United States was thus forced to resign. But in areas of Latin America, such as Chiapas, Mexico, priests and bishops who know the reasons for and have in various ways supported popular Amerindian rebellion are still quietly active.

At the turn of the twentieth century groups of *Chinese* Protestants sought independence from the government and its political squabbles and to establish some kind of unity with one another. The National Christian Council of China (a federation of churches founded 1923) and the Church of Christ in China (an organic union that emerged in 1927) were meant to provide institutions in which Christians could share their faith and life. In the background of these movements stood both the idea that making Christian practice and faith Chinese demanded a concentrated effort from all Christians, and the recognition that the growing anti-Christian movement viewed believers as people with allegiance to a foreign power and thus as a danger to China.

A series of grassroots attempts to bring the Christian gospel closer to the people showed quite different ways in which Chinese Christians envisioned their lives together. In 1922 a commune in Shantung province led by Ching Tien-ying called itself the 'Society of Holy Believers'. Six years later it took the name 'Family of Jesus' and became known to outsiders as 'Family of Jesus Communism'. Their communal ideas were in place about six months before the beginning of the Chinese Communist Party. In the Family of Jesus each person had to make or grow something that could be used by the whole community. Crops and clothing were mass-produced and distributed. When the People's Republic attacked the movement for its widespread ownership of land, it rethought its ways, organized into small groups of thirty and gave away its wealth to the poor. By 1950 when it had three hundred communes and about fifteen thousand members, the Family of Jesus included farmers and professional people, had organized itself around a vow of poverty, and had set up its own schools. They sent out groups of three or four preachers together and were often successful in founding their Chinese Bible-based communities. Their worship practice involved rising each dawn for prayer and singing – the hymns were formed of biblical verses set to traditional Chinese tunes. They did not ordain clergy but depended on group solidarity for their life together.

Some other churches, developed along pentecostal lines characterized by the definition of mystical experience in I Corinthians 14, were known as *ling-en* Christians. The Family of Jesus fitted the same pattern of intense personal conversion plus communal responsibilities. Perhaps the Christian group best known outside China was the Little Flock, led by Ni T'o-sheng, Watchman Nee (died 1972). It too had no ordained clergy and did not require baptism. Although Nee thought baptism was important, in his movement anyone who chose to be baptized (some did not) could use nearly any liturgical form. Here the desire to overcome imported denominational barriers was strongly expressed. The center of worship was the communion: a Lord's Supper of prayer, distributed bread and a single chalice, which the Little Flock thought best embodied the New Testament practice.

Nee wanted to avoid Western rituals and institutions that he thought kept people from obeying Christ. Dying with Christ, accepting Jesus' death for all people as an inner reorientation, was at the center of each true Christian. 'Walking in the Spirit' was the last of four stages in which daily life grew out of inner repentance and obedience. External activities would be judged true only if the inner changes were real. Nee made no attempt to employ Confucian tradition, but his arguments were often profoundly Chinese. He also did not approve of any Chinese theologian's attempts to make Western Christianity relevant. By 1949 the Little Flock comprised about seven hundred congregations and seventy thousand members.

In the People's Republic of China many, if not all, Christians have suffered. The constitution guaranteed freedom of religion but according to state officials the classless ideal would naturally evolve toward the shriveling of all religions. In response the Christian Three-Self Movement emerged: Christian communities were to be self-governing, self-supporting and self-propagating. Among Protestants, even at the end of the twentieth century, the Three-Self Movement was often central to life and work. In the atmosphere of the People's Republic, the indigenization of Christians' self-understanding was paramount. They could not rely on missionaries from North America or Europe. Indeed had there been no pressure from the government, it would still have been important for Christians to contextualize their message in terms of Chinese conditions. Working to understand the gospel by themselves encouraged them to demonstrate that they were not puppets of foreign powers and in some cases freed them to point out the good aspects of Chinese Communist ideals.

The very movements that did not join the Church of Christ in China or the National Christian Council of China before 1950 also did not cooperate with the Three-Self Movement. They had already forged their independence from foreign powers and missionaries as well as overarching Chinese Christian institutions. When Ching Tien-ying was arrested in 1952, charged with owning property, being authoritarian and committing adultery, the government reorganized the Family of Jesus and put an end to their style of communal living. After the arrest of Watchman Nee in 1952 and other leaders in 1956, however, the Little Flock signed on to the Three-Self Movement and even dropped its central Lord's Supper. Some of these Protestant efforts then went underground and tried to stay alive during the Cultural Revolution. At the beginning of the twenty-first century persecution remains real but it is also possible for Christian supporters of the Three-Self Movement to worship openly, many of them in previously closed church buildings.

Among Chinese Catholics similar situations have arisen. There are bishops and churches, recognized by the government, that pursue Christian existence in every way they find available to them. Heavily persecuted during the Cultural Revolution, they now occupy formerly closed buildings and make their way primarily in the open. They do not pursue policies that invite conflict, but they also believe that their Christian life and witness are true. Underground Chinese Catholics have opposed these established Catholics, have set up their own clerical leadership, and have remained true to their conviction. Their opposition to the Communist authorities is legendary; their rejection of the above-ground Catholics as traitors is occasionally bitter. One of the saddest features of Chinese Christian communities is this deep divide, which may not be bridged in the twenty-first century.

Thirty million Christians of all stripes is a small but significant minority in China. They have come through decades of persecution and are still uncertain what the future holds. The national weakening of restrictions since the 1980s continues to be punctuated by local oppression. It is difficult to say what the public suppression of the Falun Gong spiritual movement, which has no strong connections with Christianity, will mean for Christians. Many of the churches have lost their middle-aged leaders to imprisonment and death. Elderly saints are often honored and followed, but few if any know how younger adult believers will fare, particularly in the free trade zones along the coast. As Western business and culture seep into the country, threatening to become a flood, will these faithful persecuted Christians with deep spiritual experience find the dangers of materialism a situation for which they are unprepared?

There have been significant changes, however, among some Chinese believers that bode well for the future. Ding Guangxun uttered warnings well before the Cultural Revolution. Protestant insistence on 'original sin, the fallen state of the world, on the meaninglessness and absurdity of history, on the separation and antithesis of grace and nature, on the so-called pride in human works and on justification by faith could easily be turned into a sort of antinomianism which, in the name of faith, gave blessing to any sort of political stance required by the Kuomintang and U.S. policy'. These older categories should be dissolved into Chinese ones, into a transcendence in immanence, into a political and social consciousness that finds God in interpersonal relationships, into acceptance of people movements and nature. Belief and non-belief, stringent eschatology, and the harsh history of the faithful must give way to more loving and gracious interaction with all Chinese. God is not concerned only with Christians. In order for Chinese Christians to make a contribution to the world, they must give up their colonial views and their sense of being a foreign religion in China. Taking up the concerns of Chinese people, becoming thoroughly Chinese Christians, offers the opportunity of serving not only China but Christians everywhere.

Christians have needed liberation but at the same time too many liberation theologians paid attention to neither life in Christ nor the problems of absolutizing the poor. Some Christians in house churches made political statements by their silence, but any who accepted assistance from the outside needed to rethink their attempts to stay out of political life.

Ding's views, more likely to be taken seriously by the above-ground Christians, have considerable merit. A number of movements in Christian communities have not depended upon the Augustinian and European Reformation categories that have so often been expanded by Protestant divines as the sole center of life and faith. God has spoken in various people like Melchizedek, the non-Jewish priest of Jerusalem. Sinfulness must never be dropped as an inappropriate category, but the utter wretchedness of every human being and the evil of nature are not the single expression of the Christian core. Chinese Christians can encourage their neighbors to follow Christ without insisting that nothing they are or nothing in their history and culture has value.

The inner core of many free-meeting Chinese Christians – those who are certain neither that open public worship is credible nor that all of Ding's suggestions are acceptable – has depended upon exorcisms, healings and miracles sunk deeply in daily existence. Demon possession, as seen in the New Testament and experienced in the present, can destroy people. Prayer lives that empower these Christians against the fickle discrimination they experience are an absolute necessity. Hope where hopelessness reigns tends to draw even the young. The importance of family life, so Chinese at its center, has become an evangelistic principle for many of the underground Christians who meet in house churches. The care provided within the communities for the sick and the imprisoned has cracked many feelings of distrust, so common in contemporary China.

Perhaps the most striking aspect of these communities has been the clear acceptance of *suffering* as an opportunity for the fullest Christian witness. Obeying God is better than obeying humans. Some leaders may be accused of testing in less than prudent ways the toleration that now exists. But the comparison between the virtues of these Chinese Christians and those of the health and wealth gospel movement in the so-called 'first world' shows the first to be the last in the worst sense.

Many of these house churches, sadly, have separated themselves from the unfaithful. Yet in their isolation they have enjoyed outbreaks of speaking in tongues and have developed new understandings of the place of *women*. As many of the new Christians have experienced the power of God and have indicated their needs for pastoral instruction by some who are more mature in the faith, their communities have been positively affected by these energized converts. Once again, particularly in the underground Protestant and Catholic movements, both love and patience are needed to help these emerging Christians become more authentic. In the process, the 'mature' could find themselves opened to many possibilities that their staid views have kept them from considering.

The Church of *South India*, formed in the twentieth century, is one of the more remarkable efforts toward Christian unity that have appeared anywhere. It developed strong leaders with the vision, the energy and the patience to persuade local church members not merely to talk among themselves. The small conferences soon became larger meetings attended by hundreds of people who gloried in the discovery of brothers and sisters. Not all missionaries or indigenous Christians agreed to the union, but it has often served good purposes in a country where followers of Christ are such a small minority.

Surely the most horrific question about a Christian core in the twentieth century concerns how a Christian country like Germany could produce the *Holocaust* and how the leaders of other countries could support it. In terms of numbers the six million Jews who died through torture, disease and deliberate execution becomes most sickening when one discovers the banality of Nazi discussion about the concentration camps and their gas chambers and ovens. It was inefficient to shoot and bury the prisoners. A system had to be devised that eliminated them with less expense. Even excluding the numbers of non-Jews who died, this carefully planned and executed purging of Jews from Europe surpasses the death and destruction of the Crusades, not because the hatred was deeper, but because the technology was more powerful.

Christian reactions, particularly in Germany, were mixed. The settlement at Versailles after the First World War had seemed unfair to German patriots. The Weimar Republic fell to pieces amidst economic chaos. Hitler's rise to power not only promised but provided a better life for many. The barter economy became unnecessary as jobs and money with value reappeared. In some of his early speeches Hitler sounded like a hero to Christians because he insisted that Lutherans and Catholics were of the same faith and should not be at each other's throat. Hitler's cause was one of Christian unity. Particularly to the young it seemed that a new era of Christendom might emerge. Little did his listeners know that Hitler wanted a complete list for a second elimination of those with different views and values. He gained support before people learned what he had in mind. Even the opening of Dachau, that dreaded camp, was made a public event with streetcars running from Munich to see the correctional center for Communists and others who threatened the full recovery of Aryan purity. Many well-meaning German Christians had no idea what was happening. Others had local experiences that gave them a false picture. Small concentration camps were scattered in southern Germany, where rebellious youth did go for re-education. I once talked to a Schwabian farmer who was certain that the large death camps did not exist because the son of his neighbor had been in a nearby camp and came back to run the farm when his father died. There was no torture or death there, just the solid reclamation of troubled youth. Telling him about my father's experience at Dachau of walking into barracks where decaying human flesh came up over his shoe soles did not change his mind.

Classical liberal theology, so strong among European theologians, had made many contributions to the life of Christians in Europe. It had valiantly struggled for the 'brotherhood of man' (*sic*) as a major goal of Christian life. People who found traditional Christian reading of scripture and reliance on older forms of community less than what was needed, tried in every way they could to take modern thinking and problems seriously. The development of the sciences was applauded for its continuing progress. Urban poverty resulting from workers flocking to the cities for low-paying jobs was recognized and confronted. Efforts to help the homeless and the hungry were undertaken with the assistance of any who understood the need, whether Christian or not. Loving people were discovered everywhere and honored as part of the solution. Mission to other lands and those of other faiths were undertaken in helpful ways through medicine. Albert Schweitzer (1874–1965), who won the Nobel Peace Prize in 1953, wrote influential books on how Jesus and Paul had been misunderstood because their views of eschatology (the last times) were not taken seriously. Schweitzer's theological insights that found conservative views of Jesus and Paul impossible in modern times led some to acceptance and others to opposition, but his life's work in Africa impressed all. At times condescending, his 'reverence for life' and his care for diseased Africans made a stunning Christian contribution.

Yet such modern theology in the main had neither eyes nor ears for the Nazi threat. It believed that economic recovery from the First World War and the strength of European culture would stand against evil. It had often accommodated itself to the German culture as the most brilliant in Europe. Ernst Troeltsch (1865–1923) and others could not see the dangers of German science supporting this non-Christian German religion of Nazism. To be German surely meant that one was a Christian. Almost the entire theological faculty of the famed University of Tübingen thought the Nazi program against Jews to be a proper one, although few if any of them knew about life in the camps. The *Deutsche Christen*, the 'German Christians' who followed the Nazi line, defended it in their pulpits, and treated reports of Nazi sadism as misguided, then traitorous. These folk refused to believe such things could happen. Other Lutherans who fought Hitler from the beginning accepted his leadership when he was elected chancellor. Romans 13 meant that God put governments in power. They should be obeyed.

The Christians of the Barmen Declaration, and numerous unnamed people who recognized real terror in various places and tried to save Jews and others, stood against the Nazi menace. Karl Barth (1886–1968), a Swiss teaching in Germany, had already pointed out the failings in his own modern theological education and saw a connection between it and much of the church's inability to grasp what was happening. His *Dogmatics* needed little apology for its view. A natural, not revealed, theology that depended on the goodness of European Christian culture sank into the swamp of everyday events. Europe needed the revealed truth in Jesus Christ. The gospel should be described and contextualized in ways that did not sap its life. The German theologian Dietrich Bonhoeffer (1906–45) returned from safety in the United States and was killed because of his participation in a plot to assassinate Hitler. He had been a convinced pacifist but found that the situation in Germany called him to something else. His attempt to educate pastors in a small clandestine seminary, described in *Life Together*, depended on a community that stood over against much of the culture. His *Letters and Papers from Prison* tried to think through what Christian life would be like in a world apparently abandoned by God. These Christians and those who had like views were too small a minority to sway the country and its policy, but they did give witness to an authentic core of Christian practice and faith. Believing ministers and priests died in the camps while doing their best to assist other prisoners. But the modest numbers of these Christian leaders showed how many German Christians had failed to follow the example of those who held to the ideal of leading a life of virtue and service to others.

Another tormenting, but much smaller twentieth-century disruption of Christian unity is the continuing struggle of the Catholic patriots of *Ireland* with the Protestant patriots of Northern Ireland. Oppression of the Irish by the British had been a problem for centuries. That small country has had a passionate commitment to its own heritage and a disdain, if not hatred, for the British. On the other hand, the situation of the Northern Irish Protestants as a majority within their tiny country but a minority within the whole island might be described as a struggle for survival. As Irish Catholics in Northern Ireland grow closer toward being half the country's population, with the possibility of becoming the majority, the wounds bleed and fester. Both sets of people are Irish and Christian, but their insistence that the other group is heretical and malicious is buried in the bones. Children learn the fear and hatred early.

Although in the last decades some leaders and occasional majorities of those voting on important questions have wanted to lessen the danger and extract the bitterness, the hatred is for many only thinly disguised. The inability of Christian communities to siphon off the brackish water demonstrates once again how difficult it is to embody the best of Christian virtue when doctrinal issues and significant differences in liturgy and practice fill each new generation with bile. Hope for these folk lies only with Christian renewal that through embodying forgiveness can absorb the variations. With politicians and cultural leaders who will not accept the definition of the world offered by either part in this dispute, perhaps the Irish can slowly move toward peace.

Not all twentieth-century developments among Christians have led to slaughter. The *1910 World Missionary Conference* at Edinburgh gathered Protestants from round the world. In many ways it reflected the missionary expansion throughout the globe, led first by Great Britain and other European countries, and then joined by the growing energies of others, for example, Christians in the United States. Because it came on the heels of at least three similar conferences, its planners carefully selected participants and chose as its president John R. Mott (1865–1955), a leading missionary statesman from the United States. Many of the twelve hundred representatives came from Great Britain, Canada, Australia, New Zealand and the United States. That insured the predominance of English as the common language, but delegates from other lands also attended. Some Asians were present. Latin America almost disappeared from view. African concerns found their voice primarily through African-Americans and missionaries to Africa who loved the people among whom they served.

The passionate dream of the conference was the conversion of all peoples throughout the world, particularly those from the other major religions, so that by the end of the century the globe would be Christian. The goals concerned the planting of churches everywhere, the education of missionaries for such tasks, and the unity of North American and European Christians, whose resources in money and young people were viewed as essential to the task. Various papers and reports tried to make the dream of a Christian globe feasible, but there was also a learned minority of missionary theologians who insisted on the truth in other religions and the notion that the dream of world conversion was not attainable.

The conference was organized around the idea of mission that had dominated the nineteenth century – both its strengths and weaknesses. Follow-up conferences during 1913–14 were held in India, Burma, Singapore, China, Korea and Japan, but not Africa. There were fewer non-white delegates than would be the case in any twenty-first-century Christian conference. Sadly, the representatives showed almost no recognition of the developments that would lead to the First World War and the mission disruptions that would occur with the breakup of the European colonies. There was too little vision of and preparation for the cultural and political events of the century. However, the conference signified a move toward cooperation among Protestants after a long history of conflict.

Another singular effort toward Christian unity was the formation of the *World Council of Churches*. Early on a Protestant endeavor, its roots can be found in the Edinburgh 1910 Mission Conference, but the ecumenical patriarch of Constantinople had called for ecumenical conversations as early as 1920. The Life and Work Movement, concerned with Christian involvement in economic, political and social issues, held conferences in Stockholm (1925) and Oxford (1937). The Faith and Order Movement, concerned with unity among Christians, met at Lausanne (1927) and Edinburgh (1937). They joined forces in 1938 but had to wait until 1948 to form the World Council of Churches. In the last half of the twentieth century Eastern Orthodox and Roman Catholic delegates have joined the discussions. Not only deepened theological understanding but also projects to help those in need have arisen from these alliances. Conservative Protestants have questioned the council's commitment to the Lordship of Jesus Christ. At Canberra the Eastern Orthodox came close to leaving because of a Korean Minjung theologian's inclusion of native Korean spirit religion as vital to Christian faith. The decline of mainline Protestant churches in the United States has made funding of both the National (U.S.A.) and the World Councils of Churches more difficult. Were these councils to be lost, it would be a sad event unless other organizations of similar vision and accomplishment took their place.

The most notable Roman Catholic council was *Vatican II* (1962–5). Pope John XXIII was the power behind it. He was able to enlist the curia, the more conservative leaders in the Vatican, to become involved in various study questions that were to be raised. At the council, however, the bishops set their own commissions to restudy the reports from the curia and thus showed a kind of independence that Pope John graciously accepted.

The agenda that was accepted demonstrated how much the fear of discussing modern issues had faded since Vatican I (1869–70). The council offered a series of reforms that reshaped Catholicism. The use of vernacular languages in the Mass, not Latin alone, as well as other liturgical changes were meant to attract modern folk. Protestant observers found the definition of tradition more compatible. It was linked more closely to the Bible rather than holding the place of a second separate source of revelation. Other Christians were recognized as brothers and sisters, if still family members in error. Ancient antagonisms with Jews were declared shameful acts for which the church should apologize. Catholics could not abandon their mission to the world, but other religions offered values that should be respected.

With the long reign of Pope John Paul II at the end of the twentieth century, the number of cardinals has been expanded to include leaders from many countries of the South. A large group of more conservative bishops has been placed in important positions. The breath of fresh air from Vatican II has become a bit stale. The celibacy of priests and their pastoral rather than political responsibility have been reasserted. John Paul II has honored the role of women graciously and strictly at the same time that he has insisted on male leadership in the church. He has also embodied some of the important reforms of Vatican II. He has both pleaded for forgiveness from Jews by publicly confessing how badly

Christians have treated them and has confessed that the separation between Eastern Orthodoxy and Western Catholicism is sinful and based on many Catholic mistakes. He has met with leaders of other world religions to explore shared truths. Although he stands behind some quite traditional positions, probably on balance his reign has been open and very positive.

Not all world mission efforts in Europe and the United States emerged from mainline Protestant denominations or Roman Catholicism. Lettie Cowan and her husband Charles were part of a faith-based holiness mission to *Japan* in 1900 that resulted in the foundation of the Oriental Missionary Society. Mrs Cowan wrote persuasively not only about the need for the evangelization of Asia but also about the important part women should have in such work. Holiness churches regularly recognized the leadership of women as they saw their gifts in action. Lettie invited them to serve in foreign fields and to support the work financially. Having studied in a United States Bible school for training ministers, she and her husband started a school in Tokyo. Soon she insisted that Korea needed such a training institute and it was underwritten by the Oriental Missionary Society. That Holiness venture was so successful that it has led to the third largest denomination in *Korea*.

Other advances in mutual Christian understanding have occurred. At the level of scholarly research, representatives of *Middle Eastern and Silk Road churches*, divided since the fifth century over the phrase 'two natures in one person' as describing Jesus Christ, have agreed that more careful attention to the other camp's words could have softened the rabid disagreements. The emphases of Monophysite and Dyphysite Christian communities were certainly different, but political and personality problems fueled the animosity. In the most prominent instance Cyril of Alexandria (*c*. 375–444) and Nestorius of Constantinople (*c*. 381–451) might have found a common cause if uniform views had not been demanded and each of them had been more compassionate. There was a weaker emphasis on the humanity in the Monophysite churches and a lesser explanation of the unity of Christ's person in the Dyphysite churches. But the first group, even now, has little interest in denying Jesus' humanity and the second has rejected a split between the two natures.

Christian communities in the *United States* come with quite varied descriptions. The outpouring of the Holy Spirit at Azusa Street in Los Angeles during 1906 is often viewed by pentecostals as a great public manifestation of their views and practices. From the outside they seemed to be lower class people suffering under the pressures of economic, social and political deprivation. At the time their religion seemed to onlookers to be just another safety valve working to prevent disruptive revolutions of the masses. Some outsiders hoped that these people's feelings of despair and disenfranchisement would be funneled away into such practices and empower them to ask serious societal questions. Those misinformed hopes were soon dashed.

In the middle of the century charismatic outbreaks among Roman Catholics and Episcopalians, as well as many other Christian groups, changed the situation. These believers' desire for spiritual gifts could not be explained on the basis of class, education, race or any other such distinguishing factor. Thus some began to realize that this unusual happening could not be dismissed. Because the Hispanic evangelical population of the United States includes a large charismatic religious element, the work of the Holy Spirit and spiritual gifts must be included in any description of an ecumenical core of Christian practice and faith. The Roman Catholic authorities in North America have been careful to issue warnings and to lead their flocks away from dependence on charismatic gifts. So-called mainstream Protestants have developed similar approaches. But the experiences of many Christians in the countries of the South, where two-thirds of Christians now live, have given strong credibility to claims of visions, tongues and healings being a central part of Christian life.

Perhaps the most interesting change in the search for a Christian core in the twentieth century was the emergence of feminist and womanist theologies. *Women* female mystical theologians have always kept open not only their place in doing theology but also feminine images for the Christian God. But contemporary women's movements have at times found the male imagery so repulsive that they have replaced it with the Old Testament conception of 'Sophia'. The oppression of women, on many levels, has been a continuing challenge for Christians. Male and female leaders have responded in different ways to calls for women's liberation. Some Protestant conservatives have attacked Sophia theology while conceding that Christian treatment of women has never been fully adequate. Womanist theology appeared in the United States because so many feminist theologians were clearly white, upper class and educated. The major contributions of these efforts have been the consequent theological argumentation and the focus on real advancements for women.

The central themes of spirituality, evangelism and service have had remarkable witnesses in the *United States* alone. Two major twentieth-century prophets of Protestantism in the United States were Billy Graham (born 1918) and Martin Luther King, Jr (1929–68). The first, a rousing North Carolina evangelist who drew much early attention in California revivals, has preached throughout the world a simple gospel that attempts to mute denominational strife. He insists on repentance and a close relationship with God and leaves baptism and the Eucharist to be handled by local congregations. His evangelistic campaigns have brought renewed strength to many Christian groups and have been particularly successful in awakening former Christians to reinvigorated life and faith. Only in his failing years, however, has he recognized how imprudent his choice of the word 'crusade' was for his evangelistic campaigns; he had paid too little attention to Christian–Muslim relations. But despite this failing, in his twilight he still shines.

The second, a vaunted Alabama civil rights leader who nonviolently led blacks and whites toward racial reconciliation, joined a line of Christian martyrs through his assassination. As a young and inexperienced pastor he provided leadership that few expected he could muster. He kept the gospel and the church at the center of some of the most distressing civil strife of the century. The streets and jail often served as his pulpit. A powerful speaker and fearless guide he showed how much Jesus and Gandhi had in common in their rejection of violence; in the process he won a Nobel Peace Prize. He was the stalwart, though flawed, figure among a cadre of significant black church leaders. He lived a liberation theology that was also thoughtfully supported in his publications.

Thomas Merton (1915–68) learned the twisted ways of life first as an orphan, then during his secular education in France, England and finally at Columbia University in New York City. He was interested in many things: philosophy, politics and literature – indeed he demonstrated a prodigious writing talent. By the time that he drifted toward Catholicism and made his way to the Trappist Monastery at Gethsemani, Kentucky, his life had begun to turn around. He knew the failings and strengths of pre-1939 secularism and atheism. When the story of his spiritual journey, *The Seven Storey Mountain*, was published in 1946 any reader could recognize that another giant of mystical theology had appeared. He gave all his energy to the practice and explanation of spirituality. Tragically, he was electrocuted by accident at a conference of Buddhists and Christians in Thailand. For Merton, the life of the soul was the common interest of all religions.

At her death Dorothy Day (1897–1990) was praised as the most important figure of Catholicism in the United States. She founded the *Catholic Worker*, the newspaper of a lay movement that depended on prayer, personal sacrifice and heated debate. She and her colleagues served the dispossessed and worked for justice and peace. Day did not mind being called a Communist or suffering for her faith (Jesus had), but she thought talk of her as a saint marginalized her efforts. An unwed mother, her pregnancy involved a conversion experience; she vowed to and did raise her child as a Catholic. Those experiences and others led her to a sharp sense of the need for a Christ-like social order. She became a pacifist and followed that path through the Second World War and the Cold War until her death. For her the church was a community that had to counter what she saw in the world.

CONCLUSION

Two World Wars eroded the sense that European culture demanded Christian faith at its base. Christendom tottered and fell to its knees. Parts of it still function, but much is gone while other aspects are out of favor. A German might argue for keeping the tax that supports Lutheran and Catholic hospitals and social agencies while never intending to participate in Christian community.

During the Cold War, the United States' conflicts in Korea and Vietnam led many to question governmental institutions and decision, but the place of Christians in the culture has never been as hotly contested as it has been in Europe. Yet involvement in Christian congregations in most U.S. urban centers is greatly reduced, hovering at 1 percent in a large city like Seattle. In spite of Evangelical Protestant revival, Christian faith and practice are often marginalized. At the same time Islam is growing in popularity, especially in urban areas, and will soon become the second largest religion in the country.

Around the globe Christians have become more vital, especially south of the equator where two-thirds of them live. African Independent Churches that grew up without missionary leadership have become strong. Christians in Latin America have struggled to see how established Catholicism will handle various social, economic and political problems. The rapidly growing groups of Evangelical Protestants, many of them charismatic, have added another element. Christians in Asia also deserve recognition. Korea has a substantial Christian community and has sent missionaries throughout the world. Thirty million persecuted Christians in China now test the waters to see if the terrors are gone or only hiding. Christianity is maintainng itself as one of the world's great religions, but Christians have not conquered other faiths as they sought to do at the beginning of the twentieth century.

CONCLUSION

The practice and faith of Christians worldwide are far more variegated than this short presentation could make clear. The history of only a few of the minorities who survived pressure and persecution from the majority established religions in their countries indicates that established Western Christendom is not the norm. Western Christendom has offered many beautiful and helpful aids. I spent almost all the daylight hours of my thirty-fifth birthday in Hagia Sophia. Its present existence as a Muslim museum in Istanbul cannot totally blunt its effect. Being there was a moving, unforgettable experience. The stained glass windows of Marc Chagall (1887–1985) commissioned for the Fraumünster at Zurich focus the soul. Many English speakers find that the Anglican *Book of Common Prayer* poetically guides a life of worship and service. Ancient and modern lectionaries – lists of biblical texts to be used each Sunday – help even conservative Protestants work through more scripture than their favorite, memorized passages. And mainline Protestants, Roman Catholics and Eastern Orthodox have often offered themselves to the poor and homeless of countless cities.

All true. But this book has not been a story primarily of established dominance and power, whatever their creative influence. Could it not be said that the churches that grew to rely on economic and political preference have often been at their best in the midst of persecution? This volume has been concerned with how many Christians' daily lives have been marked by suffering rather than privilege. I have for some time thought this tale should be told, but I was deeply moved by a Chinese

Christian who sadly noted how little can be learned for the lives of Chinese Christians from typical Western church histories. Such volumes too often speak primarily of majority establishment as if that is the only goal; almost anything that assists its achievement is considered an authentic means. Those histories sometimes claim that Asian Christians would have been much better served had they lived under a ruler like Constantine who would have given them the preference that leads to establishment. Such sentiments are false. Chinese Christian art, which never originated in a fully established majority community, is stunning. Building a church structure in twentieth-century Malaysia always required getting permission from the Muslim authorities. Many times local officials allowed Christian communities to buy the land and purchase the materials, only to refuse final authorization. But a cruciform church with worship and education facilities in the long beam of the cross, with legal aid on one side of the cross beam and medical assistance on the other, was built. Too few ecclesiastical worship centers in cultures where Christianity is established have thought through their mission carefully enough to plan and erect such a facility.

So many Christians have lived as persecuted minorities for so long that their narratives must be given attention as examples of authentic discipleship. Their inculturation of practices and faith that are part of their broader culture at the same time that their efforts are often counter-cultural does not make their contextualization of the gospel inauthentic.

It has been useful to follow the three questions of Christians' relationships with people of other faiths, their ability to interact creatively with many cultures, and their differing ideas of what a Christian core should comprise. Christians all over the globe have fought people of non-Christian religions, while others have found in every religion – the major ones and the local traditional ones – wisdom and virtues that could be emulated. Christians have lived within many distinct cultures, at times refusing almost all of the practices and values of the host culture or taking on so many of their ways that those believers could honestly say that their culture's best customs were fulfilled only in Christian community. Some Christians have insisted that they know the Christian core so well that their creeds and books of discipline administered by their properly ordained clergy exclusively describe it. Other Christians have limited 'the core' to belief in Jesus as Lord, a series of ethical practices in line with his life and teachings, and the building of vibrant communities.

Readers interested at first in following only one of these questions could move through the book more quickly. There are, however, historical individuals and movements that are most interesting primarily in terms of more than one of those questions. But treating the three as transparencies that should overlay each other has offered yet another feature. The best Christian leaders are those who have something to say about each of these topics. Augustine and Origen qualify. Augustine had been a practicing Manichaean before he became a brilliant Christian theologian. Origen attacked the Graeco-Roman religions, including astrology. His description of Buddhism is sound, perhaps learned from a Buddhist teacher; indeed a twenty-first-century Zen Buddhist could have an intriguing lens through which to read Origen's texts. And Origen was doubtless the only early theologian who was a match for Augustine.

The oddity of these two leaders lies elsewhere. The first, who set out many lines of proper practice and faith followed by Latin Western European Christians, is often viewed as defining globally what it means to be a Christian. The second, who formed so many practices and understandings of belief among Eastern Orthodox Christians and may have been the first bona fide Christian missiologist, was too often viewed as a heretic. Both tell us who a Christian is.

The Chang'an (Xi'an) stele, with its clear story of what some Chinese Christians believed and its tale of those who graciously served others, must be recognized as a major template for who Christians are to be. Written in such good Chinese with an appropriation of some Buddhist, Confucian and Taoist teachings, it has one major failing: its optimistic longing for more governmental approval and support that never came. The Dunhuang documents, discovered in a Buddhist Chinese library, are similar. Even when they at times seem to stretch Christian faith beyond its boundaries, they always labor to demonstrate that no one need fully renounce being Chinese in order to become a Christian.

Thomas Aquinas was a great doctor of the church, not because he wrote an unparalleled systematic theology based on what appeared to be the universal human logic of Aristotle, but because his genius was applied to helping Dominicans learn how to engage in dialogue with Jews and Muslims. The age in which he lived and his own gifts encouraged him to speak clearly to any humans he knew about Christian faith and practice. The decision of the Roman Catholic Church in 1970 to declare Teresa of Avila another doctor of the church suggests that mystical theologians with love for others and leaders with disciplined spiritual lives must be recognized as authentic theologians.

By contrast the Magisterial Reformers, Martin Luther and John Calvin, lived in times and places that cramped their visions. They reacted with wisdom and power against the Roman church of Europe that so needed drastic change. But they are lesser figures for guiding Christians in the twenty-first century because they have so little to say about living among the other great religions of the world. Their definitions of the Christian core are tethered to the questions that bound their attention. Much the same is true of Anabaptist theologians of the period, although their understanding of Christian community, so marked by continuous persecution, can advise Christians in this present century who live as minorities without hope of establishment. No definition of who Christians are could avoid the Reformation emphasis on a majestic God, people justified by grace through faith, or the importance of a community practicing the faith. But each of those aspects may be stated and lived out in varied ways.

A series of Roman Catholic catechisms, most clearly that of Alexandre de Rhodes for the Vietnamese, tell us important things about all three questions. They emphasize the character of the major Eastern religions met by Christians, the cultures that have shaped and are shaping the inhabitants of different lands, and the insight gained into what a core of Christian practice and faith looks like within the pursuit of mission.

Various persecuted Christian communities have outlived their predicted demise. The hidden Christians in Japan, now disappearing in the climate of freedom after nearly five hundred years of persecution, had been expected to die out in the seventeenth century. Being free without painful oppression can destroy. At other times Christian communities have been exterminated without leaving so much as a trace. In the Middle East, East Syrian (Nestorian) Christians have battled for their existence – nearly to vanish in the twentieth century. In 1905 Addai Sher found in Seert a full Syriac translation of Theodore of Mopsuestia's *On the Incarnation*, an important text of which we have only translated fragments quoted in other treatises. That document was not the only thing that perished during the terrors of the First World War. In the 1960s a German scholar went to Seert to look for the manuscript, but discovered that no one even remembered when any Christians had lived there.

In this new century most Christians are non-Western and thus are not desperately threatened by Western post-Christendom views. Leonardo Boff of Brazil helps inspire Christian communities that have little similarity to Christendom and yet truthfully tell the Christian story to the downtrodden and those who keep them down. He argues that ecology is a Christian theme, present in premodern theologies and directly related to poverty and wealth in the contemporary scene. Kwame Bediako of Ghana sees vibrant theology in the prayers of a Ghanian woman, Afua Kuma, who can neither read nor write. She spells out her Christian sense of things with metaphors from African daily life. Bediako insists that each culture, not the least African ones, will have characteristics that so enhance parts of the Christian core that all should see how much each community needs the ecumenical work of others living in a very different milieu. The Korean Moonjang Lee, who teaches in Singapore, counters Korean Minjung theology as depending too much on ancient spirits but seeks to sink Christian life and belief deeply in Korean culture. He insists that Asian Christian traditions look at the gospel in ways that all the world needs. Revived interest in Christian practice and faith has occurred in North America and Europe through the discovery that those regions are inhabited by people who have religious questions neither limited to nor rooted in Christian community. Living out discipleship by focusing on the practice of virtue in life together once again seems to be the way through the present situations on any part of the earth. It involves communities of believers who think of themselves as empowered by the Holy Spirit and called to serve the oppressed, the poor and the diseased as well as the rich broken by life. Christian churches that never merit enough attention from their neighbors to be in conflict or suffer persecution may not deserve the name 'Christian'. At the same time followers of Christ who make no attempt to listen to Christians with different views and who can neither admire people of other faiths nor respect significant aspects of their cultures do not yet understand Christian practice and belief.

Christians will continue to be members of one major world religion. But they will be most able to claim authenticity when the growing witness of their communities in the South becomes the norm. The Christians of the South deal regularly with people of other faiths, live out their own faith in the careful embodiment of their culture and thus reveal both old and also strikingly new conceptions of a Christian core both to the outside world and to their brothers and sisters in the North. As it was at the beginning, Christian practice and faith represent a non-Western religion that appeared on the western fringes of Asia. Christians should know and students of Christianity should be taught that the religion's dominant phase in the West, as impressive as it was, was never more than part of the story. Many views of Western Christians, doubtless some held by the author of this book, now represent weak minority opinions.

INDEX

what might be called 'manners' were spelled out in detail. Wealth and its trappings endangered the soul. The force of his work was so strong that he also thought he should make clear in a different book that rich folk could be saved, certainly a question raised in the Bible and in response to his detailed account of the Christian life.

Tertullian of Carthage in North Africa spelled out a series of *social careers* that Christians should not pursue. Stone masons, plasterers and painters made statuary or pictures of idols and thus supported idolatry. Craftsmen like cobblers or makers of dinnerware might be accepted, but only with careful investigation. They too often made frivolous pieces that signified misspent wealth. Tertullian and others could hardly stomach the growing urban thirst for entertainment, in either the less expensive theater or the gaudy circus. Large amounts of money were spent in collecting animals to fight with each other and with humans. City rulers held such 'games' throughout the empire, not only in Italy and North Africa. Gladiatorial contests began to look shameful to Christians; they seem not to have been as frequent in Constantinople – the city of Byzantium renamed and expanded after Constantine's conversion. Jesus urged Christians not to kill. Even contemplating it amounted to defeat before temptation.

Tertullian did not want Christians to be soldiers, but Eusebius (*c.* 260–*c.* 339), the church historian, tells us of a third-century legion composed primarily of Christians who served well. Jesus had not rebuked the Roman centurion for his professional work but admired his sense of how commands needed to be obeyed. Christian principle against killing, whether in war or in other circumstances, was strong, but some believers tried to justify their involvement in taking human life as part of their duty.

Christians adopted another institution from the Jewish and Graeco-Roman cultures surrounding them: the conclave or *council*. Only a few years after Jesus' death, leaders assembled to talk about what was central to their faith. Such discussion began in Jerusalem when Jewish Christian leaders there wanted to hear about the apostle Paul's practice and preaching. In Asia Minor (Turkey) during the second century, a regional council gathered to determine the truth of prophecies collected by Montanists, Christians who thought that the spiritual life of the church was drifting and that prophecy was just as important as ever. The assembled bishops said that prophecy was not the question – ecstatic prophecy was. It had no claim to authenticity. But the way was opened to view most prophecy as ecstatic and thus not a Christian practice.

The same kind of ambiguities faced Christians when they considered *gender roles and family*. The *pater familias* of Roman life began to strike disciples of Christ as overbearing. The power to decide whether or not a newborn lived was too dreadful a decision for a father to make. He was the head of the house as Christ was the head of the church, but Christ gave up his life for that church. Abortion was viewed in similar ways; it was infanticide. Taking various medicines for that purpose or performing manual surgery was forbidden. Children were gifts from God.

God ordained marriage for the creation of family. Divorce was not allowed even as it had been under Jewish law. Women were highly valued, but the dominance of males in the relationship was usually often viewed as divinely sanctioned. Early on Christian marriage was administered by civil authorities and blessed by the church. Only later did it become a church ceremony that had ecclesiastical status.

The writer of the New Testament epistle to the Ephesians – some say Paul – pointed out that marriage is a partnership in which both the man and the woman are to submit to one another in reverence for Christ. The author assumed that women knew submission from their culture, whether it be primarily Jewish or Graeco-Roman. But he demanded that men think about loving their wives in the same ways that they loved their bodies. Christ loved the church and died for it. So should they love their wives. This represented a deep challenge to the *pater familias*. If in Christian marriage the partners lived in mutual submission because of their sense of what Christ did for people, then female children and women could emerge as more significant.

Women appear to have been more important among early Christians than is sometimes supposed. The Virgin Mary holds place as the significant parent to the point that some speculatively posit an early death for Mary's husband, Joseph. The passage in Luke's Gospel that is called the Magnificat depicts her as a deeply virtuous disciple who knew how to serve by bending humbly to God's will. Rich women supplied the money to keep Jesus and his band alive and teaching. Paul has been read as always keeping women silent and placing them in positions of servitude rather than leadership, but he recognized important women in his circle and others. Phoebe was a deacon in a church at Cenchreae near Corinth, a powerful patron and supporter of others. The woman Junia was of note among apostles like Barnabas (not one of the twelve), a Christian before Paul was converted. Priscilla, along with her husband Aquila, taught Apollos a fuller understanding of the faith.

There is evidence from Jewish inscriptions that some Jewish women were leaders in Hellenistic synagogues. They had both the social position and the money to serve in those capacities. It is thus likely that a wealthy woman like Lydia, a seller of purple in Thyatira, was a leader in her local Christian congregation. The four prophesying daughters of Philip must have practiced their gifts in services of study and worship. Women martyrs could be quite influential. As pentecostal communities the world over have experienced, various spiritual gifts evidenced in women empower them to take positions of leadership. There is even a little evidence that as the church developed the pattern of bishops, presbyters and deacons as the primary levels of authority, some women were presbyters and at least one was a bishop. The Montanist movement, so dependent upon prophecy, had women leaders. Its success and thus its threat during the second century formed part of the background in which women in Christian communities were squeezed out of positions of public influence. The other important source of this suppression was the penchant of some Christian male leaders for taking over the description of women in ancient Greek writers like Aristotle who saw them as unstable and irrational. The depiction of the husband in Roman society as the sole head of the family also encouraged the diminishing of women's role in Christian groups

Most ethical codes from Christian sources call for the support of widows and orphans. The insistence upon watching over them indicates a recognition of their vulnerability within Graeco-Roman societal structures. Worship manuals include comments on how to care for widows. They often spell out provisions for their welfare under the direction of a bishop or presbyter and under the watchful eyes of deacons. Widows were not to be immediately enrolled among the widows cared for by the church; they should be encouraged to remarry and were expected to be free to do so. Gossiping and backbiting among women were anticipated but frowned upon. How much that small catalogue of vices also depended upon Graeco-Roman views of women is difficult to say.

The earliest glimpse of Christians shows that they were viewed as a Jewish sect and thus shared some of the privileges and tensions that Jews faced under Roman rule in Palestine (Israel). Because Jesus' ways and words appeared to be threats to both Jewish religious authority and Roman political power, he was crucified as a criminal. The cross was a mark of shame. Jesus attacked some of the Jewish leaders for, in his eyes, abandoning their faith and becoming lax in their concern for the common folk. True worship of God was his goal. But he also said just enough for a case to be made depicting him as a political rebel. He rejected the Jewish Zealot party's hope of driving the Roman armies into the seas. The loss of that hope, however, may lie behind his apostle Judas's betrayal of him. With Jesus' death his followers were marked as troublemakers. Thus the Christian faith first preached at Pentecost appeared dangerous to safely ensconced political leaders. Some of the apostles were imprisoned in Jerusalem. Paul, the missionary, was beaten in various cities where he traveled; once he had to be let down from a wall in order to escape because the gates were being watched.

Although Christian groups grew rapidly, they continued to incur random *persecution*. Their earliest legal standing occurred in some of the empire's cities, particularly Rome, as burial societies. They were illegal as a religion. Jews represented an ancient faith with certain rights in various metropolitan centers, but Christians struggled with their Jewish heritage. At the turn of the second century, Ignatius, bishop of Antioch, was arrested by the Roman authorities and taken to Rome. Evidently the political powers thought that by removing the identified leaders of Christian groups, they could suppress them. Ignatius believed he would be eaten by lions in the famed city and looked forward to such a death as an opportunity to demonstrate his faith. In this period martyrdom became a debated pattern of Christian life. Should faithful followers of Christ seek death as a witness to life? Should they become inconspicuous or should they flee? Much depended on the ways in which Roman law was stated and enforced. Often, provincial governors distant from Rome did not want to search out and imprison or kill people who they thought were basically harmless. Pliny the Younger, governor in Bithynia (northwestern Turkey), was convinced that the Christians could be crushed if necessary.

One difficult problem for Christians was that some caesars were insistent upon seeing their predecessors or even themselves as gods. Many Roman leaders thought that the authority of the state depended upon the Graeco-Roman pantheon, which individual caesars could join and then be worshipped. They tolerated nearly any religion that would offer sacrifice to the gods who protected the state. Even Jews were treated in many cities as those who embodied an ancient religion that depended deeply upon continuous sacrifices. But a religious group like the Christians, who did not give allegiance to those gods and did not offer animal sacrifices to their own god, threatened the state.